BARBARA POLLACK is an award-winning journalist, art critic and curator who is one of the world's leading authorities on contemporary Chinese art. She has written extensively since 1994 for such publications as *Vanity Fair* the *New York Times*, the *Washington Post*, *Departures*, the *Village Voice*, *ARTnews* and *Art in America*. Her previous book, *The Wild, Wild East: An American Art Critic's Adventures in China*, was published in 2010. Pollack curated the groundbreaking exhibition *My Generation: Young Chinese Artists*, which opened at the Tampa Museum of Art and Museum of Fine Arts, St Petersburg in 2014 and traveled to the Oklahoma City Museum of Art and the Orange County Museum of Art in 2015. She has lectured extensively, including as a featured speaker at the World Economic Forum "Summer Davos" in Tianjin, China. In recognition of her contribution to this field, she was awarded two grants from the Asian Cultural Council and is a recipient of the Andy Warhol/Creative Capital Arts Writers' Grant.

"*Brand New Art from China* is frank, honest, and full of passion ... The author offers a rare and precise insight into a nation and culture that is often described by so-called outsiders with an imbalanced view or by confused misinterpretations. Her writing is realistic and clear at the same time ... an attractive analysis of this mysterious culture and society."

Ai Weiwei

"The last 30 years have been a singular, rich time of invention for contemporary art in China. But what will happen now for a new generation, growing up after the extraordinary changes through which the artists of this earlier moment lived? In this new book, Barbara Pollack starts to chart this emerging terrain and the new questions, at once artistic, institutional, and curatorial, that it poses – a key reference for art in China today."

John Rajchman, Department of Art History, Columbia University

"Barbara Pollack's book is the first systematic study on a new generation of Chinese artists born in the 1980s and 1990s whose artistic practices are indicative of what's to come next. Born and grown up in a unique sociopolitical space and time, for these millennial-generation artists, art-making is both a personal reaction to the immediate

realities in which they live and a public statement that points to a certain universality and humanism of the twenty-first century. Pollack approaches the new art form from the perspectives of art history, socio-economy and geopolitics, and through her tireless first-person encounters with the artists and art professionals, her insatiable curiosity and intellectual quests, she's able to contextualize and decipher for us a very vexed and complex moment of art history in the making."

Adrian Cheng, founder of K11 Art Foundation

"Barbara Pollack has done the hard work of making contact with hundreds of artists, curators, critics, gallerists, and collectors of Chinese art and making sense of this complex and rapidly changing landscape for readers in English. In this book, her focus on millennial, post-Mao, post-internet and even 'post-passport' artists challenging traditional ideas of 'Chinese-ness' provides an invaluable contribution to global art history and criticism."

Martha Schwendener, art critic, *New York Times*

"For anyone interested in what's happening in China's art world, Barbara Pollack's *Brand New Art from China* is both a must-read and a joy. Pollack builds upon her work as a curator and journalist to create a compelling treatment of the artists, collectors, and art market forces that are shaping the world's liveliest contemporary art scene. In her signature style and drawing upon almost two decades of research and personal relationships with the artists included, she weaves together thoughtful insights on the question of identity for a new generation of artists born in China after the death of Mao. Her analysis of the tension between Chinese-ness and post-passport identity lies at the heart of her discussion, and her consideration of the emergence of new individualism within this generation offers a significantly fresh perspective."

Todd D. Smith, Director and CEO, Orange County Museum of Art

"Profiting from years of reporting on contemporary Chinese art, and based on extensive conversations with the artists, Barbara Pollack's new book offers a fascinating account of members of a new generation of Chinese artists seeking a trans-national identity outside the traditional dichotomy of China and the West."

Bruce Altshuler, Director, Program in Museum Studies, New York University

"Pollack's intimate reflections deftly contextualize the state of contemporary art in China today. Her deep knowledge and passion for the subject provide a nuanced roadmap to not only understanding the next generation of art world leaders but the complex society in which they have been forged."

Michelle Yun, Curator of Modern and Contemporary Art at Asia Society Museum

Brand New Art from China

A GENERATION ON THE RISE

Barbara Pollack

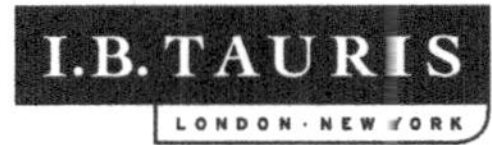

Published in 2018 by
I.B.Tauris & Co. Ltd
London • New York
www.ibtauris.com

ISBN: 978 1 78831 313 1
eISBN: 978 1 78672 412 0
ePDF: 978 1 78673 412 9

A full CIP record for this book is available from the British Library
A full CIP record is available from the Library of Congress

Library of Congress Catalog Card Number: available

Typeset in DanteMT-Regular (Screen) by OKS Prepress Services, Chennai, India
Printed and bound in Great Britain by TJ International Ltd. Padstow PL28 8RW

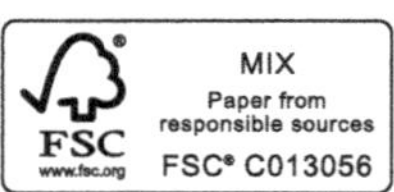

CONTENTS

ACKNOWLEDGMENTS

Little did I know when I published the article "China: The Next Generation," in *ARTnews* in 2011, that this topic would become my primary focus over the next six years. But from that initial encounter with young Chinese artists, my curiosity was sparked, and I could not resist the lure of the questions raised in these first interviews. Already I had met artists like Yan Xing and Sun Xun and it has been my great pleasure to watch their careers blossom and grow with each successive year. But most importantly, my initial insight that this would be a generation of artists profoundly influential not only in China, but also in the global art arena, has proven true.

From that initial research, my work too blossomed into an ongoing inquiry, resulting in two exhibitions: *My Generation: Young Chinese Artists* (which opened at the Tampa Museum of Art and the Museum of Fine Arts, St Petersburg in June 2014 and traveled to the Oklahoma City Museum of Art and the Orange County Museum of Art through 2015) and *WeChat: A Dialogue in Contemporary Chinese Art* (which opened at the Zilkha Gallery of Wesleyan University and traveled to Asia Society Texas in 2016).

For those opportunities, I must thank Todd Smith, director of the Orange County Museum of Art, who was the chief instigator behind *My Generation*, accompanying me to China and meeting these artists himself. I also must thank Pamela Tatge at Wesleyan University and Bridget Bray at Asia Society Texas for the help with WeChat. These exhibitions helped further my investigation in profound and productive ways. Additionally, I am grateful to Budi Tek of the Yuz Museum for asking me to curate *Sun Xun: Prediction Laboratory* in November 2016 and Jill Snyder of MOCA Cleveland for inviting me to organize *Lu Yang: Delusional Mandala* in June 2017.

I also have to thank the Asian Cultural Council for awarding me a grant in 2015, following a previous grant in 2008, specifically funding research into a new generation of Chinese artists. Cui Qiao of the Beijing Contemporary Art Foundation also provided me with generous support. Several individuals in both China and the USA also helped fund this project, including Heather and Andrew Rayburn, Amy Gao and Qiao Zhibing and Tsai Lihsin. But this book would not have been possible without numerous commissions for articles and catalogue essays, and I acknowledge Barbara Macadam of *ARTnews* and Barbara Graustark of the *New York Times* for all their assignments and their great insights.

Certainly, I know that I could not have continued my research without the generosity of the artists I interviewed for the book, more than 100 located in various parts of China, but primarily Beijing, Shanghai, and Hangzhou. They invited me into their studios and homes and accompanied me to exhibitions and nightclubs, allowing me unfettered access into their lives and art-making practices. These experiences would not have been possible without the assistance of three people—Sammi Liu, Sophia Bingqin Cao, and Norbu Zhewen Peng—who served as translators and guides on my many trips to China. Additionally, Banyi Huang of Columbia University helped me with my research and further translations when I returned to New York.

I would not have gotten far without the advice of numerous dealers and curators, specifically Philip Tinari, director of the Ullens Center for Contemporary Art in Beijing; Lauren Cornell, director of the graduate program at the Center for Curatorial Studies at Bard College and chief curator of the Hessel Museum of Art, formerly curator at the New Museum; Alexandra Munroe, Samsung Senior Curator, Asian Art, and Senior Advisor, Global Arts at the Solomon R. Guggenheim Museum and Foundation; Xiaoyu Weng, The Robert H. N. Ho Family Foundation Associate Curator of Chinese Art at the Guggenheim Museum; James Elaine of Telescope and Leo Xu at David Zwirner Hong Kong, formerly of Leo Xu Projects. Adrian Cheng and the K11 Art Foundation were particularly helpful, arranging studio visits and providing me with essential background information. Meg Maggio of Pékin Fine Arts went above and beyond in assisting me, providing me with a base in Beijing and opening endless doors for me. I also thank Lorenz Helbling of ShanghART Gallery, Arthur Solway of James Cohan Shanghai, Alexia Dehaene of MadeIn Corporation, Lu Jingjing of Beijing Commune, Natalie Sun of Platform China, Leng Lin of Pace Beijing and Joe Baptista of Pace New York, Christophe Mao of Chambers Fine Art, David Lehmann of Lehmann Maupin, Sean Kelly and Janine Cirincione of Sean Kelly Gallery, Simon Wang of Antenna Space, and Theresa Liang of Long March Space. All of these people gave me solid advice and arranged interviews with their artists that were invaluable to this project.

In preparation for this book, I researched many other important publications which must be credited, particularly *China's Millennials: The Want Generation* by Eric Fish (Rowman and Littlefield, 2015) and *Little Emperors and Material Girls* by Jemimah Steinfeld (I.B.Tauris, 2015). My thinking was sharpened and framed by the renowned work of Hou Hanru, Artistic Director of the MAXXI in Rome and Wu Hung, Harrie A. Vanderstappen Distinguished Service Professor of Art History, East Asian Languages and Civilizations at the University of

Chicago and consulting curator at the Smart Museum of Art. I was also deeply influenced by readings assembled by John Rajchman for his courses at Columbia University.

Throughout this process, there have been a few individuals who encouraged and supported my work, even when I myself doubted the future of this project. Ellen Scordato of Stonesong went well beyond the duties of a literary agent, urging me to proceed whenever I encountered obstacles. My son, Max Berger, was at times an integral part of this research, accompanying me to China in 2014 and filming many of the artists featured in this book. And of course, I must thank my husband, Joel Berger, who missed me when I was away in China and gave me confidence to go forward every step of the way back at home.

INTRODUCTION

In 2013, a young woman artist from Shanghai created a character called Uterus Man. Part-superhero, part-feminist icon, Uterus Man was ostensibly male but wore a slick, pink jumpsuit and rode around in a chariot in the shape of a pelvis; he lassoed enemies with an electric umbilical cord and soared through the air on a magical sanitary napkin. Undoubtedly humorous but also viscerally disturbing, Uterus Man was presented as the lead figure in an animated film as well as the protagonist in a fully operational video game.

Instead of movie theaters and gaming arcades, this work of art was intended to be shown in galleries and museums, and it quickly circulated on the international art circuit. Critics and curators adored the way the project blurred gender identity, presenting an androgynous superhero with estrogen-driven powers. But *Uterus Man* not only addressed gender roles. It also blurred cultural identity, in that nothing about it looked like it came from China. If anything, it looked like it was produced by a Japanese anime company.

When I showed this artwork to students of mine at Shandong University in Jinan in May 2016, they were shocked and surprised.

Uterus Man might be art in some Westernized radical universe, but how could this possibly be *Chinese* art? To them, a Chinese artist had a responsibility to deal with 5,000 years of Chinese culture, simultaneously bolstering national pride and global prestige. A Chinese artist could not abandon his or her Chinese identity. To do so would be not so much an act of treason as a serious aesthetic shortcoming. After all, why would you want to abandon a culture that had contributed so much to the world?

In some ways, these students—who were studying at a provincial university with limited access to contemporary art—had missed out on 40 years of art history, unaware of not only international trends, but also the advances made by their own country's artists. Art that diverged from calligraphy, from appropriations of Ming Dynasty furniture, from Pop Art renditions of Cultural Revolution icons, seemed so strange to them that it might as well have come from a foreign country. They might have been tempted to accuse the artist of selling out or catering to Western tastes. But, to their credit, they stopped short of this position and tried instead to wind their brains around the fact that someone who was their age and not that different

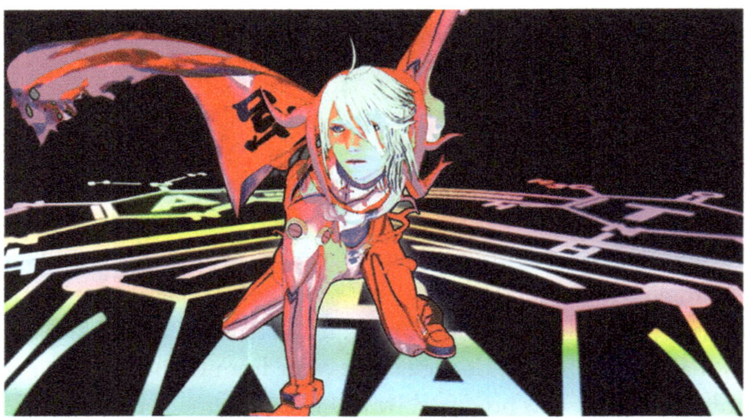

LU YANG, *UTERUS MAN*, VIDEO STILL, 2013. COURTESY OF BEIJING COMMUNE.

from them was making work that challenged the very notion of identity, transcending the limitations of Chinese characteristics.

This sense of confusion is not limited to Chinese audiences. Back in the USA, I am often faced with American audiences who can be equally perplexed by the work being made by a new generation of Chinese artists. Accustomed to viewing art from non-Western centers as a kind of souvenir of foreign travels, they are confounded or, more accurately, a bit disappointed not to find more "China" in an exhibition of Chinese contemporary art. Reviving Cold War differences, they can appreciate an artist who stands up to the authoritarian power of the Chinese government, which explains in large part the popularity of a renegade like Ai Weiwei. They can also savor recycled Chinese materials, such as gunpowder or Chinese characters, which is why artists like Cai Guo-Qiang (who has had a 2008 retrospective at the Guggenheim Museum in New York City) or Xu Bing (who was awarded a 1999 MacArthur "Genius" grant) have met with such great success in the West. But these are

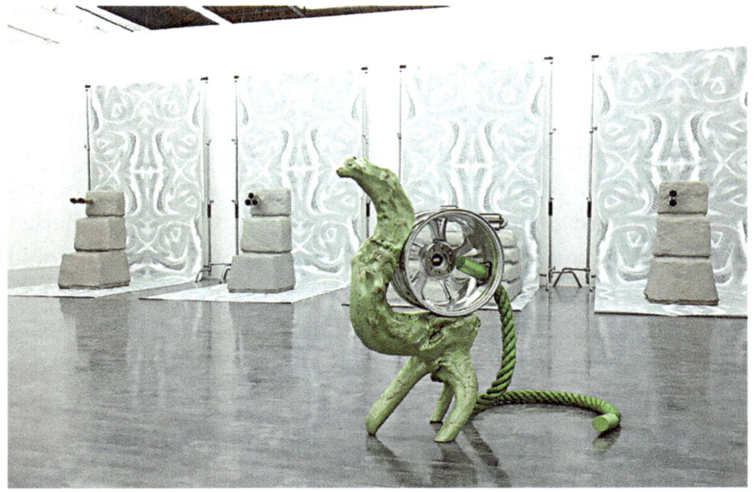

GUAN XIAO, *BASIC LOGIC*, INSTALLATION VIEW, ANTENNA SPACE, 2015. COURTESY OF ANTENNA SPACE.

artists of an older generation, one that emerged in the 1990s when Chinese art was first being introduced in the West.

A New Generation

Since 1976—the year that Mao Zedong died and the repressive Cultural Revolution ended—China has undergone the most rapid development of any country on the planet. In 40 years, China has gone from a developing world country, isolated and impoverished, to a major superpower, fueling the global economy and participating in international cultural exchange. At the same time, China's art scene has evolved from an underground movement, disavowed and censored by the government, to one of the biggest art markets in the world, with thriving galleries and museums, and artists who are world-class superstars.

I was intrigued to discover what life in this express lane would mean to artists born after 1976 and how these artists, in turn, would express such drastic changes through their creations. Would Chinese artists experience a kind of whiplash effect from watching their lives spin around so fast? Would they merely succumb to global pressures and make a kind of homogenized art to integrate into the international art world? Or would they come up with an entirely unique kind of art indigenous to this new global environment? It appeared that by studying a new generation of Chinese artists—those born in the 1980s and 1990s who grew up with the advancement of the new market economy—I could possibly discover an art movement that would lead the way for twenty-first-century artists worldwide. Just as Picasso and Kandinsky had made some of the seminal works of modernism in the first decade of the twentieth century, perhaps I could find pioneers among this group of emerging artists that would point the direction of art for the new millennium.

As citizens living in the epicenter of globalization, young Chinese artists represent prime candidates for launching such a movement, and it is important to recognize the ways they differ from an earlier generation of artists in China. Their predecessors, born in the 1950s and 1960s, bore the brunt of the Cultural Revolution, a period when art-making and everything else was strictly state-controlled, permitting little personal freedom. In contrast, these younger artists grew up with the emergence of a market economy where everything available was a matter of choice. While the previous generation struggled within a China that was culturally isolated, these new artists were direct beneficiaries of the Open Door Policy, which flung open China's borders to McDonald's, Mickey Mouse, and a whole host of global influences. And while the pioneers of Chinese contemporary art did not emerge until the 1990s and for decades developed their work in a country where contemporary art was forced underground, the artists who are the focus of this book came of age post-2000 when China already had a full-fledged art infrastructure with hundreds of galleries and museums. They have been able to establish gallery careers early on in their development, both within China and throughout the world.

To fully understand the differences between these two generations of Chinese artists, one has to imagine them growing up in two different countries and in different centuries, even though they all come from the same place, even the same cities. So, it is not surprising that there is a distinct difference in the artworks they make, particularly when it comes to expressions of Chinese identity. Whereas the previous generation self-identified as "Chinese artists," this younger generation more often seeks to escape this category, describing themselves as "global artists."

This self-defined worldliness is a particularly prominent trait among the artists I researched for this book. Although all of the artists that I interviewed were born in China, none could be said to live in isolation. Some were educated in the West, others had chosen to move to the USA or Europe to pursue their careers. All—even those who went to school in China and continued to live there—were adept at the internet, able to circumvent government censorship to access information on global art trends. And all had ambitions that soared beyond the borders of China, making art that could be read by a wide variety of audiences, with a determination to build high-profile careers in international art.

In fact, many described their work as "universal," a term that I thought had gone out of use during the 1990s when art historians and critics dismissed it as glossing over the substantial differences between Western and non-Western cultures. These artists didn't seem to mind blurring such distinctions, preferring a much more fluid approach to East–West dynamics. They embodied a new turn of phrase, namely "transnationalism," a hybrid identity formed from the many places they had lived and influences they had studied.

Post-Passport Identity

Artists like Lu Yang—who created *Uterus Man*—are determined to express their reactions to life in a decidedly post-Mao China. They grew up in a China populated by skyscrapers and superhighways with a post-internet culture in which an encyclopedic range of influences collide at the speed of light. The artworks by this new generation of Chinese artists are products of this twenty-first-century China, the epicenter of globalization, where remnants of local culture are rapidly evaporating. Their artworks are refreshingly original and free from the nagging stereotypes and iconography that dogged earlier periods of contemporary art from China. There are no more depictions of Mao, no more references to Imperial China or acknowledgments of the Cultural Revolution.

For this generation, the label "Chinese artist" is an uncomfortable burden, imposed by curators, both foreign and Chinese, who are sorely behind the times. As ever more of these emerging artists exhibit their work internationally, they are discovering the pitfalls of categorization on the basis of one's passport. Shows of "Chinese contemporary art" often ghettoize artists, preventing them from fully emerging as unique individuals in their own right. More importantly, the term conjures up stereotypes of what that art might look like. For example, the solemn portraits of Zhang Xiaogang and the grinning satyrs of Yue Minjun, two market leaders who emerged in the 1990s, had saturated the West and dominated the public's imagination about new art from China. This earlier work, while often an earnest attempt at defining a Chinese identity, smacks of a kind of self-orientalization; that is, an internalization of the exoticism attendant with an appreciation of Chinese culture. To these young artists, nothing could be worse than to be associated with such pioneers, who are not seen as mentors or role models, but rather as authority figures that need to be challenged. Post-passport identity assumes a new cosmopolitanism. It is not exclusive to Chinese artists but it is especially pronounced in the works of this new generation who bristle at any boundaries defined by nationalism.

"Anyone can be a Chinese artist," said Xu Zhen, a rebellious provocateur who is a leader in the Shanghai art scene. By this he means that anyone—even an American artist—can throw together images of Mao, maybe some dragons and pagodas, and imitate the look of many Chinese contemporary artists of the older generation. He himself cynically recycles Asian stereotypes in his work, but blends them seamlessly with icons from Western art history, such as the Winged Victory in the Louvre or nineteenth-century political cartoons by Thomas Nash. Xu Zhen is afraid of flying and doesn't travel, so he has not seen these works in person but has found them by endlessly surfing the internet, a cornucopia of imagery presented in a jumbled, anti-chronological order. Likewise, Lu Yang got the idea for *Uterus Man* from an online news story about a Japanese man who had had his sex organs removed to be truly androgynous. She later met the man and had him perform as a cosplayer dressed as her character, appearing at conventions and other public venues. To Lu Yang, Chinese identity is a misnomer, since she views herself as living on the internet where she has no need to identify herself by her country of origin, but can instead slip into various personae, leaving ethnic identity behind.

So, although I use the term "young Chinese artists" and will continue to employ it frequently as a shorthand for this younger generation, I have come to think of them as "post-passport." By this I do not mean that they have entirely rejected their Chinese identity, but that they interpret it through the lens of a postmodern society in which the Forbidden City and Rem Koolhaus's CCTV headquarters reside simultaneously. They are not unaware of Chinese history and have been thoroughly educated in the 5,000 years of Chinese art, but much of this knowledge seems irrelevant in comparison to the exciting possibilities of their present-day lives. "Post-passport," therefore, is not a negation of Chinese identity but an embrace of new identity forged in a collision of forces that characterize present-day China.

My use of the term "post-passport" is influenced by the 2001 groundbreaking essay by Thelma Golden, director of the Studio Museum in Harlem, who curated the exhibition *Freestyle*, and called the participating artists "post-black."[1] By this, she did not mean that they had transcended race relations or had achieved unquestionable parity with white artists. What she meant was that *Freestyle* artists had integrated the achievements of previous generations of African-American artists (who by necessity had had to position their cultural identity at the forefront of their work) and had come up with a more fluid approach that permitted multiple interpretations of self to exist simultaneously. Similarly, the Chinese artists that I have interviewed for this book are not ignorant of, nor do they reject, Chinese culture out of hand, but acknowledge how their own life experience contrasts with more outmoded notions of "Chinese-ness." As such, they are re-evaluating Chinese identity in ways that contradict and supplant criteria that have been used to evaluate Chinese art for the past 40 years.

The End of Chinese-ness

"Chinese-ness" is a term that is slippery to define, because Chinese identity means many things to many people and has often been employed for divergent political and cultural agendas. A combination of nationality and ethnicity, "Chinese-ness" can apply to both people living in China and overseas Chinese living in the ever-broadening Chinese diaspora. It implies a unified culture, erasing the distinctions between China's many ethnic groups and dialects. It is rooted in the assertion of a shared past and belief in an ascendant future, which has been adopted by political institutions to bolster a unified authoritarian state.

At the same time, "Chinese-ness" is an honest attempt to evaluate one's identity at a moment when it is threatened by outside influences. Many Chinese artists of the 1980s and 1990s explored this identity intensively in their work, in order to figure out just who they were and what they might express that would be uniquely their own. This was particularly important to Chinese artists living abroad, who wanted to insert elements of personal heritage into an international dialogue about "multiculturalism." At a time when women artists were exploring feminism, black artists were addressing racial identity, and gay artists were confronting the AIDS crisis, Chinese artists were reflecting on their own roots to further a cross-cultural conversation about East–West differences.

Up until 2000 and beyond, "Chinese-ness" was considered an essential element in Chinese contemporary art, for better or for worse. The phrase was not only present in evaluations by Western curators but central to many debates in Chinese curatorial circles. As early as 1980, leading critic Li Xianting wrote, "It is critical for us to be able to express the thoughts and feelings of the Chinese people in our art, even if the form we use is indiscriminately borrowed,"[2] meaning that while artistic expression may borrow formal considerations from Western art practices, the work must be an expression of Chinese values. His words carry with them an urgency to retain Chinese characteristics, even as Chinese artists emerged on the international scene.

But this strategy of employing Chinese symbols and iconography to convey a sense of identity was later seen as a facile tactic, calculated to win favor from Western curators looking for an alleged authenticity in Chinese art. On the occasion of the Shanghai Biennale 2000, reactionary critic Wang Nanming delivered a paper criticizing Chinese artists either living or showing their work in the West as trading deliberately in Chinese symbols to attract foreign audiences. "By appropriating simple motifs or symbols left behind by tradition, they formulate these motifs into some 'essential' markers of Chinese-ness," he stated.[3] In only 20 years, "Chinese-ness" had transformed from a positive expression of local culture to a calculated strategy worthy of criticism.

To complicate matters further, Western curators and collectors employed the term "Chinese-ness" to acknowledge the accomplishments of Chinese artists who emerged in the 1980s and 1990s, complimenting them for bringing awareness of a local culture into a global arena. When Uli Sigg, the world's leading collector of Chinese contemporary art, put his trove on view at the Kunstmuseum Bern in 2005, the accompanying catalog contained several essays pointedly addressing the issue of "Chinese-ness."[4] In this book, Sigg asked each of the participating artists to address how this quality impacts their work. Many expressed confusion and annoyance at the question, answering that, since they were born in China, their work is inherently Chinese. Yet, the exhibition was curated in such a way as to reinforce "Chinese-ness" as an organizing principle, focusing on depictions of Mao or contemporary use of calligraphy to assert that expression of Chinese identity was the primary quality present in the diverse works on view.

I myself experienced this issue of "Chinese-ness" firsthand when I first began interviewing Chinese artists who were living in New York in the late 1990s, such as Cai Guo-Qiang, Xu Bing, and Zhang Huan. In conversations with them, I often felt that Chinese identity presented an impenetrable barrier, one that I could not cross without knowing a great deal more about China. The works often included references to Chinese folk tales, Ming Dynasty furniture, calligraphy, and Buddhism, requiring a crash course in Chinese culture to begin to understand their meaning. Yet, the impact of these works was undeniable, arousing my curiosity, rather than shutting down discussion. Looking back, I have to admit that I was as enthralled with the exoticism of the work as the next curator, feeling as if I were transported to a place that I only vaguely knew about from news reports and novels. I was undeniably persuaded to investigate Chinese contemporary art by the "Chinese-ness" of these early artworks.

A New Vision, A New Art Movement

Fast forward to 2012 and my first interviews with a younger generation of Chinese artists, when I was equally charmed but in a very different way. In the hand-drawn animation of Sun Xun, the abstractions of Liu Wei, the internet avatars of Cao Fei, and the homoerotic installations of Yan Xing, I saw a vision for the future, one that was global in its aesthetics and its ambitions. Here, there

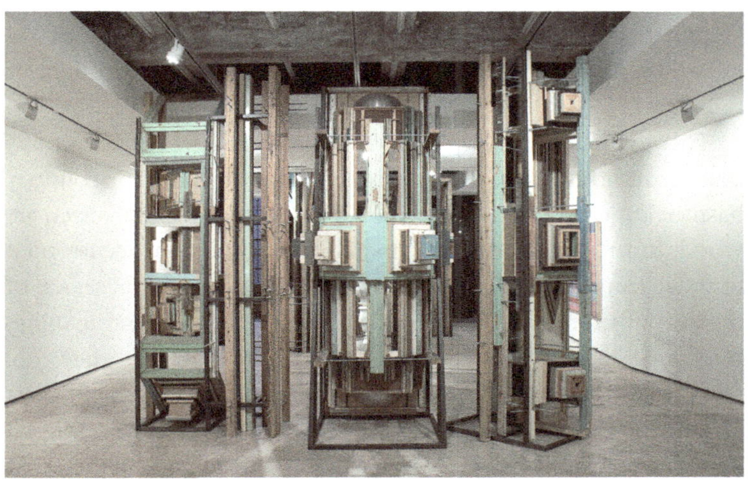

LIU WEI, *MERELY A MISTAKE II NO. 6*, 2009-11, INSTALLATION VIEW, LEHMANN MAUPIN NEW YORK, 2013. COURTESY OF THE ARTIST AND LEHMANN MAUPIN, NEW YORK AND HONG KONG.

was a sophisticated incorporation of current art trends and a sharp departure from predictably Chinese references. Yet, the work was resolutely rooted in Chinese economic and cultural conditions, addressing recent history, politics, and art developments in complex and subtle ways.

For example, Liu Wei has made a series of towering sculptures from the cast-off architecture of demolished Beijing housing projects, using the industrial green walls and windows with chipped wooden frames indicative of state-run developments from the 1960s. Walking through these futuristic structures felt like stepping into a time machine, capable of bringing viewers back to the past or forward in time simultaneously.

Cao Fei invented the digital *RMB City*, an imaginary location in "Second Life," the online community and 3D virtual world that allows individuals to adopt personas to interact, converse, and even have sex in cyberspace. In *RMB City*, her avatar, named China Tracy, flies past landmarks of a New China from Shanghai's Pearl TV Tower to Beijing's CCTV headquarters, while other participants trade in high-end real estate. Nominated for the Guggenheim's prestigious Hugo Boss prize for the work, Cao Fei herself seems to jet-set from one museum to another throughout the world.

These works bring into sharp focus conditions of life in a post-Mao economy, retaining just enough local elements to counterbalance the risk of homogenization present in a post-globalized art world. In this world, curators and collectors are now accustomed to flying from biennial to biennial and art fair to art fair in search of the next big thing. And yet, they do not want to see the same thing, the same bland cultural McDonald's, everywhere they go. Sometimes mistaking tourism for art appreciation, they still want to have an enlightened encounter with just enough foreign signposts to make their trip worthwhile. While an older generation of Chinese artists gave them plenty of that, the new generation of young Chinese artists delivers something more sophisticated and at times more subtle. They provide the sensation of entering a postmodern experience, a juxtaposition of international influences, that offers a glimpse of what it means to try and transcend national boundaries.

In recent years, there has been a backlash to globalization, expressed in political movements throughout the world, from the ascendance of ISIS and radical fundamentalism to Brexit and even the election of Donald Trump as president of the USA. In China, this rise in nationalism and Chinese pride is even more pronounced, promulgated by Xi Jinping and enforced by the current government through educational policies and cultural programming. Chinese youth have been influenced by this nationalist campaign and frequently express anti-Western sentiments. But, at the same time, they have been profoundly influenced by Western brands and advertising, more so than any generation that has come before them. The result is a conflicted sense of identity, one that places an extreme value on homeland, yet knowing that adaptation is necessary to excel in a global economy.

To a large extent, a vast number of Chinese young people under 40—now numbering over 750,000,000 citizens of China, or

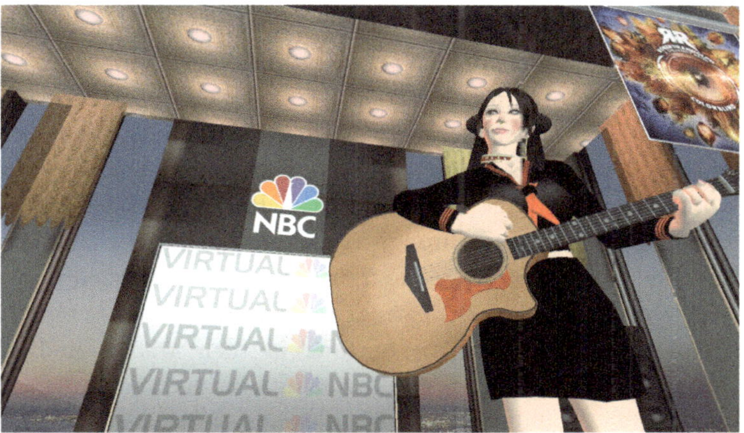

CAO FEI (SL AVATAR: CHINA TRACY), *I. MIRROR*, 2007. MACHINIMA, 28. COURTESY OF THE ARTIST AND VITAMIN CREATIVE SPACE.

more than half the population—are struggling with this identity crisis. Somehow, they must learn to hold their own country in the highest esteem, despite what they have learned about freedoms afforded in other nations that they have encountered when studying and traveling abroad. Meanwhile, the Chinese government grows increasingly repressive, censoring the use of the internet, accompanied by a pronounced crackdown on dissidents and their supporters, in an effort to maintain control despite the invasion of outside influences.

As I witnessed firsthand when I taught at Shandong University in Jinan, the Chinese government has succeeded to a large extent in persuading its youth to support its policies. These students knew that they needed to toe the party line in order to obtain teaching positions and job security. But beyond their immediate career goals, they seemed firmly convinced that Chinese culture was superior to Western imports and entirely believed that success should not sacrifice commitments to one's own heritage.

In contrast, the young Chinese artists that I interviewed in Beijing and Shanghai were a long way from this position. They were acutely aware of government pressures, but were adamant that this would not influence their art-making or philosophical outlook. They were much more concerned with the pressures of the art market, a demand for work that had a global reach and could be shown, appreciated, bought, and sold anywhere in the world. Through education and travel, through residencies in foreign countries, and through exhibitions in Europe and the USA, they had been exposed to the benefits of a globalized world and were eager to participate as leaders, not just bystanders. As such, they spent a lot of time in their studios and in conversations with their peers, discussing what such an art would look like and could be.

Although I had been educated to reject such broad values as "universal" and "international"—thrown to the wayside by much politically correct theory of the 1990s—I had to admit that the art I was encountering in China was fully engaged with such ideas.[5] When I interviewed the painter Qiu Xiaofei in 2016, on the eve of his first New York show at Pace Gallery, he described his process as paralleling that of a DJ, mixing cultural influences as if they were snippets of music. In conversation with Beijing animator Sun Xun, it turned out that his films, while rendered in the brushstrokes of traditional ink painting, were equally influenced by the writings of Aldous Huxley and George Orwell, which explains their pointed critique of recent Chinese history. Time and again, an artist surprised me with the depth of their knowledge of Western history and philosophy, often coupled with superlative technique imparted in a Chinese art academy. Or alternatively, even when the artist employed Western conceptual art practices, their target was often Chinese social issues. These artists shuttled back and forth between cultural vocabularies, even when they had only a rudimentary grasp of English.

"Post-passport" better describes this artistic practice than the overused "universal," in that the artworks come from a variety of cultures and functions in a wide range of locations, even when the artists choose to remain in China. Yet, many of them argued with me that their core issue was the struggle to address "universal values," rooted in a belief in a humanity that transcends national boundaries. While somewhat naive and unspecific, they seem open to a new definition of global culture, one that allows for a penetrable identity. They have come to this belief not through academic study in postmodern theory, which is why some of their ideas seem at first glance unsophisticated. They have reached this conclusion through their own individual life experiences and their personal reactions to a society that once functioned in total isolation.

Individuality is key here and there are as many individual responses to "post-passport identity" in this generation as there are mobile phones. By summarizing how crucial the issue of identity is to this generation, I do not mean to say that there is one aesthetic or trend that dominates their production. These artists work in a variety of mediums, from the traditional modes of painting and sculpture to post-internet productions of 3D animation and digital coding. Also, they address a wide array of issues, from intimate concerns of loneliness and family pressures to sociopolitical issues, ranging from the One Child Policy to the state of China's polluted cities. That is to say, there is not one fixed approach to art-making among these artists or even one identity. In accordance with their varied experiences, there are a full panoply of identities. If anything is a unifying principle, it is their ongoing struggle with the notion of Chinese identity, the notion that a nationality or ethnicity can determine an artist's options.

Obviously, "post-passport identity" does not solely affect Chinese artists but is a force in the lives of many artists throughout the world. I would also argue that it has inalterably changed the way that critics, curators, and collectors look at and experience art. As such, any art movement of the twenty-first century must be inspired by this sociocultural phenomenon to have any lasting currency. If that is the case, the Chinese artists that I have met are at the forefront of such a movement, leading the way for others in these most confusing times. They are particularly adept at dealing with such confusion, given the upheavals in their own country during their brief lifetimes. Certainly, they know a great deal more than we might expect about how to form an identity in the midst of a tsunami of cultural influences.

Young as they are, these Chinese artists are already role models in negotiating a sense of identity at the intersection of global forces. The fact that many of them have figured out how to incorporate localized issues and specifics of biography into their works rescues them from merely imitating and replicating discoveries of Western artists. Their artworks are not derivative, but transitive, fluently conversant in a variety of artistic vocabularies. They embrace history and contemporaneity, the local and the worldly, oriental and occidental, craftsmanship and conceptual strategies. Hopefully, you will find their artworks as original and startling as I have. At the minimum, you may find that something is originating in China that will have lasting impact on our appreciation of contemporary art, both there and here.

1
THE LAST CHINESE ARTISTS

Any assessment of the new generation of artists emerging in China must first begin with an overview of the generation that came before them, those who emerged in the late 1980s and 1990s. They were among the first artists to begin careers after the Cultural Revolution, the first to have exhibitions in China, the first to be acknowledged abroad, and the first to make records at the world's auction houses. In their capacity as ambassadors for a post-Communist yet still relatively isolated and remote country, they carried the burden of explaining China to the rest of the world. And for this reason, among others, their artworks were viewed through the prism of Chinese identity whose artistic merits played second fiddle to their role as guideposts to a new China.

Known for his solemn portraits of Chinese families, Zhang Xiaogang is an artist who has broken all auction records but remains humble and reticent when talking about his life. Born in 1958 and raised in Sichuan Province, he has experienced the upheavals in China over the last six decades, from the Cultural Revolution to its current booming art market. Yet, when he speaks about his paintings, he always talks about them as very personal memories, despite the fact that they have been widely interpreted as political commentary.

Sitting across from him in an elegant room in his Beijing studio, I watch his carefully composed expression as he answers my questions, always considered and considerate without ever quite breaking into a smile. We have known each other a long time, ever since 2007, when he was still chain smoking and drinking as he worked on his canvases late into the night. That was seven years before *Bloodline: Big Family No. 3*, a 1995 painting that sold for over $12 million at Sotheby's Hong Kong, a record for Chinese contemporary art. Today, after a recent heart attack, he lives a much more sober life with no cigarettes in sight, and he works at a slower pace due to doctor's orders. But his success has not ceased, including a 2016 exhibition pairing him with American minimalist artist Sol LeWitt at Pace Beijing, the China outpost of the world-renowned Pace Gallery.

"So much has happened over these past decades that it is hard to summarize in a few words the differences between these two

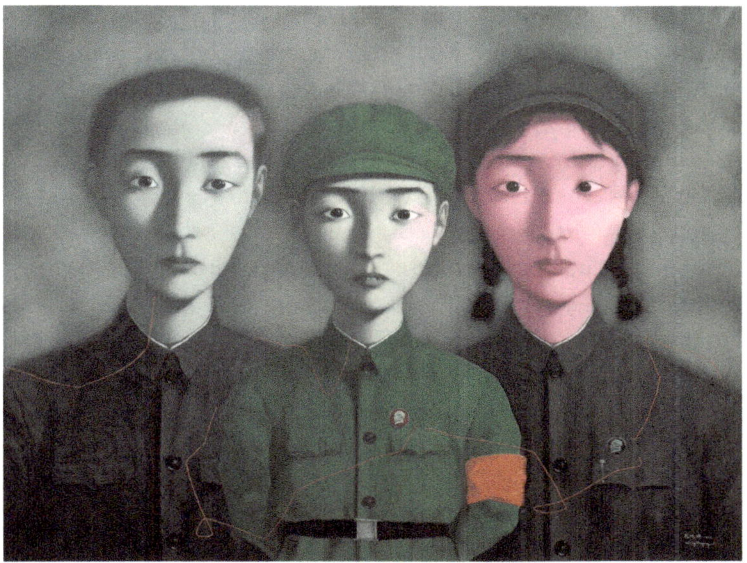

ZHANG XIAOGANG, *BLOODLINE: BIG FAMILY NO. 3,* 1995. COURTESY OF PACE GALLERY.

generations," he begins, when asked to comment on the changes he has observed between his generation and the younger artists that he teaches at the Sichuan Academy of Fine Arts. He was a student there himself in the late 1970s in one of the first classes to graduate after the end of the Cultural Revolution.

Zhang Xiaogang experienced the injustice of the Cultural Revolution firsthand, as an eight-year-old whose parents were sent away for "re-education," living with his brothers under the care of an aunt for most of his childhood. Later in 1976, he was sent to the countryside himself, like so many youth, but he had already picked up the habit of drawing, which allowed him to enter the academy after it reopened its doors when the Cultural Revolution ended. His years at school, and following his graduation, were a heady time, exposing him to Western masters from Impressionists to Surrealists, despite the fact that information was still limited and fragmentary.

"Our hopes, aspirations and value systems at the time are clearly not enough for today," says Zhang. "The knowledge we acquired then seems fairly old now, even though it was really fresh and exciting to us at the time. People were passionate then. Today is the era of information overflow."

It is almost impossible to comprehend the changes that Zhang Xiaogang is commenting on without a brief overview of Chinese contemporary art history. For while it may seem that he was among the first Chinese artists with exposure to Western art trends, the history goes back much farther and is rich with contradictions. In this context, Zhang's resolution of Chinese and Western influences, and his success both on the global stage and within China, are all the more remarkable.

The history of Chinese contemporary art is brief in comparison to art histories of the West, beginning as it did in 1976 with the end of the Cultural Revolution. But the struggle to discover a Chinese modernity goes back much further, at least to the May 4th Movement of 1919, which spawned a New Cultural Movement rooted in Western ideas and opposing traditionalist values. While the history of this period is complex and contradictory, leading eventually to the rise of the Communist Party, the artists of that era are best known for widespread experimentation, drawing from Cubism and post-Impressionism in opposition to the ornate craftsmanship and classical scroll paintings of the Ming and Qing dynasties.

Unfortunately, the Communist Revolution of 1949 put an end to much of this free-spirited expression. Under Mao, art was reformed to serve the people through an endless state-controlled production of propaganda and history paintings glorifying happy peasants and heroic soldiers and formal portraits that idealized political leaders. This political kitsch came to a head with the Cultural Revolution, a period from 1966 to 1976 in which all forms of expression came under attack as the remnants of bourgeois society with the potential to undermine the transformation of Chinese society to a Communist regime. The fallout from this period is well documented, including nearly a million deaths and the complete eradication of an intellectual class, with artists and writers regularly sent to the countryside for what was considered re-education. Even when art schools reopened after 1976, students were still taught to mimic the conventions of Socialist Realist painting, a practice that continues to today.

However, by 1985, Chinese artists, like Zhang Xiaogang, had regained much ground during a period of liberalization leading up to the pro-democracy movement at Tiananmen Square. During the '85 New Wave movement, artists began to smuggle in catalogs from Western art exhibitions and a few prominent artists from the USA and Europe began having shows in China, most notably Robert Rauschenberg and Gilbert & George. Chinese artists leapt on an entire art history kept from them during the Mao era, digesting in one gulp everything from abstract expressionism to Pop Art. This period of experimentation culminated in the landmark *China/Avant-Garde* exhibition, held in 1989 at the National Gallery of Art, now known as the

National Art Museum of China in Beijing. Displaying everything from installation art to performance art, the exhibition had a brief run just months before the crackdown at Tiananmen Square.

By 1990, government censorship forced Chinese artists back underground, but the progress that had been made could not be suppressed. In subsequent years, artists held exhibitions in unofficial places, such as apartments, studios, and empty temples. By the mid-1990s, some of this work had begun to circulate at international art exhibitions outside of China, and Zhang Xiaogang had his first shows abroad. Several leading Chinese artists, such as Cai Guo-Qiang, Xu Bing, Huang Yong Ping, and Zhang Huan, relocated to New York and Paris, finding a warmer reception in foreign cities than in their hometowns.

By the time we come to examine those artists who emerged in the 1990s, such as Zhang Xiaogang and Cai Guo-Qiang, Chinese attitudes towards identity and culture had gone through several transformations and meant many contradictory things. For those artists which remained in China, the questioning of identity was a form of individual expression in opposition to an enforced notion of China imposed by the government during the Cultural Revolution and in the post-Tiananmen era. For government officials whose job was to regulate these artists, Chinese identity was fixed and certain, unquestionably serving political forces that did not tolerate negative portrayals of China. For a new generation of Chinese art critics, "Chinese-ness" was an essential inherited condition, rooted in Confucianism and classical art forms that could be modernized but must remain forever on guard for dilution from Western influences. And for Chinese artists living abroad, Chinese identity was a negotiable state of being, a component of their individuality that could be inserted into a global dialogue.

This variety of ways of expressing identity were not set in stone, and often conflicting ideas could be read into the work of a single artist. For example, Xu Bing made his groundbreaking work *Book from the Sky* in Beijing in 1988, shortly before leaving

China for the USA in 1991. This installation fills a room with scrolls covered in thousands of characters that look like ordinary Chinese, but on closer inspection, turn out to be unique letters invented by the artist; it is impressive in its volume but impossible to read. This work has been interpreted in diametrically opposite ways by two different critics, Gao Minglu and Norman Bryson, in the catalog for the exhibition *Inside Out: New Art from China*, held at the Asia Society and PS1 in 1998, in which it was included.[1] According to Gao, the work represents an emptying of meaning, in keeping with Buddhist notions of negative space, opening a door to viewers' interpretations. To Bryson, the work is a reaction to political and economic forces occurring in China that are breaking down unification in society to the point where shared understanding is impossible. Both interpretations are valid but reflect very different notions of "Chinese-ness," with

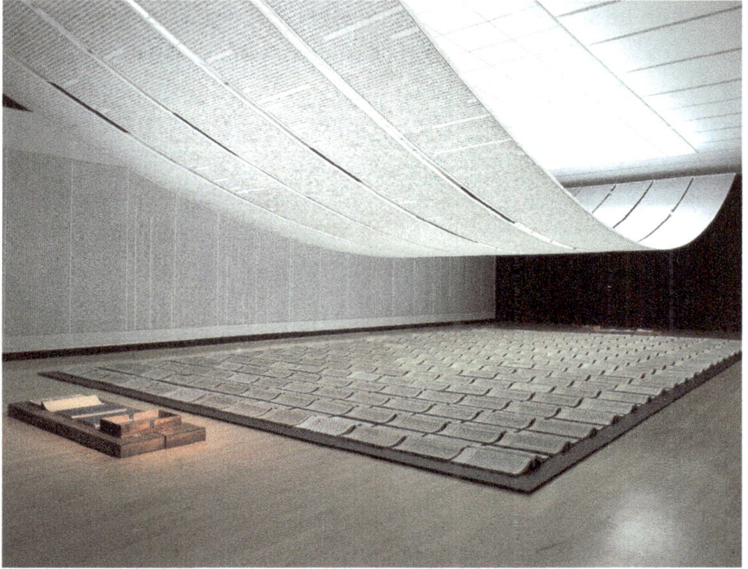

XU BING, *BOOK FROM THE SKY*, 1987-91, INSTALLATION VIEW, NATIONAL GALLERY OF CANADA, 1998. COURTESY OF XU BING STUDIO.

Gao Minglu finding the work to be essentially Chinese because there is a continuity between this contemporary creation and a traditional Chinese outlook, while Bryson regards it as a form of political expression particularized by conditions in China.

Similarly, Zhang Xiaogang has one idea about how he came to make his famous *Bloodline* series, but curators and critics have interpreted the work quite another way. In this series, nuclear families—mother, father, and child—are presented in frontal poses, facing the audience with blank, emotionless expressions. In some, the family appears in Mao jackets, the omnipresent garb of the Cultural Revolution; in others, a thin red line and sheer patches of color connect the figures. These monochromatic compositions, as austere as black-and-white photographs from another era, are similar to Rorschach tests, inviting viewers to come up with their own interpretations not only of the artworks but of recent events in China.

When he started the series in the early 1990s, Zhang Xiaogang had no idea that these solemn characters would become the face of Chinese contemporary art. In 1995, Zhang Xiaogang presented his *Bloodline: Big Family* series in an exhibition entitled *The Other Face: Three Chinese Artists* as part of the larger international exhibition *Identità e Alterità*, installed in the Italian Pavilion during the 46th Venice Biennale. Since then, they have appeared in hundreds of exhibitions and on the cover of auction catalogs, an instantly recognizable iconography that is easily dispersed and understood globally. "This is as strange to me as it is to you," Zhang says to me. "Frankly, I was just concerned with what work I should make to continue being an artist."

Indeed, the *Bloodline* series was the result of a crisis of faith when Zhang Xiaogang saw that he had to reject Western influences in his work such as Surrealism and expressionism to come up with something original. Stymied in his development, in 1992 he fled to Europe, where he stayed for three months, visiting 20 or 30 art exhibitions. In the end, he returned to China, determined to find something authentically Chinese to express in his work. He found it while flipping through old photographs in his parents' house dating back to the 1960s and 1970s, capturing the family at the time of the Cultural Revolution.

"In the 90s, it was important to discover one's own identity. As it was the transition period from Chinese communism to a capitalist market economy, the immediate crisis for me was a crisis of identity," says Zhang. "I was very lost at the time. This difference in identity prompted people to choose between two paths: either join in with international standards, or go back to traditional culture to find one's roots. I chose to delve into contemporary history to discover my own cultural legacy."

Upon further reflection, he uncovered three strains to Chinese identity that he considered essential, namely "western modernism, socialism and traditional Chinese culture." After his sojourn as a foreigner in Europe, he came to realize that "it was very important for a Chinese artist to be conscious of his or her identity, because China was way too different from the rest of the world." This realization allowed him to delve into a more intimate approach to art-making, one that transcended abstract theories and burdensome art history. "My biggest gain from the trip was the realization that art is life—it was an overwhelming feeling," he says.

So, Zhang Xiaogang's emphasis on a Chinese identity is not the result of isolation and ignorance of Western art practices, but a reaction to his initial embrace of those trends. In Europe, he faced his crisis head-on by seeing the masterpieces of Western art history and feeling as if there was nothing more he could add to that legacy. Back in China, however, he was surrounded by a new cultural experience that could not be captured through Western iconography and symbols. His rejection of the West was not total. Instead, he embraced an approach that allowed for innovation in both Western and Chinese traditions for art. This can be seen as a series of abandonments: firstly, a rejection of the Socialist Realism that he studied at the academy; secondly, abandoning his reliance on Surrealism and expressionism; and finally, synthesizing aspects of Surrealism and Western oil painting with imagery derived from recent Chinese history in order to develop his own unique vocabulary.

Because the figures in his paintings are clearly Chinese, even when they are not in Mao suits, it is almost too easy to use them as an example of "Chinese-ness." Far more fascinating is the fact that Zhang Xiaogang felt that he had to struggle to find a Chinese identity in order to continue making art and came to the belief that his work should reflect the Chinese experience. Though not unique to China, and certainly evident in the works of artists from many cultures around the globe, this search for identity underscores how confusing life in post-Mao China was in the 1980s and 1990s, where the fanaticism and idealism of the Cultural Revolution was supplanted by the greed and competition of a capitalist economic system. Many of the artists emerging in the 1990s shared Zhang Xiaogang's dilemma and devoted their time to exploring the meaning of Chinese identity.

"I remember that I gave a lecture in the US around that time and I talked about the fact that China is so young, only 30 years old, but it was a very lonely country and it is this loneliness that I sought to convey through my family portraits," he explains. But often, these paintings were given a pointedly political meaning, either as a critique of the Cultural Revolution or of the emotional harm caused by the One Child Policy. To this artist, these meanings were not his initial intention, though he does not object to people finding evidence of recent Chinese history and political conflicts in his work. "Maybe the day when our historical reality overlaps with that of Europe, there would no longer be any Chinese elements in our artworks," he says. "Chinese elements cannot be seen as simplistic visual codes, but rather something more profound. Sadly, many artists today superficially play with so-called Chinese elements."

Zhang Xiaogang's experience and point of view is framed by the fact that his career rose with the advent of two major art movements in China—Political Pop and Cynical Realism—which captured the disappointment felt after the failed idealism of the democracy protests and the repression of Tiananmen Square. These movements were among the first Chinese art that garnered attention in the USA and Europe, riding a crest of curiosity about China in a post-Cold War era. Often, exhibitions and specialty auctions featuring artworks from the 1990s exoticized China, despite best intentions to the contrary. In this atmosphere, Chinese contemporary art was viewed as standing in opposition or at least in parallel to Western art movements, causing curators and collectors to value art that highlighted "Chinese-ness" over more conceptual projects.

Or, as the leading international curator Hou Hanru, who left China post-1989 and moved to Paris, put it in a 1996 essay:

> These images, because of their "Chinese characteristics," have become ideal commodities for consumer/spectacle society (while the really serious researches of artistic freedom through linguistic/conceptual innovations are largely overlooked and ignored because of their lack of "Chinese characteristics"). In other words, this kind of "Avant-garde" is gradually entering the game of more and more internationalised logic of Western consumer/spectacle society becoming like slogans or news titles which appear and disappear in a twinkle [. . .] In this process, the real beneficiaries are art dealers, journalists and so on.[2]

As if responding to this very criticism and offering a sharp departure from an essentialist view of Chinese identity, the Solomon R. Guggenheim Museum has organized the groundbreaking 2017 exhibition, *Art and China after 1989: Theater of the World*, with Hou Hanru as its curatorial advisor. This exhibition proposes that "Chinese artists have been both agents and skeptics of China's arrival as a global presence, and seeks to reposition a Sinocentric art history in a way that sees China as integral to the emergence of the global contemporary." According to Alexandra Munroe, Samsung Senior Curator of Asian Art at the Guggenheim and chief curator of the show, much of the focus on Chinese identity during the 1990s and early 2000s was the result of market forces, with auction houses and art galleries that specialize in Asian art playing a key role in constructing the way that Chinese art would first be interpreted outside of China. "Auction houses wanted identity, galleries wanted identity and collectors wanted identity," according to Munroe.

This impulse was further bolstered by some of the early exhibitions featuring Chinese art, such as *Magiciens de la Terre* at the Pompidou Centre in Paris in 1989, which set out to counteract the ethnocentricism evident in the vast majority of exhibitions of contemporary art at the time. Offering 50 percent Western artists and 50 percent artists from Asia, Africa, and the Middle East, *Magiciens de la Terre* sought to introduce a host of new identities to the panoply of international contemporary art, but, in so doing, often repeated colonialist gestures that exoticized and estranged artworks from newly emerging art centers. This way of thinking about art from places like China was also reflected in many of the curatorial efforts in the advent of the international biennial circuit. Despite sincere efforts to offer alternatives to the history of postmodernism as developed in the USA and Europe, many of these exhibitions placed particular emphasis on new identities as ready evidence of a multicultural perspective. Posited as progress, these exhibitions played an unwitting role in reinvigorating the importance of cultural identity, a mandate experienced as an imposition by many Chinese artists.

I sat down with two artists, husband and wife Wang Gongxin and Lin Tianmiao, pioneers of the Chinese art scene who had spent ten years in New York in the late 1980s, returning to China in 1994. While they were living in Williamsburg, they attended many gallery and museum exhibitions and were fully familiar with the trend towards multiculturalism at the time, which was not only impacting Chinese artists but was also bringing attention to feminist artists, gay artists, and African-American artists. During their stay in New York, they were not yet able to incorporate this into their artworks, but on returning to Beijing, they found that they were surrounded by experiences and materials that could inform their projects.

"I don't call myself a Chinese artist but an artist working in China—artist comes first," says Wang Gongxin, born in 1960, who makes video installations that often reflect conditions in his homeland. "Our generation cared about the social political pressure, so we will always bring this kind of information into our work. We want to use all those messages from our experience to get a different angle to think about the whole global experience," he says. Having shown internationally for the past three decades, including a retrospective at the National Gallery of Victoria in Australia in 2014, he openly resents the way he was pigeonholed during the 1990s. "If a Chinese artist wanted to participate in a big show, the curators would try to ask you to make something

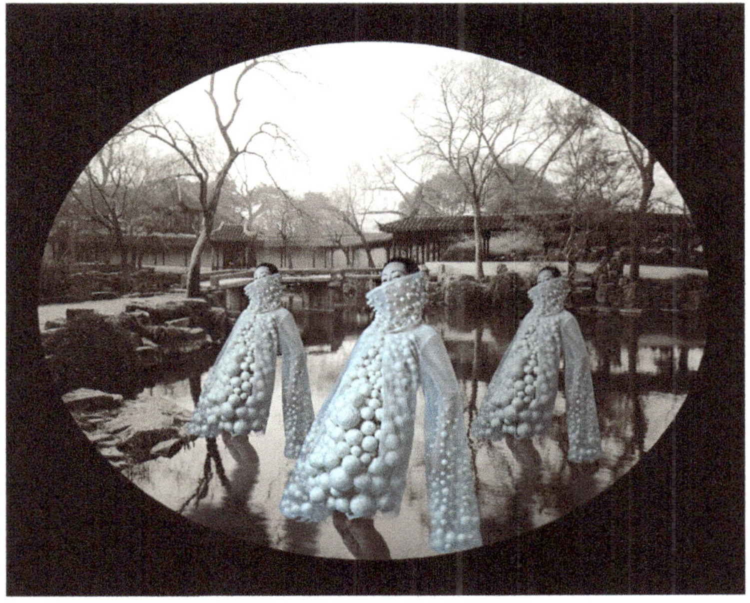

LIN TIANMIAO AND WANG GONGXIN, *HERE OR THERE,* NO. 1, 2002. COURTESY OF GALERIE LELONG.

that outside people could easily realize is by a Chinese artist," he explains.

Recalling a conversation with the late-artist Chen Zhen, who lived in Paris at the time, Lin Tianmiao relates that the artist compared entering exhibitions to attending a dinner party in Europe. "The first sentence is always, where are you from?" says Lin, adding, "Even if you live here twenty years, they suddenly bring you back to where you came from."

Born in 1961, Lin Tianmiao is probably the most famous woman artist in China, with a retrospective at Asia Society in New York in 2012. Her sculptural installations often involve silk thread that is meticulously wound around mundane objects, from bicycles to human bones, a practice she first learned as a child by her mother's side. She admits that she was profoundly influenced by the work of Kiki Smith and other feminist artists whose work she saw in the USA. "I learned that I could approach my work from inside myself," she says. "I am not so concerned with cultural identity but with human identity."

"In the 1990s, that's the period even American people try to use identity themselves, because that period is also politically correct with political messages brought into the art," Wang Gongxin recalls. "We tried to involve ourselves with the art world and we tried to show people our work, but I can feel that they always push you to the corner of Chinese identity so if you did not talk about the subject, they never choose you." But on returning to China, he found an environment rich in material about his personal experiences that he wanted to incorporate into the work. He did this not to emphasize identity but to develop a global dialogue around the circumstances of contemporary China. "Of course, you can look at my work and see my background and my education because there are a lot of images from China, but the artwork doesn't really talk about identity," he says. "It is really about social issues and global matters."

Munroe concurs that for many of the Chinese artists living in the diaspora during the 1990s—Cai Guo-Qiang, Chen Zhen,

Huang Yong Ping—the use of Chinese material was not so much an assertion of identity per se, but an insertion of an alternative history into the conversation about postmodernism that was taking place in the West. By bringing in Chinese artifacts, such as references to Chinese medicine, feng shui, or Qing Dynasty furniture, these artists were not merely establishing their identity as representatives of China, but were offering an alternative to an art history that for centuries had marginalized their culture.

Groundbreaking theorists such as Edward Said, Homi K. Bhabha, and Hou Hanru went a long way in the 1990s toward breaking down the difference between "the center" and "the periphery," calling for a notion of identity that addresses "hybridization" or claims of authority from exiled or nomadic artists. Hou Hanru specifically calls for a concept of identity that goes "beyond" or operates "in-between," a situation that he could particularly identify with having moved to Paris in the mid-1990s, after having established a reputation as a curator in Beijing in the late-1980s. He asserts that China, which defined itself as "the Middle Kingdom" and the center of the world throughout its history, has experienced the twentieth century as a series of attempts to reclaim that position. But, as he recommends upon experiencing the work of Chinese diaspora artists,

> Rather than a "re-centralization" of a "national identity" split within art, artists prefer to expose their inert and inevitable contradictions and conflicts to shake established conception and values, so as to tell the truth; now, we must learn to live in permanent and paradoxical transitions of cultural identities and differences.[3]

A key figure in this discussion is Cai Guo-Qiang, born in Quanzhou in 1957, who left China for Japan in 1986, later relocating to New York in 1995. Known mainly for his experimental fireworks explosions, Cai Guo-Qiang has also created gunpowder drawings and mammoth installations in museums around the world, including a retrospective at the Guggenheim Museum in 2008.

That same year, he designed the fireworks display for the Summer Olympics in Beijing. But he had made a name for himself from early on in his career, receiving the Golden Lion at the 48th Venice Biennale in 1999 for his recreation of the *Rent Collector's Courtyard*, an icon of the Cultural Revolution that he had built from scratch over several months at the biennial. Six years later, he was the curator of the first China Pavilion at the 51st Venice Biennale. On June 15, 2015, Cai realized his most recent explosion event, *Sky Ladder*, off the coast of Huiyu Island, Quanzhou – the subject of a recently released documentary film.

If any artist could be accused of promulgating "Chinese identity" or brandishing Chinese elements, it could be Cai, who has turned the ancient Chinese invention of gunpowder into his primary material. But, from my first meeting with him in New York in the late 1990s, I can assure you that he always viewed himself as a global player, telling me that he was making works for "extraterrestials," including explosions of mushroom clouds in Nevada or an extension to the Great Wall of China with a string of firecrackers stretching several miles in the Gobi Desert. As he told me in an interview in his New York studio in 2015,

> For a long time, people didn't talk about the Chinese theme in my art, but when I participated in the *Inside Out* exhibition curated by Gao Minglu, I executed *Borrowing Your Enemy's Arrows*, which is now in the permanent collection of the Museum of Modern Art.[4]

Borrowing Your Enemy's Arrows, 1998, is a dramatic work in which a full-scale wooden boat hangs from the ceiling, pierced with hundreds of white-feathered arrows. In case the cultural identity of the artist is lost on viewers, there is a miniature Chinese flag waving from its bow. "There is a lot of attention on China, the world is thinking about China, so in a way my piece symbolized a new era where China is sailing into a global arena," he explains. "On the one hand, the boat appears to be hurt and attacked by all these different values and cultures from the outside, but on the other hand, it appears full and soaring into the air."

Cai created the work in 1998 just as China was opening up to foreign investment and becoming an export country in the global market, but his true inspiration was a Chinese tale about a legendary military general. According to the story, the emperor ordered him to produce 100,000 arrows in two days or be killed, so he came up with a plan to extract the arrows from the clutches of his enemy. He launched a fleet of ships into a fog with straw figures on their deck. As the enemy's army shot at the boats, his men collected the arrows, more than 100,000 of them, and brought them back home. His life was spared and the enemy was defeated. One can imagine that Cai, like the general in the story, devised a way to leave China and gain in strength, rather than accept defeat by the outside world's expectations of a Chinese artist.

Perhaps weary of the unrelenting corner that Chinese artists of his generation found themselves in, Cai Guo-Qiang himself

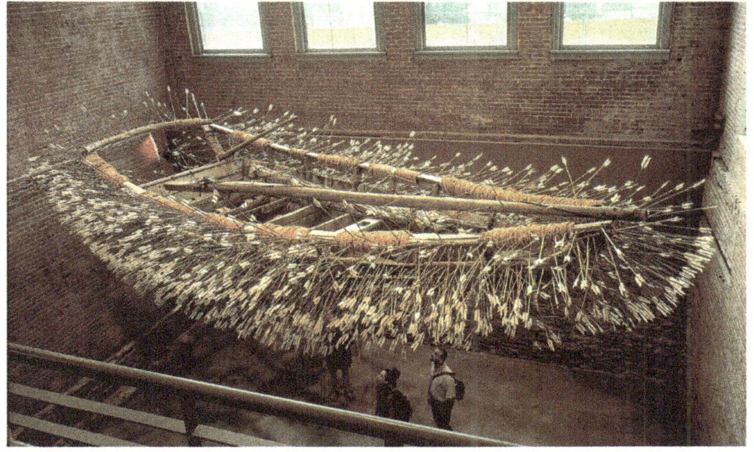

CAI GUO-QIANG, *BORROWING YOUR ENEMY'S ARROWS*, 1998, INSTALLATION VIEW, PS1 CONTEMPORARY ART CENTER, NEW YORK, 1998. PHOTO BY HIRO IHARA, COURTESY OF CAI STUDIO.

curated an exhibition of Chinese contemporary art for a museum in Doha in 2015.[5] Featuring leading Chinese artists, from Liu Xiaodong and Yang Fudong to Liu Wei and Xu Zhen, the exhibition was pointedly titled, *What About the Art?*

"What I thought was missing [from the discussion of Chinese contemporary art] was the artists' individual creativity and I wanted to single that out because a lot of these other exhibitions focused on the socio-political situation, Chinese culture and history," says Cai.

> Of course, these artists were inventing their own creativity and practice. They are investigating their artistic expression and language. But still the focus seems to be the cultural context of China—the history of calligraphy, traditional Chinese paintings, Chinese written language—it's rare that exhibitions truly delve into how they developed and reinvented their own artistic methodology.

As this artist goes on to explain, Chinese artists have entered an international art world that is still dominated by a Western perspective that positions them as the "other"—his words—emphasizing familiarity with the cultural context but ignoring experimentation or creativity. This placed Chinese artists at a disadvantage in relation to artists from other parts of the world, according to Cai. "If you are an artist from Denmark or the UK, when you come to New York, you can't just talk about where you are from or your biography—you have to talk about your expression, your concept, and your methodologies," he says.

"Cai has come to realize that the contemporary Chinese art world has been hijacked by the auction houses and the art market. It has become monolithic with very little nuance or criticality and there is less and less tolerance on the part of the international art world for this phenomena that has been packaged in such a heavy handed way," Alexandra Munroe told me at the time of the Doha exhibition.

> Curatorial practice and critical thinking has been secondary to the market activities in this entire region and in how it is perceived abroad. So Cai asks "what about the art?" and proposes that we look at Chinese artists not as representatives of a nation-state that implausibly would have a single style of art and go back to looking at individual artists and individual practices and what the art says about being alive today.

For better or for worse, Chinese artists of this older generation are themselves in part to blame for playing up their role as ambassadors, rather than individuals, highlighting Chinese identity in their work, sometimes at the expense of other qualities. Even among their peers, a few will acknowledge that by trying to fulfill the expectations of curators and the market, they focused on Chinese cultural elements not only to placate powerful gatekeepers but also to create a bridge between their personal experience and the somewhat limited knowledge of their audiences in the West. They often fused Chinese materials with contemporary art practices, described at the time as a merger of the East–West dichotomy and heralded as a breakthrough in a global dialogue about colliding value systems.

However, over time, this reliance on Chinese characteristics—either as a re-evaluation of identity provoked by vast changes taking place within China or as a sign of resistance to claims of universality propounded by ethnocentric Western art theorists—became a self-limiting strategy that Chinese artists are now rebelling against. Even artists of that older generation, such as Cai Guo-Qiang, Wang Gongxin, and Lin Tianmiao, no longer want to be seen as "Chinese artists," preferring simply "artist." Even Zhang Xiaogang, whose infusion of Chinese imagery into Western painting practices was his innovation, would prefer attention in his own right, rather than as a logo of a brand of "Chinese contemporary art." But even with this newfound struggle, they have not quite managed to escape the nomenclature of Chinese artist; have not quite been assimilated with international art trends.

The dilemma facing so many of this first generation of Chinese artists is that the assertion of identity ultimately leads to a certain kind of invisibility. On the one hand, it can help to secure much-needed critical attention for artists to tap into the widespread interest in China's emerging position on the world stage. On the other hand, it sets Chinese artists off on a separate trajectory, reifying rather than erasing differences between the East and the West. Recent scholarship has tried to rectify this conundrum by shifting the focus away from cultural identity to concepts and innovations by artists in China and the Chinese diaspora. But the advent of a new generation of artists—who are experimenting with the very notion of identity and are redefining what it means to be Chinese—goes much further in bridging cultural divides and making a mark on the global contemporary art world. This new identity embraced by young Chinese artists is rooted in globalization as a personal lived experience, reframing their understanding of country, family, art, and self.

2
ANYONE CAN BE CHINESE

About an hour south of the center of Shanghai, there is an industrial park; like many in China, it is relatively new but already a ruin, with dozens of empty office buildings separated by parking spaces and bald patches of grass. Outside one of these forlorn structures is a lone dog, unhappily yapping in a pen, though there seems to be no one around to pay him any attention. But just inside the adjacent building is an artist's studio packed with assistants and production equipment, five times the size of Andy Warhol's Factory. It belongs to the provocateur Xu Zhen, an artist who has wielded influence in China and abroad since the late 1990s.

Xu Zhen is a pivotal figure in the Chinese art scene, straddling the divide between the older generation of artists that emerged in the early 1990s and the younger generation, many of whom were born after 1980. Born in 1977, Xu Zhen is still quite young himself, but he has been showing so long and with such potency that he is already considered a leader and a mentor for younger artists. Bypassing art school, he began his career in Shanghai with a series of provocative videos. Today, he is known as an artist who has worked in practically every medium—painting, photography, video, sculpture, and installation.

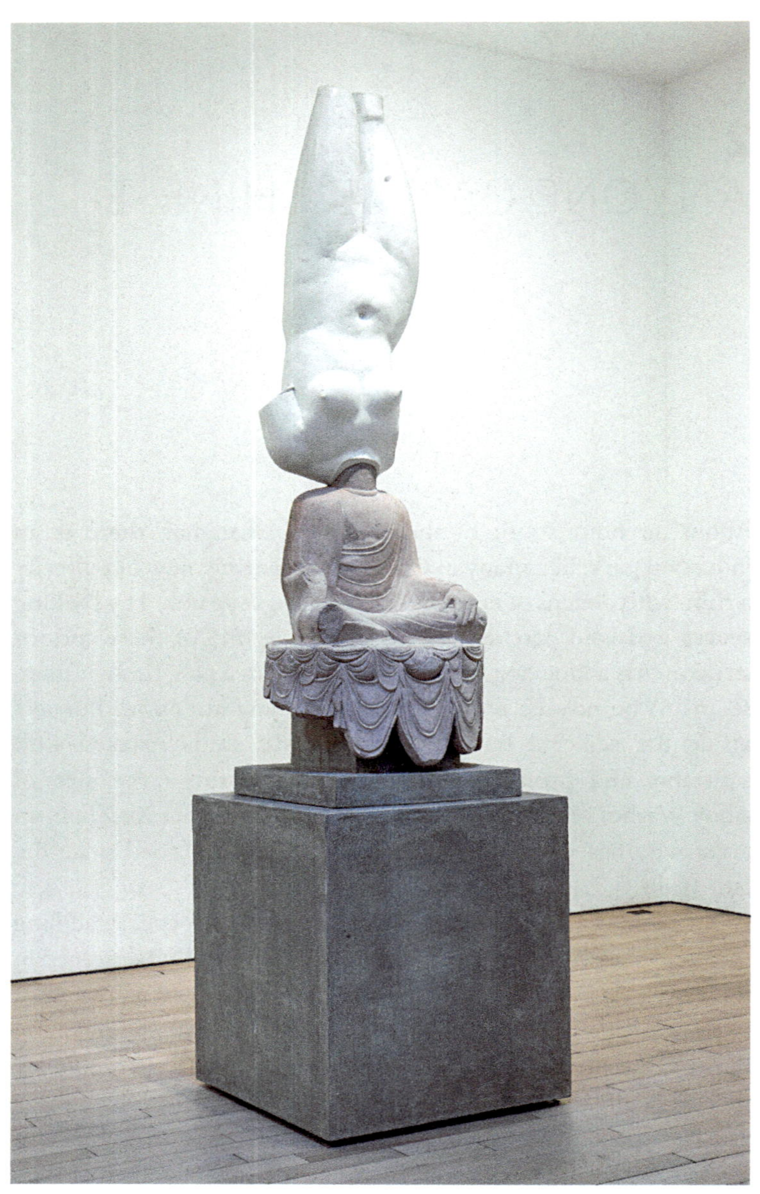

XU ZHEN, *ETERNITY-APHRODITE OF KNIDOS, TANG DYNASTY SITTING BUDDHA*, 2014. COURTESY OF JAMES COHAN GALLERY.

In 2009, at the age of 32, Xu Zhen relinquished his identity as an artist and proclaimed himself CEO of an art-making company, humorously titled MadeIn, after the commercial labeling "Made in China." With already a decade of art exhibitions under his belt, he knew that a Chinese artist could barely escape the pigeonholing of foreign curators and the expectations that his work should bear the markings of Chinese culture. Yet from the start, he seemed to be trying to defeat this categorization, and now with MadeIn, he could certainly stand such stereotypes on their head.

Which is what MadeIn literally did at its most recent exhibitions. Visitors to their shows at the Ullens Center in Beijing in 2014 and the Long Museum a year later encountered mammoth sculptures, amalgamations of Greek and Chinese antiquities, contorted and combined in ways that made a joke of the whole concept of East meets West. A replica of Winged Victory rested upside down atop a headless bodhisattva, the two statues joined at the neck. In another, a line of Greek warriors were reconfigured as a multi-armed god. These were not just inspired revisions of classical icons, East and West, but more of an Animal House game, playing on the expectations of viewers to find something from either culture in works by artists who aspire to go "global." Yes, at biennials and art fairs throughout the world, there were dozens of artists, especially Chinese, who had built careers by merging cultural artifacts. But when MadeIn did the same thing, it was more as a critique of this practice, rather than an homage, a satire sometimes lost on those first encountering the works.

"I have a complex relationship with Chinese traditional culture," Xu Zhen told me once at an interview just before the opening of the MadeIn retrospective at the Ullens Center for Contemporary Art in Beijing. "It's like your parents—you love them but there must be some conflicts in the real life. I think these statues are able to carry many complex emotional aspects." But Xu Zhen, with his long face framed by chic rectangular eye glasses, offers these remarks with a laugh. He speaks Chinese, but no other languages, and never gets on an airplane to travel, so he remains landlocked in China. Yet, more often than not, he has shrugged off his Chinese identity, telling me that, "to be called a global artist is an insult, but to be called a Chinese artist is an even bigger insult."

There are many occasions when Xu Zhen has eschewed references to Chinese culture entirely or mixed up symbols so seamlessly that the only reaction could be total confusion. At one of MadeIn's first exhibitions, the company produced an entire survey of "art from the Middle East," combining aesthetic strategies from conceptual art practices with just enough stereotypes of the war-torn, Islamic-dominated region to evoke a Middle Eastern identity. There were mosques made of Styrofoam and Charlie Hebdo political cartoons woven into tapestries. There were sculptures made of barbed wire and a field of broken bricks set on an invisible waterbed, so the ground seemed to move like a silent earthquake. When these works were shown at James Cohan Gallery in New York in 2009—with the title *Lonely Miracle: Art from the Middle East*—most visitors had no choice but to assume these were products of a collective of Arab artists, which was exactly the point. In this globally driven art world, it is easy to fake ethnicity. All it takes is a bit of irony and just enough cultural references to add locality to the mix.

"Anyone can be a Chinese artist," Xu Zhen once told me. "An American artist can be Zhang Xiaogang," referring to the Chinese art star known for his somber depictions of one-child families and Cultural Revolution devotees. Knowing full well that Western viewers were seeking souvenirs of their trips to the Far East and evidence of their global sophistication in their art acquisitions, Xu Zhen chose to play with these expectations rather than simply feed the market. And if anyone can be Chinese, anyone can be Xu Zhen, which he has proven by allowing MadeIn to be the producers of his artworks.

"MadeIn takes the factory idea of Andy Warhol a step further," states Philippe Pirotte, director of the Kunsthalle Bern where MadeIn showed in 2011.

> Xu Zhen's formation of MadeIn as a company is conscious and self-reflective about the potential power China now has as a world market leader. When the Western world criticizes the Chinese art world as more market than discourse, Xu Zhen answers by saying that the only form of creative collaboration possible in China is a company.

In this particular company, Xu Zhen serves as CEO, overseeing different departments including management, research and development, production, and distribution. In his factory building, he has entire floors devoted to each aspect of this plan, including one floor populated by elderly women stitching surreal images on tapestries and another with young assistants squirting florets of oil paint on canvases like icing on a wedding cake. When asked if renaming MadeIn as the author of his works could be the death of his art career, Xu Zhen shrugs and says, "Bill Gates is as famous as Microsoft and Steve Jobs is synonymous with Apple."

The notion of forming a company, especially one named MadeIn, makes perfect sense in the context of the booming Chinese art market, where artists are known by auction records rather than by retrospectives. For the decade preceding Xu Zhen's founding of MadeIn, an era when auction houses flourished in China while galleries and museums developed at a slower pace, the economics of the art market overshadowed aesthetic appreciation of much of the art activity. Leading Chinese artists, who saw their prices increase exponentially each year, were often better known for their markets than for their artworks. In fact, Western criticism of Chinese contemporary art often looked askance at this boom, labeling it a bubble unjustified by the questionable quality of the artworks involved. In this context, Xu Zhen anticipated such criticism by openly declaring himself involved with a commercial operation, albeit one that often contradicted market trends in its choice of production. Sure, MadeIn made paintings, tapestries, and sculptures that could be easily sold at galleries in China and abroad. But the bulk of their projects, like the Middle Eastern exhibition, were

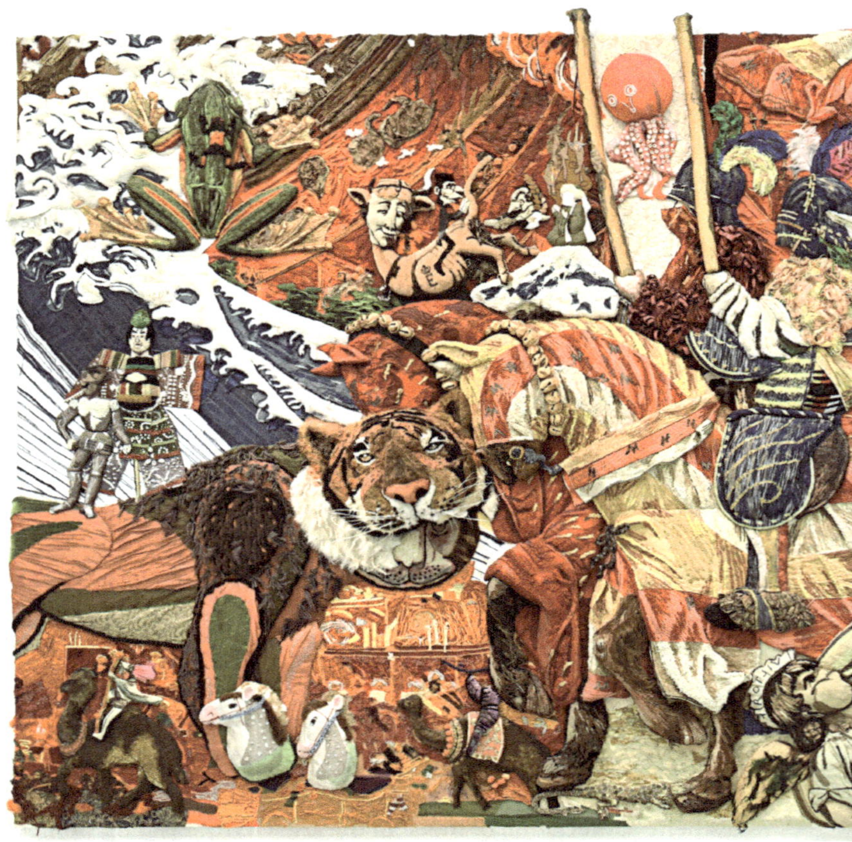

XU ZHEN, *TRIUMPH*, 2015. PRODUCED BY MADEIN COMPANY. COURTESY OF MADEIN COMPANY AND JAMES COHAN GALLERY.

more intent on confusing audiences than satisfying collectors' buying sprees.

For example, MadeIn thoroughly fooled those who attended their 2011 exhibition in Bern. In lieu of artworks, they assembled an exercise routine, *Physique of Consciousness*, based on a combination of the physical actions taken during prayer by all of the world's religions. There were vitrines and posters and videos to demonstrate these routines, and workshops were held with

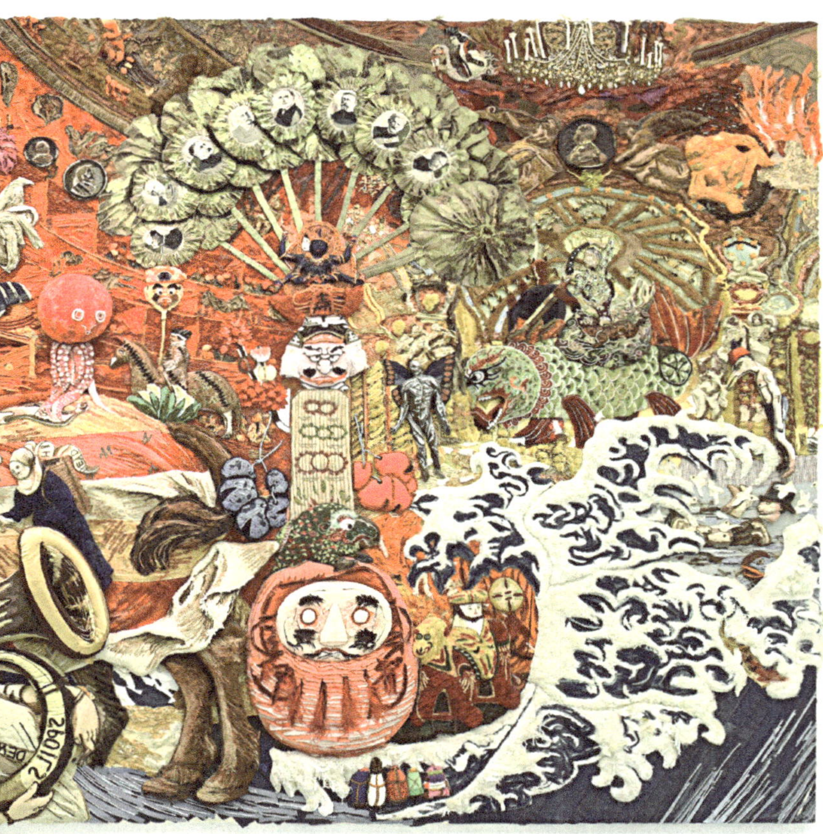

instructors on site to guide participants. In fact, many people did not think it was an art exhibition at all, but rather thought that the museum had turned itself over to a yoga studio for several months.

At the Ullens Center retrospective in 2014—presented under the title *Xu Zhen: A MadeIn Company Production*, as if the artist had become a brand of a multinational corporation—a jumble of artworks were brought together, often contradicting each other.

To enter the exhibition, one had to walk through a replica of a supermarket, complete with goods on shelves and a working cash register at the exit. If you picked up a container of milk or a pack of cigarettes, you discovered that this was mere packaging, entirely empty. In fact, every object had been fabricated by MadeIn specifically for the installation, with every item for sale for no greater cost than milk or cigarettes would carry in an actual supermarket. MadeIn employees were happily ringing up sales at the opening, further blurring the distinction between art and commerce.

This project, in fact, recalled the very first art exhibition staged by Xu Zhen, back in 1999. In that instance, in a Shanghai that had yet to boast any galleries or museums, the young artist, along with a group of friends, staged a show in a shopping mall. "Beijing was then the city of culture and Shanghai was a commercial center, so it made sense to have art in a shopping mall," he explained. The exhibition was short-lived. After a few days, the police shut it down, not because the site was inappropriate, but because one work, an early video by Xu Zhen, was deemed pornographic. Shown on three screens, it depicted a young man and a young woman in their underwear, sniffing each other as if looking for the source of a noxious smell. Today, when so many works have gone much further, this video would probably go unnoticed by authorities. But at the time, and in such a public place, Xu knew he was pushing the envelope.

Testing limits and crossing boundaries seems to be part of Xu Zhen's DNA. Born in a Shanghai yet to be filled with skyscrapers and superhighways, he attended Shanghai Arts and Crafts Institute as a teenager, but did not pursue higher education at an art academy. Instead, encouraged by his father, a carpenter and factory worker, Xu Zhen moved to Beijing to see if he could be part of the emerging art scene there. However, he never met Zhang Xiaogang or any of the other artists that were already achieving stardom in the early 1990s. Hanging out with poets and musicians, he pursued a bohemian lifestyle, but soon grew bored and returned to Shanghai to start his career in earnest. With no training in painting or traditional skills, he turned to video, quickly making a series of works that soon gained him attention at a very young age. In 2001, when he was 24, he was featured at the Venice Biennale with *Rainbow*, a video of a man's bare back turning bright red from a beating, though the violent slaps were never shown on screen. He had already made a not necessarily positive reputation for himself with *Not Doing Anything*, 1999, which shows him slamming a dead cat against the floor until it turns into a bloody pulp. It was removed from an exhibition in Italy, a very immediate reminder to the artist that censorship does not only happen in China.

By 2004, Xu Zhen had grown tired of waiting for a gallery scene to open in Shanghai. At the time, there was but one main gallery in the entire city, ShanghART, which has represented the artist since the beginning of his career. Together with a young Italian expatriat David Quadrio, he set up one of China's first nonprofit alternative spaces. They named it, or, more accurately, misnamed it Bizart, knowing full well that it could never be profitable. Instead, the founders worked day jobs, most often as graphic designers or sometimes as tour guides, funneling their salaries back into the gallery to keep it afloat. Adding the title of curator to his many roles, Xu Zhen used the space to organize many experimental art exhibitions, creating a space for the city's many emerging artists to show when there were few other available venues. Two years later, in 2006, he founded art-ba-ba, an online community that distributes information and reviews about shows, both in China and abroad, with a message board that encourages online discussions. This website is broadly credited with bringing the international art world into the consciousness of a generation of Chinese artists.

"Not only does Xu Zhen work as an artist, as an artistic director, and a curator, but also as a collaborator, as an accomplice, a broker of all sorts, an entrepreneur, an activist, a philosopher and definitely as a tastemaker," says Defne Ayas, director of Witte de With Center for Contemporary Art in Rotterdam who for many years was an independent curator in Shanghai. Xu Zhen was not the first Chinese artist to wear multiple hats. Ai Weiwei, for one, took on the role of ringleader in Beijing during the 1990s when he first returned from a decade in the USA. Bringing with him knowledge of the East Village art scene and the thriving alternative spaces in New York City at the time, Ai Weiwei set up the China Art Archives & Warehouse and edited a series of groundbreaking books documenting the performance art taking place in China at a time prior to the existence of galleries. As a self-taught architect, he built his own studio and designed several homes of artists and later many of the galleries in Caochangdi, a village outside Beijing that became a burgeoning art district. Indeed, Ai Weiwei's studio complex became the go-to place for all visitors seeking information on the Beijing art scene, and for a time, before he ran into problems with the government, he acted as a mentor to many emerging artists.

When asked if he was like Ai Weiwei, Xu Zhen demurred, stating that without an international reputation on par with the master, taking political action would be impossible. But, Xu Zhen's art projects intersect with politics in interesting ways. Movement Field, for example, is an interactive installation in which visitors are encouraged to walk different pathways through a field of grass and trees, each of which are based on routes of famous protest marches. In 2013, when it was originally shown at Long March Space, a gallery in Beijing that often represents MadeIn projects, the indoor space was filled with mounds of dirt and sod, artificial trees, and bushes punctuated by statues commemorating each march. How did MadeIn get away with presenting a work of such political potency? Carefully and conscientiously, by specifically excluding Tiananmen Square from the list of protests.

For Xu Zhen, commenting on politics is a particularly sensitive matter, not because of the threat of censorship, but because it is so expected of Chinese artists. The entire older generation of artists that came before him incorporated political references—Mao, Tiananmen, the Cultural Revolution—into their paintings and sculptures, to the point that it almost became cliché. Even when such references were entirely absent from the artworks, Western commentators often read political meanings into them, finding it impossible to believe that a Chinese artist could participate in an avant-garde without commenting on the oppression of the Communist Party. For younger artists like Xu Zhen, the pressure to be political had become a type of cage, as oppressive as the political system itself. The temptation for many is to become entirely apolitical, turning their attention to pop culture and social issues, rather than focusing on the political system. But for Xu Zhen, the issue of the political is really one of aesthetics. His artworks invite us to question whether it is possible to be able to see China without consideration of its political culture. As he knows full well, the answer for most is a resounding "No."

"Whether I am looking at politics or religion, I am considering people's reactions to something that has influence on each other and forms our history," says Xu Zhen. "Religion is an invisible route, but protests, which are more visible, are often rooted in people's beliefs as well. It looks like they're not related, but they are all tracked in people's behaviors." In considering how to address such weighty issues in his art, Xu Zhen starts by designing an experience that may later cause people to question their beliefs.

> You have to have the physical sensation before you can make a decision. For example, as Chinese, we never actually vote, so if now we give you the right to vote, how do you make the choice? If you don't have the experience, it's hard for you to know which way to take. My values come only after I see something or experience something. I think that response is more responsible. So a big feature in our artworks is to open your sense of feelings and then you can make your own judgment.

At the same time, Xu Zhen and the artworks by MadeIn seem calculated to make viewers doubt their own judgments. One of Xu Zhen's most famous works is *8.848-1.86*, referring to the height of Mount Everest minus the artist's height in meters. The installation, shown in 2006 at ShanghART, was a faux documentary account of scaling the world's highest summit and hacking off the peak to bring it back to Shanghai. There in the gallery in a refrigerated, oversized vitrine was the top of the mountain, a snowy peak encased in glass. Other items in the gallery included a video of the expedition, oxygen tanks and other equipment used to make the trek, photographs and detailed entries in a travel log. It was so convincing that many reviewers writing about the show accepted that the climb had been made and that Everest was now a bit shorter.

"It is conceptually witty, it is provocative, it deals with all kinds of things in a lighthearted way," says Simon Groom, who included the work in an exhibition at the Tate Liverpool in 2007. "This work really played into foreign perceptions of China's insensitivity to surrounding countries. It is about what is

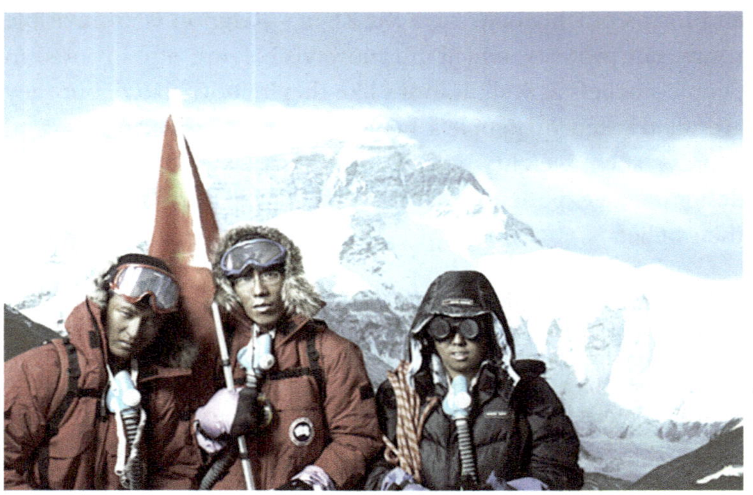

XU ZHEN, *8.848-1.86*, 2005. COURTESY OF JAMES COHAN GALLERY.

authentic in a country where you have selective truth and yet the country is changing so fast that the concept of truth itself becomes a slightly misleading term."

Xu Zhen's last show as an artist, before he became CEO of MadeIn, was his most provocative. For his 2008 installation, *The Starving of Sudan*, he turned the white box of Long March Space into the scene from the 1963 Pulitzer Prize-winning photograph by Kevin Carter of an emaciated African child being eyed by a vulture waiting for him to die. In the gallery, Xu Zhen stationed a real child near an animatronic stuffed vulture, insinuating visitors into an act of callous voyeurism. Impromptu photographers whipped out cell phones to capture the scene, thereby reenacting the questionable neutrality of the photojournalist in the first instance. The installation generated heated discussion. Foreigners raised issues of exploitation, fearing for the welfare of the child performer. Chinese viewers, however, thought it was a bitter commentary on China's incursion into Africa and the broader exploitation taking place on the global stage.

Both of these works demonstrate Xu Zhen's complex approach to truth and reality in the Chinese context. In a country where censorship still plays a dominant role, and where many artists self-censor to avoid controversy, this artist seeks to make works that cannot be accepted at face value. He challenges viewers to sort out for themselves what is real and what is fabricated, what is truthful and what is deception. Magically, he skirts the censors' control even as he references Tibet, in the case of Mount Everest, or China's incursions into Africa, as with the *Starving of Sudan*. And yet, he has often been considered rude or impolite for raising these topics at all. It is precisely by placing the responsibility of interpretation on the viewers that he manages to get away with it all.

Likewise, Xu Zhen deflects easy summation of his work as the product of a Chinese artist by complicating his presentation of reality. Realism is historically the *sine qua non* of Chinese art, evolving in the present era from the influence of Socialist Realism during much of the twentieth century. Even those artists who emerged in the 1990s, all of them trained in hyperrealistic painting techniques, were directly influenced by the dominance of realist painting, even as they did their best to evolve from that restrictive style. So, in an earlier period, depictions of Chinese cultural symbols, ranging from Cultural Revolution iconography to Ming furniture, could be read without irony as references to Chinese reality. Xu Zhen, representing the new and younger generation, refuses such simplistic correlations, challenging the very way viewers might read an artwork and relate it back to a Chinese context.

"It's not about the East–West collision per se," explains Phil Tinari, director of the Ullens Center for Contemporary Art. "It's about the received notion of the East–West collision. It's about the fact that it's such an obvious and easy way to look at things and yet one that still holds so much sway." He compares Xu Zhen not to Warhol, but to Jeff Koons, especially with the artist's interest in the "lingering power of cliché," noting that even the notion of a Chinese context has also become a cliché. "If we didn't have this idea of some difference between East and West, I don't think that globalization would make sense to most of us, and Xu Zhen is poking fun at this strictly bipolar way of looking at things." This is especially interesting coming from an artist based in China, where the one-party system marks a definitive schism with much of the West. Instead of critiquing the political system directly, according to Tinari, this artist goes deeper, investigating the roots of absolutism, which lies in the misconception that an individual's beliefs are reality. A mistaken belief in the real—whether it is from a Chinese perspective entailing an absolute acceptance of government-sponsored information, or from the West and its confident expectation of difference—is Xu Zhen's actual target.

In fact, what Xu Zhen is actually questioning is the very meaning of a "Chinese context," given the massive impact of globalization on his home country. The Shanghai of his youth no longer exists, and, if anything, his definition of identity is rooted more firmly in a borderless internet culture than in Imperial dynasties or communist iconography. It is important to see how Xu Zhen, an early adopter of the internet with the establishment of art-ba-ba.com, understood from the outset the influence that online culture can have on his generation. "We no longer think of ourselves as Shanghai artists, or even Chinese artists," he says. "Whether you are in New York or London or Beijing, you share the same culture. Like it's absurd to ask a hacker which country he comes from." And, like a hacker, Xu Zhen is an avid internet surfer, scooping up icons and images he finds online and recycling them in many of MadeIn's art projects.

In the tapestry *Fearless*, 2012, for example, a large phoenix, complete with feathers, soars through the center of the work, surrounded by Friedrich Nietzsche, John Nash's cartoons, medieval revelers, and a mammoth snake—all taken from Western art history, without a dragon or Mao in sight. It is MadeIn's intention to defy expectations regarding which images a Chinese artist might appropriate, and what this all has to do with China at all. In doing so, the project speaks volumes about what is real in China today, a country flooded with knock-offs of Western brands and where illegal DVDs are sold on every corner. In this context, perhaps the most genuine thing that can be found in China is not a contemporary rendition of ink-and-scroll painting, but an uncanny replication of foreign iconography. For Xu Zhen, the genuine in China is a matter of artifice in the extreme.

Given his role as trickster and organizer, it was surprising yet perfect that Xu Zhen was chosen to be the honored artist at the 2014 Armory Show in New York. Each year, the fair selects a country or region to celebrate, and that year, China was featured with 17 galleries specially invited to participate. MadeIn was recruited for a year-long engagement, developing logos and signage for the event and creating a singular work of art to be exhibited among the booths of commercial galleries. Realizing that the occasion required a degree of spectacle, MadeIn presented *Action of Consciousness*, 2011, a ten-foot enclosed cube in which 50 arbitrary objects are tossed high in the air by two hidden performers. The items range from a soft sculpture model of Tiananmen Square to a bust of van Gogh, and viewers outside had only a second or two to observe them. "I think this artwork will be perfect against the backdrop of the Armory Show because at a fair people move very quickly to browse and only look at the art for a second," Xu Zhen said at the time, suggesting how the work is as much a critique as a celebration.

"I think it is particularly fun to work with an artist who questions the very nature of being an artist," said Tinari, who served as curator of the Chinese participants and selected Xu Zhen for this prestigious position. However, Xu Zhen wasn't there to gauge audience reaction. After experiencing severe turbulence on a flight from Berlin in 2005, he refuses to fly. Instead, staff members from MadeIn were called in to install and

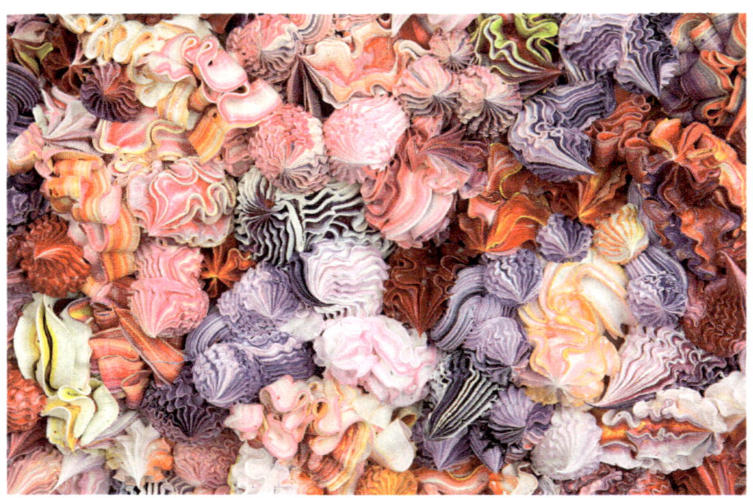

XU ZHEN, *UNDER HEAVEN—3208NH1409* (DETAIL), PRODUCED BY MADEIN, 2014. COURTESY OF JAMES COHAN GALLERY.

perform while the artist followed coverage over the internet, as usual. To confuse matters all the more, MadeIn also manned a booth, like a commercial gallery, showing works by two lesser-known emerging Chinese artists.

Absenting himself from the proceedings could be interpreted as a self-destructive move by another artist. After all, the Armory Show, with all its attendant publicity, would be a prime opportunity for a Chinese artist to introduce himself to an American audience. But, it seems to be part of Xu Zhen's plan to eliminate his visage as much as possible, allowing MadeIn to take center stage. It is a calculated move, since his participation, with the necessary translator at hand, might come off as introducing an unavoidable note of exoticism and difference, when MadeIn's main goal is to eliminate such stereotypes. *Action of Consciousness*, itself just a big box with objects flying upwards for a second or two, further defeated any celebration of Xu Zhen as an individual artist. According to Xu Zhen, he is now just a brand, like Marc of Marc Jacobs, and even then he refuses to be advertised. Increasingly anonymous, he is becoming more famous still, the beneficiary of unparalleled opportunities.

"This is now, this is now in China, and his work, more than anyone else I can point to, combines a humanism and a confusion that is the order of the moment," says Tinari "We no longer are sure what we believe in—and it is not cynical. It is a step beyond cynical." Knowing full well that what Westerners are often looking for in their search for artists from other cultures is a degree of authenticity, Xu Zhen authentically refutes this desire. His strategic complication of identity defeats any stereotyping of himself as a Chinese artist. Anticipating the critical dismissal of Chinese contemporary artworks as derivative or second-rate, as is so often the case in the West, he abandons the nomenclature "Chinese artist" entirely, preferring to describe himself as "based in China but working in a global context." Just what that means has yet to be defined by this artist, or any of the artists working in the younger generation in China. But as Xu Zhen proves, this does not mean merely abandoning China for the West, or eliminating Chinese references. It may very well mean adopting a complexity, sophistication, and wit that encapsulates the many contradictions in present-day China, while confronting a narrow-mindedness still dominant in the West.

3
CHINESE ABSTRACTION

While Xu Zhen seeks to sow confusion about cultural categories by creating a mash-up of East and West, many other artists of his generation try to transcend that basic dichotomy entirely. Abstraction would seem like the likely vehicle for achieving this goal given that art without figuration or representation offers the possibility of universal understanding, but that remains an unfulfilled ideal. In point of fact, the history of abstraction in China diverges greatly from its evolution in Europe and the USA and may need to be understood in a different context, which has led several influential Chinese art critics to insist that there is a genre called "Chinese abstraction," standing in opposition to the practice in the West.[1]

Despite this ongoing debate, abstract art is on the rise among young Chinese artists. When the American collectors Don and Mera Rubell opened their exhibition, *28 Chinese*, at their family museum in Miami in December 2013, ten of the artists chosen were abstract practitioners. These ranged from Lan Zhenghui and Zhu Jinshi, representing an older generation, to Zhao Yao, Liu Wei, Li Shurui, Shang Yixin, Wang Guangle, and Xie Molin, all new artists on the scene. While some of these artists may be viewed as representative of "Chinese abstraction," far more favor abstraction for its global reach and its ability to transcend national boundaries.

Born in 1976 in Fujian Province, Wang Guangle is a transitional figure in this debate. Entering his industrial studio on the edge of Beijing, I am confronted with canvases that look like narrow hallways leading to blacked-out destinations. These rooms with no exits are an illusion created by the systematic application of paint in rectangles from the edge of the canvas to the center. The frightening sensations that these paintings evoke are no accident. Wang hit upon this method of making work from a ritual of painting coffins that he witnessed in his childhood, whereby a layer of lacquer is applied each year until the intended recipient dies. Nothing could be farther from the realist painting he studied at school at the China Academy of Art in Hangzhou, graduating in 2002.

"When I create my works of art, it is other people who call them 'abstract,' not myself," he claims, even though he has been heralded as the leader of the new abstraction emerging in China at this time. In the West, abstraction is also on the rise among younger painters, with one critic, Walter Robinson, describing the trend as "zombie formalism," meaning that it is merely decorative work devoid of deeper meaning. In some ways, the art emerging from China in recent years can also be accused of such superficiality. But, in the case of Chinese artists, this is a hard-earned choice to *be* superficial, and in so doing, to be unleashed from the burden of history and politics.

Wang Guangle denies a connection to Western abstraction, insisting that he is unschooled in this history and came upon his signature style in a very different way. "Even though my work looks abstract, it isn't really abstract," he says, explaining that, although he is aware of the work of Mondrian and Mark Rothko, he hadn't seen their paintings in person until he came to New York for his first exhibition at the prestigious Pace Gallery in 2012. He insists that, in contrast to their use of forms, his work comes out of a practice of ritualistic repetition. "I have a daily routine, such as getting out of bed, brushing my teeth, or catching the bus to work; I abstract time from this series of activities, and eliminate the specific content, using repetition to convey meaning," he explains.

According to the esteemed curator Gao Minglu, this is an example of "Chinese Maximalism," a phrase he coined in 2003 to contrast developments in Chinese art with American Minimalism.[2] What he saw in the work of Chinese artists emerging in the 1990s was a practice that resulted in abstract forms but was actually an encapsulation of mundane repetitive actions. He applied this term to artists ranging from Ding Yi and his obsessive use of squares and crosses to Zhu Jinshi, who troweled onto his canvases piles of oil paint until they looked like waves of lava. According to Gao, this use of repetition instilled in the artworks a fundamental relationship to spiritual concerns, as found in classical Chinese painting, rather than the concern with form evident in Western abstract paintings.

> From the perspective of pure visual language, "Maximalism" has developed the conventions of "process," "replication," "continuation," "movement," "dispersion," and "arbitrariness" present in Chinese traditional art, just as it has preserved and developed the harmonious relationship between the artist's mentality and the works' mentality that is a hallmark of Eastern aesthetic thinking. All in all, "maximalism" as a methodology, whether seen in its traditional elements, or in its contemporary critical insights, has an obvious "Chineseness" as its essence.

This insistence on a Chinese essence is a defensive posture, calculated to address accusations that the abstractions of these artists were merely "derivative" of Western techniques. Of course, by the time Gao wrote this thesis, Western abstract art had already undergone a century of development, producing Kandinsky, Mondrian, Pollock, de Kooning, Frankenthaler, Rothko, Reinhardt, LeWitt, Martin, and Stella, to name but a few. Chinese artists might be seen as playing "catch-up" or, worse, lagging far behind their peers in the West.

To counter such accusations, an argument developed that China invented abstract art centuries ago when literati painters experimented with unique forms of calligraphy;[3] and that claims that abstraction began in the twentieth century overlook a myriad of forms created by other cultures that have often been disregarded by Eurocentric historians as "tribal" or "craft."[4] No one knows what would have happened if experimentation in calligraphy and brush-painting continued unabated to contemporary times. But this practice was halted suddenly with the advent of Mao in 1949, who advocated for an art that served the People, namely, state-controlled production of Soviet-style Socialist Realism. Art forms like calligraphy were viewed as counterrevolutionary and artists trying to further this tradition were forced to go underground.

At the same time, many mid-century emigré Chinese artists abroad intentionally merged Asian and Western approaches to abstraction. The most famous of them is Zou Wou-ki, who emigrated to Paris in the 1940s and had a long career combining cross-cultural influences on canvas. Zou Wou-ki and other artists were particularly fascinated with bringing techniques from calligraphy and ink painting into the vocabulary of postwar abstraction, an innovation still rooted in an East–West dichotomy. Not exclusively Chinese, many American and European masters appropriated ideas and forms from Asian art and philosophy, from action painting rooted in calligraphic gestures to minimalist works referencing Zen Buddhism.

With the end of the Cultural Revolution in 1976, a new swell of artistic activity burst forth in China, culminating in the '85 New Wave movement. A flood of material on Western art movements in magazines and in catalogs flowed into China, everything that artists had been missing in the previous decades, from abstract expressionism to Pop Art to Minimalism. Instead of the linear evolution from movement to movement that ostensibly happened in the USA and Europe, Chinese artists instantaneously dove into a sea of abstract styles—from action painting to

Minimalism—as a route out of state-dominated political art. Abstract art was not the dominant art form of the 1980s and 1990s. Political Pop, which ironically combined Andy Warhol with iconography from the Cultural Revolution, received far more attention. And after the impact of the Tiananmen Square crackdown, another movement called Cynical Realism, featuring somber and sarcastic depictions of life in a repressive China, also attracted the spotlight. Those artists who had been trained in realist paintings in the newly opened art academies retained a connection to figuration. But, at the same time, abstract artists emerged, far less commercially successful, though more recently gaining market attention. These artists are the focus of Gao Minglu's essay on Maximalism, artists who he insists were not merely imitating advances from the West but were redefining abstraction in purely Chinese terms.

A prime example noted by the eminent art historian Wu Hung, a professor at the University of Chicago, is *Assignment No. 1: Copying "Orchid Pavilion Preface" a Thousand Times*, 1995, by contemporary artist Qiu Zhijie. As Wu asserts in his essay, "Negotiating with Tradition in Contemporary Chinese Art: Three Strategies":

> Following the traditional method of calligraphic learning, [Qiu Zhijie] copied ancient masterpieces, often in the form of ink rubbings reproduced from stone steles. Assignment No. 1 utilized this traditional method of studying calligraphy, but it is also a deconstructive analysis of China's cultural heritage and of the artist's own artistic experience. For three years, from 1992 to 1995, Qiu Zhijie continued copying the preface of the Orchid Pavilion, the most celebrated masterpiece of Chinese calligraphy, on a single sheet of paper. This tedious exercise produced two concrete results: a piece of imageless calligraphy and a video that records the gradual obliteration of the original text.[5]

The final work therefore has the black smudges and dark clouds of a Cy Twombly, yet is rooted in Chinese practice and philosophy.

A work like *Assignment No. 1* complicates the bifurcation between Chinese painting (*guohua*) and Western art (*xihua*), a division that has existed in China since the end of the Cultural Revolution.[6] This categorization of art is so entrenched that it governs academic training, professional criteria, and even art criticism. The challenge for many Chinese artists emerging in the 1980s and 1990s was how to modernize *guohua* without entirely succumbing to *xihua*. The solution for a number of them was what has come to be called "experimental ink painting," which has spawned its own brand of abstraction, where calligraphic gestures without textual meaning can be evaluated as nonrepresentational art. Several of the leading practitioners of "experimental ink"—Zhang Yu (b.1959), Wang Dongling (b.1945), and Yang Jiechang (b.1956)—were featured in the Metropolitan Museum's groundbreaking 2013 exhibition, *Ink Art: Past As Present in Contemporary China*, curated by Maxwell Hearn and Wu Hung. Though this exhibition employed a very wide definition of "ink art," including photography, sculpture, installation, and new media in addition to painting, it still operated in a way as to reaffirm the vitality of the *guohua–xihua* division, bordering on a celebration of contemporary *chinoiserie*.

While experimental ink painting is a growing field, excelling at auction houses and galleries, many of the younger artists now emerging on the international scene entirely reject the division between Chinese and Western painting, choosing instead to transcend the East–West dichotomy by embracing influences from either direction to make bold, unique statements.

Wang Guangle might have grown up with limited exposure to Western abstract painting, but many of his peers are thoroughly conversant in multiple art histories. For them, the search for a universal language is not a pipe dream but a wholesale rejection of the categorization first presented to them in art school that forced them to choose between majoring in *guohua* or *xihua*. Now, in an age where so much of art falls in neither category—especially as photography, video, and new media are on the rise in

China—their goal is to globalize their artworks as much as possible to take advantage of international opportunities.

Born in 1972, Liu Wei is a pioneer in the new type of abstract art emerging in China in the last decade. As he has expanded his exhibition career internationally—with recent exhibitions at Samsung Museum of Art in Seoul (2016); Ullens Center for Contemporary Art in Beijing (2015); Museum Boijmans Van Beuningen in Rotterdam (2014); and Minsheng Art Museum, Shanghai (2011)—he has developed his multidimensional practice from provocative videos to installations with sociopolitical underpinnings to geometric canvases generated by computer programs to his most recent environments based on phenomenological theories.

"Liu Wei has a really ambitious scope of ideas that he is thinking about," says Asia Society chief curator Michelle Yun.

> You can look at his work in a microcosm and how it relates to his kind of experience growing up in this modern day China but you can also look at it in terms of how all societies have evolved. They are very timely in one way, but because they are very universal, they are also timeless.

In a 2016 show at PLATEAU, Samsung Museum of Art, Liu Wei created an installation, *Panorama*, from the cast-off doors and walls of industrial buildings that were being demolished in Beijing. The final sculptures were full of off-kilter geometric designs that entirely incorporated the ready-made materials. This and earlier installations in this series have been interpreted as a critique of the urbanization of China's cities; a study of the erasure of memory as development wipes out all traces of traditional architecture. But in a more recent exhibition, at Lehmann Maupin's two galleries in New York in the fall of 2016, he eschewed even this level of identifiable references for a more radical approach to installation. In the first gallery, he turned the place into a funhouse maze by bifurcating the space with an enormous mirrored cube that viscerally altered the sense of the architecture. Viewers had to renegotiate the gallery, confronted at every level with new reflections of themselves. In the second gallery, he created a kind of obstacle course that incorporated mirrors, odd-shaped objects, skewed, and curved canvases and a platform covered in olive-green military material. The sensation was akin to walking into a three-dimensional cubist painting.

"There is no dichotomy between the abstract and the figurative in my work; the abstract can be figurative, and vice versa. The most fundamental element of everything we see is abstract in nature," Liu Wei told me on the eve of his New York opening. Explaining that he is no longer interested in globalization, he offered that his recent work is more about a new way of seeing by creating "realities" that can alter the viewers' point of view. His earlier work could be ostensibly linked to Chinese realities while maintaining an abstract form, yet his recent work entirely liberates him from this interpretation,

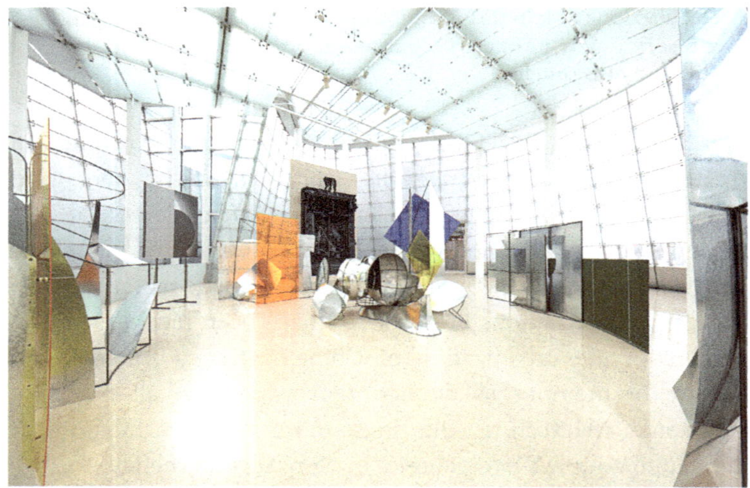

LIU WEI, *PANORAMA*, INSTALLED AT PLATEAU, SAMSUNG MUSEUM OF ART, SEOUL, 2016. COURTESY PLATEAU, SAMSUNG MUSEUM OF ART, SEOUL, KOREA, THE ARTIST, AND LEHMANN MAUPIN, NEW YORK AND HONG KONG. PHOTO: SANG TAE KIM.

addressing more individual psychological states in the act of seeing and experiencing art.

When asked about whether the work has an inherent "Chinese-ness," he provides a complex answer:

> Why does it have to be Chinese? "Chinese-ness" is more rooted in your value systems and philosophy, not superficial symbols. In that way, the presentation does not have to be manifestly Chinese. This is a problem plaguing Chinese artists. Contemporary art is a Western concept, and is supported by a different philosophical system. For Chinese artists, it's very different, because we grew up in a different social-political reality, with our own education systems, aesthetic standards, value systems, and so on. But it's not a matter of simple appropriation. Admittedly, this is a dilemma for Chinese artists, because you constantly question whether you are abandoning traditions for something completely Western.

Liu Wei is discovering ways to eliminate the conflict between Chinese and Western experience by concentrating on individual visual responses. Yet, it is telling that as an artist who was born at the tail-end of the Cultural Revolution and who experienced the total overhaul of his society, he retains the visceral sense that there is a difference between his and a foreigner's appreciation of the world. Younger artists have almost totally abandoned even this tenuous connection to "Chinese-ness," insisting that it has been replaced by a much more global identity, particularly well expressed through abstract art.

Norwegian jazz-electronic band Supersilent are cited as the favorite group of Chinese artist Qiu Xiaofei, born 1977, who plays their music for inspiration as he paints in his studio on the outskirts of Beijing. Like this musical troupe, which never rehearses and mixes noise and improvisational sound freely at their concerts, Qiu takes layers upon layers of art history, both East and West, and mixes them freely in his large-scale, brightly colored canvases with waves of luscious brushstrokes, punctuated by solid geometric forms, such as spheres, cones, and spirals.

In one, *Temple Base*, 2014–15, a spunky green pine tree stands out atop a pile of chaos, with no clear indication of a Buddhist retreat. In another, *Zero Gravity No. 1*, 2015, a line of three-dimensional balls roll across a forest floor, combining abstract forms and a pastoral setting.

"In my work, you can find realism, abstract expressionism, and other contemporary elements, like spray paint, and all this friction adds excitement to the work," he tells me through a translator. "A traditional artist would concentrate on distilling down to one iconic style. But I have a more democratic approach, borrowing from a lot of styles and points of view to interact with each other on one canvas." Qiu Xiaofei would never claim to be directly rebelling against such pioneers as Zhang Xiaogang or Cai Guo-Qiang, who placed Chinese elements prominently in their works. Instead, he would say that every facet of his art history education—from his training as a realist painter in school to his early exposure to Robert Rauschenberg and his most recent appreciation of abstract expressionism—can be discerned in his multilayered paintings. Nothing is discarded or disregarded in works that blend art history with personal neurosis.

Born in Harbin in 1977, Qiu's exposure to Western art came at an early age. His father, a newspaper editor, was an avid fan of art who encouraged his son to take drawing lessons as a child. He remembers going to art exhibitions with his father, including the groundbreaking exhibition of Robert Rauschenberg's work that opened at the National Art Museum of China in 1985. Although he couldn't understand the work at the time, it had a transformational impact on him, as it did so many Chinese artists of that generation.

As a teenager, he entered the preparatory school of the Central Academy of Fine Arts, where he remained through college and graduate school. There, in the school's library, he encountered da Vinci and Duchamp, in no particular order. "I did not learn Western art history sequentially, but all of it, all at the same time," he recalls.

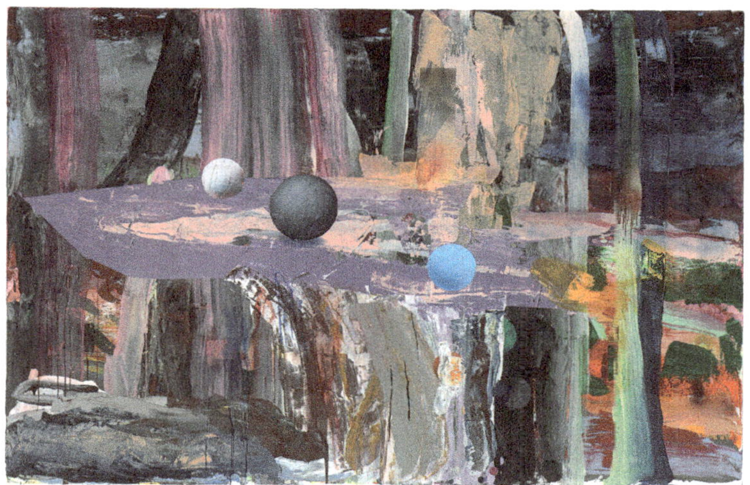

QIU XIAOFEI, *ZERO GRAVITY NO. 1*, 2015. COURTESY OF PACE GALLERY.

Trained in realist painting, as is required at Chinese art academies, Qiu Xiaofei quickly turned to a more expressionist style rooted in personal memories and recent news headlines. In his breakthrough work, *Utopia*, 2010, he depicted a post-apocalyptic cityscape featuring a headless statue with an outstretched arm—similar to the hundreds of statues of Mao found in China—overseeing a field of severed heads. It is a perfect encapsulation of the shattered idealism of his generation, who grew up in the aftermath of the political zealotry of the Cultural Revolution. But, he was also already experimenting with installations and incorporating found objects into his work, very much influenced by Raushenberg's assemblages and combines, best exemplified by his work *Dissipate Drunkenness*, 2014. Assembled in a seemingly haphazard fashion, the installation's studied casualness and improvisational spirit challenged conventional notions of "realism" by juxtaposing found elements and the artist's paintings. It injected a dose of playfulness in a Beijing art scene that at times takes itself much too seriously.

In the course of this development, Qiu Xiaofei moved away from any remnants of realism and dove headlong into abstraction, sometimes employing calligraphic brushstrokes, other times something closer to graffiti. "The shape this takes needn't be something he has seen or imagined before; instead, it can be a more subconscious object or creature," writes Iona Whittaker in her catalogue essay for his 2014 Pace Beijing exhibition.

"My paintings are oftentimes inspired by random thoughts. Maybe I am inspired by a picture, a sentence or a poem, I would start making a painting in a quite random situation. However, during the process, I would paint based on a stream of my own consciousness," he explained. "Thus, to some extent, contemporary art is self-experiential. It is neither propaganda nor a type of education. It is politics that is individualistic and personal, not the kind of politics carried out from the top down."

Another artist dealing with universality in a more explicit way is Zhao Yao. Born in 1981, he studied design at the Sichuan Fine Art Institute and his training is evident in his geometric compositions—a bold and colorful array of circles and triangles—painted in acrylic on found fabric. One recent series was titled *Painting with Thoughts*, which could also be translated as "The Thinking Painting," as if the work itself had a mind of its own. It is his intention to encourage viewers to think about the logic within a painting, not as an act of art appreciation, but as a kind of self-interrogation. His works make one think about our predetermined expectations of art, instigating an examination of cultural biases.

In his studio, a vast industrial space filled with many differing kinds of artworks, Zhao Yao shows me a book of brainteasers, mazes, and puzzles that inspired his recent work. "The reason why I selected it is that abstraction is more universal across all cultures; it is not like figurative representation, which is imbued with all kinds of cultural-specific narrative and emotions," he explains. I ask him about his relationship to the history of abstraction, given that some of his paintings look like they've been influenced by Malevich and the Russian Constructivists. "I don't pay a lot of attention to the specificity of art history. I am more interested in how to add on new meanings to ready-made imagery."

Still, certain dimensions of his work could only be realized in China. In his series *Spirit Above All*, which he began in 2012 and repeated in 2016, Zhao Yao brought works to Tibet to be blessed by Buddhist monks. In November 2016, a mammoth painting measuring 116 meters wide by 86 meters long was transported to the Moye Temple in Qinghai province where, with the help of Chakme Rinpoche and 100 local villagers, it was installed at the mountain top. Part performance, part abstract painting, this arduous endeavor was undertaken, according to the artist, to instill an aura of spirituality to the work. It is not so much a labor of love as an ironic gesture, given that he is well aware that this claim to a spiritual component has been made by artists throughout the history of abstraction from Mondrian to Robert Ryman, with little impact on the well-being of mankind. "Why would we imbue a geometric shape such as a square with infinite spirituality and individuality? If I were to make changes to existing forms and concepts, would I be able to do the same?" Zhao Yao asks me rhetorically.

"I realized that abstraction is really directed towards individuality and spirituality, yet it is able to induce a collective understanding of something," says the young artist, repeatedly using the term, "universal." It is an interesting choice of word for a Chinese artist and one used frequently by artists that I interviewed for this book, a remnant, perhaps, of the fact that it once was used as a way of erasing creative accomplishments from all parts of the world outside of Western Europe and the USA. In this Eurocentric point of view, it was assumed that European and American artists could make "universal" statements, while artworks by artists from Asia, Africa, and other regions were considered ethnographic artifacts with localized truths.

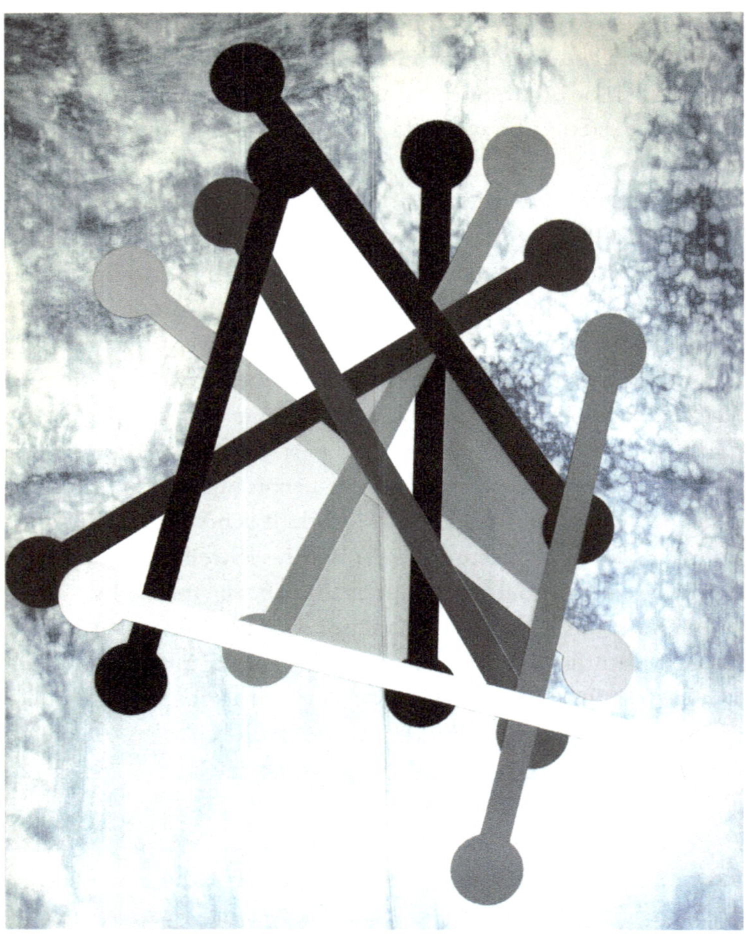

ZHAO YAO, *SPIRIT ABOVE ALL I-10*, 2012. COURTESY OF PACE GALLERY.

And yet, these young Chinese artists embraced the term "universal" as something within their grasp, given their ambidextrous abilities in both Eastern and Western art practices. For them, all art histories were readily available, particularly in the age of the internet. More importantly, with art careers now taking them to every place on the planet, it was essential to make work that could be readily understood in a variety of locations. Still, I had the nagging suspicion that I would interpret the work of Zhao Yao differently than I would an American abstract artist of the same age. Whereas I might dismiss the trickery of turning brainteasers into canvases if the artist was based in New York, I read a deeper meaning—perhaps about political resistance, perhaps about rebellion against the realist painting of his academic training—into the work made by a Chinese artist.

Even though Zhao Yao intentionally pursues the universal, I am not quite sure that audiences abroad would grant him that privilege: like myself, they would probably insist on reading the work through the prism of cultural identity. I ask him how he responds to this suggestion:

> On the one hand, you shouldn't want to be singled out as a Chinese artist. On the other hand, you have to reconsider the cultural resources available to you due to the special position you occupy. To take my trip to Tibet as an example, it is a part of the social-cultural environment that we grew up with. So you can't intentionally avoid it. In this way, you can truly face the relationships you have with the outside world.

Globalization is the undeniable backdrop to this new way of conceiving of "the universal." China has undergone political, social, cultural, and economic transformations during the lifetime of these young artists. They grew up in cities where the presence of Starbucks, McDonald's, and KFC were taken for granted. For them, the daily deluge of global brands has fundamentally altered their relationship with the wider world—universality can be accessed through a swipe of a credit card. Moreover, these artists have been able to travel and even enjoy an education abroad, seeing with their own eyes parallel art histories in ways denied to their predecessors.

To use terms like globalization and universality interchangeably may be deeply cynical, yet this is the reality for many young people today, not only in China. Qu Xu is an artist who explores the convergence of these terms by literally turning money into abstract paintings. In his best-known series, *Currency Wars*, he magnified the patterns found on paper bills from around the world and turned them into large, brightly colored geometric compositions. By revealing the source of his designs, Qu Xu unveils the deeply commercial nature of contemporary art while simultaneously advancing its circulation. In keeping with this concept, these seemingly abstract works have been shown in China, the UK, France, Belgium, Thailand, and Australia, with worldwide distribution.

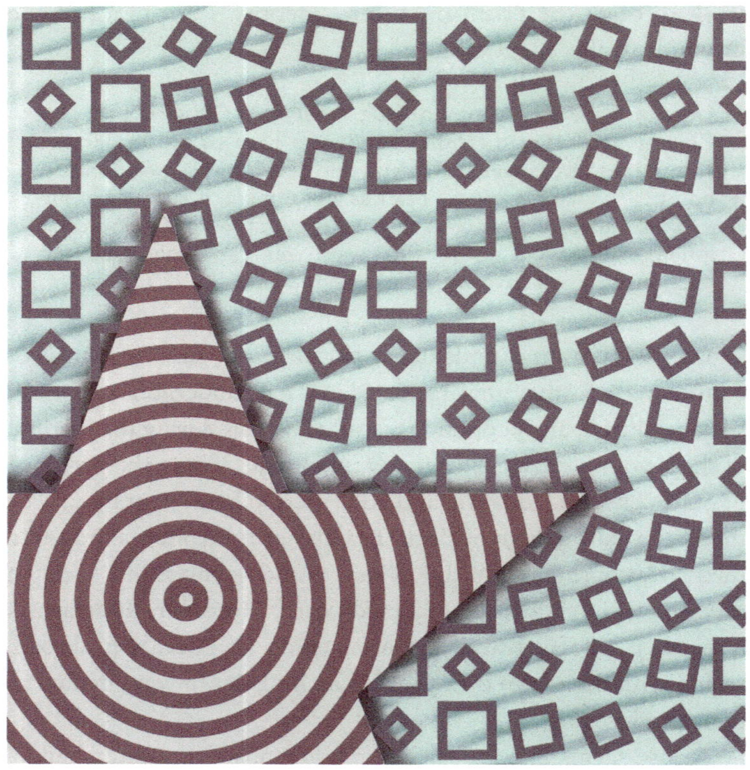

QU XU, *CURRENCY WARS, EURO 500 OLD AND NEW*, 2016. COURTESY OF THE ARTIST AND ANTENNA SPACE GALLERY.

The concept for this work comes directly from the artist's personal binational experience. Born in 1978 in Suzhou, he moved to Germany in 2004 after graduating from the Nanjing Art Institute. In Germany, he came under the tutelage of pioneer Swiss artist John Armleder while studying at Braunschweig University of Art. After completing that course in 2007, he continued studying with Armleder in a postgraduate study program for another year. Qu Xu went to Germany specifically to study with Armleder because he found his approach to art completely different to that which he had learned at home. This was an interesting choice for a Chinese artist. Armleder began his career as a member of Fluxus, a loose collective of artists influenced by Dada, Marcel Duchamp, and John Cage, which created performances, installations, and other works that invited audience engagement. He has since gone on to make, by his own definition, "intentionally meaningless" artworks, ranging from randomly composed abstract paintings to sculptures made from reconfigured furniture. His influence on Qu Xu is apparent, not only in the younger artist's choice to make a game out of making art, but also in Qu Xu's use of installation, often displaying his *Currency War* paintings in pairs, back-to-back, on freestanding structures.

"In recent years Chinese artists have excelled overseas with their abstract works and have been hailed as the new generation of artists," says Qu Xu as he explains the reasoning behind his *Currency Wars*. "I feel like it's more important to know that, once collectors get their hands on the works, the price skyrockets. Collectors may gain knowledge about art and society through the purchase of artworks, but it is primarily a transaction of capital. To put it crudely, it is using money to buy money."

Qu Xu believes that, by appropriating money through his art, he is situating himself somewhat outside the circle of influence that he describes. Yet he fully acknowledges that he is both critiquing the system and advancing within the system simultaneously. When asked pointedly about this and the meaning of the work, he retreats into the observation that this is just a way of making people notice "the beauty in every day life." But when I bring up the topic of Chinese identity, he laughs and tells me that when visitors to his studio raise this issue, he simply shows them his most gruesome video, *Zebra*, in which a butcher flays a horse until his skin resembles zebra stripes. He showed this work when the team from Louis Vuitton came to visit, shocking them with its brutality, while he chuckled over the fact that they all were carrying leather bags.

"I feel that now there isn't really the distinction between Western artist and Chinese artists. We are all implicated in one system of art and have to engage with the same conceptual problems," Qu Xu says, emphasizing that there is no longer the need to make a distinction between artists, given that, regardless of their place of birth or practice, they are all now confronted by a similar market structure and deluge of information from the internet. By extension, he is insisting on a commonality between audiences, who for the most part share the main objective of acquiring the work and reselling for profit.

Whereas Liu Wei, Qiu Xiaofei, and Zhao Yao are almost idealistic about the possibility of a universal understanding engendered by their artworks, Qu Xu sees himself as a player within the globalized art world. He is reaching international audiences by adopting an iconography readily understood by all. His is not a hypothetical universal but one rooted in the concrete system of commerce. It raises the question of whether it is too late for abstract art to claim supremacy in purveying universal truths, since that task has been overtaken by a market-driven economic system that assures every person the means to access a Big Mac and a smartphone.

Whether they agree with this premise or not, most young Chinese artists are products of this system, and as such, readily view themselves as "global artists" rather than homegrown ones defined by national identity. The impact of this trend can be seen in their artworks, especially in the field of abstract art, where they can raise questions and offer experiences, relieved of the burden of recent Chinese history. For all of these artists, this has required a 180-degree turn away from the realist painting they were taught in art school, a turn that may, therefore, be seen as an act of rebellion. More often, however, it comes from the simple desire to fully join the art world that they no longer see as divided along national boundaries.

4
THE ME GENERATION

Every year in December since 2002, Art Basel Miami Beach opens its doors to over 70,000 visitors, turning a string of Art Deco hotels and a mammoth convention center into the highlight of the art world for just under a week. There are now three Art Basel art fairs, including the original in Switzerland, founded in 1970, which sells out $10 million masterpieces before it even opens its doors, and the newcomer Art Basel Hong Kong that opened in 2013 and introduced Asian buyers to the hoopla of a world-class art bazaar. But the one in Miami is the most fun, with a dozen satellite fairs dotting the city and dozens of parties taking place every night, with patrons trying to traipse across the sandy beach in their Christian Louboutins.

Nothing can seem farther from China than this affair, in which only a handful of the 210 dealers hail from Asia and, until recently, few mainland buyers could be found. Art fairs can be exhilarating, but they also can be cruel, alienating affairs and Chinese collectors often find themselves treated as outsiders in this clubby atmosphere. Though a few of them always come to the fair, armed with translators and art advisors, they clearly prefer Art Basel Hong Kong, which is like an annual class reunion of the newly minted billionaires, private museum founders, top-selling art stars, and cross-cultural curators who make up China's art scene.

In contrast to some of his compatriots, conceptual artist Yan Xing does not appear to be even remotely out of his element at major international art fairs. I run into him at Art Basel Miami Beach in December 2016 and he swiftly takes over, boldly guiding me through the aisles as confident as any of the fashion-forward collectors that filled the Miami Beach Convention Center. Tall, slim, and beaming confidence, the 30-year-old proudly brandishes his in-depth knowledge of the participating galleries, saying hello to dealers that frequently intimidate me and pointing out works by new emerging artists that were completely unfamiliar. He was just six months away from his own international debut, a solo show at Kunsthalle Basel in June 2017, which attracted a stellar crowd because it coincided with the original mega-fair Art Basel that took place at the same time.

This encounter in Miami brought me back to when I first met Yan Xing in Beijing in 2010, charmed by his over-the-top personality and his innocent enthusiasm for his own ambitions. Beijing gallerist Meg Maggio brought him to my attention as one of the few openly gay artists in China. He had just staged a performance in her gallery, Pékin Fine Arts, which had riveted audiences. Yan Xing stood facing a corner, his back to the crowd, and recounted his childhood in a searing work called *Daddy*. In this monologue, he confessed that he grew up in Chongqing, raised by an absentee mother preoccupied with her business career and abandoned by his drug-addicted father. His life was a series of affairs with temporary father figures, according to this half-true, half-fictional account.

"When I was growing up I was not close to my parents, so I was a lone, only child," he told me when we met a short time afterwards. Without a trace of shame or embarrassment, he told me that by the time he was 12 years old, his mother had set him up in an apartment and gave him an allowance, forcing him to fend for himself while she pursued business opportunities in a coastal city. This had not stymied his growth or wounded his spirit. He went on to graduate from the prestigious Sichuan Fine Arts Institute, Zhang Xiaogang's alma mater, moving to Beijing in 2009 when he graduated. As I listened to this somewhat startling biography, I grew concerned for this young man who had gone through so much on his own. He assured me that there was no need to worry. Already he was as well known, if not better known, for his micro-blog, *Fuck Off*, which documented his nightly clubbing and promiscuous love affairs. "It is not difficult being gay in China," he insisted, adding "It's just difficult finding a lasting love relationship."

By 2015, Yan Xing's evident state of loneliness had been resolved. He had met and married UCLA professor of Chinese archaeology Lothar von Falkenhausen and was now splitting his time between Los Angeles, Beijing, and a series of artists' residencies that took him from the Ukraine to the Dominican Republic. In the meantime, he had been named Best Young Artist by the 2012 Chinese Contemporary Art Award, nominated for the Future Generation Art Prize from the Pinchuk Art Centre, and featured in the Focus on Talents Project from Beijing's Today Art Museum. His multifaceted installations, incorporating photography, sculpture, video, and performance, were never as confessional as *Daddy* again. Instead of blatantly brandishing his gay identity, he made works that questioned the veracity of any display of self and interrogated factual accounts as mere storytelling opportunities.

In early works, Yan Xing may have revealed more of himself. In the video *Sexy*, 2011, for example, he lay naked on a rocky landscape and masturbated for the camera. But this rawness quickly evolved into something far more sophisticated in his video *Arty, Super-Arty*, 2013, in which groups of young men pose silently in scenes straight out of Edward Hopper paintings, the latent homoeroticism underscored by the absence of women. By the time he created the installation *Two videos, three photographs, several related masterpieces, and American art* in 2013, he appropriated the look of Robert Mapplethorpe portraits, but only to make a point about the underlying violence and eroticism of contemporary art, not to disclose a personal preference—or at least that's what he says.

"I think the concept of the identity of the artist is very outdated and has reached its limit because it depends on how we observe this identity," Yan Xing tells me just months before his project in Kunsthalle Basel, which he describes as a faux exhibition organized by a fictional curator. When I ask if this imaginary curator is Chinese or Western, he quickly replies that such divisions do not matter. And though there will be a backstory about a foot fetish and even a video involving a sexual act, this work has nothing to do with his being gay. "I think as a professional artist, you have to work on how much of your personal identity you want to reveal to the public," he says. I giggle at this reply since, in person, Yan Xing needs no encouragement to reveal the most personal details of his life.

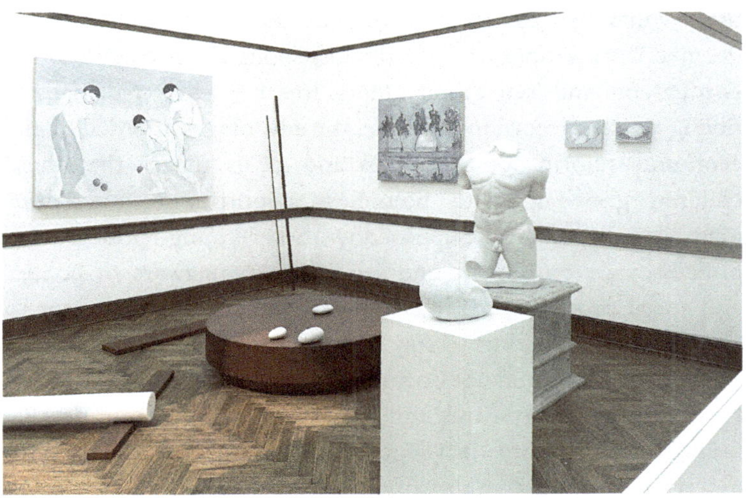

YAN XING, *LENIN IN 1918*, INSTALLATION VIEW, GALERIE URS MEILE, 2013. COURTESY OF THE ARTIST.

Yan Xing is too much of an individual to be considered representative of an entire generation but, in a way, this is the key characteristic of many artists in his generation. Products of the One Child Policy, they grew up as distinctive individuals without the challenges of integrating into a multi-sibling home.[1] This is perhaps the first generation in China with such an emphasis on individuality. Most obviously, such an impulse was repressed during the Cultural Revolution, when family ties were replaced with work units and individual desires were subjugated to the needs of "the People." Even afterwards, the artists who emerged in the 1980s and 1990s seemed to have inherited this vocation to work collectively and often introduced themselves in terms of movements or networks. But with this younger generation, I met artists more akin to those I knew in the USA, resolutely determined to be seen as unique and original, rather than part of a collective or movement.

Ironically, the One Child Policy, introduced in 1979 and phased out in 2016, is the single most significant factor in the lives of this young generation of Chinese artists, connecting them more than they would like to admit. In China, these children are often deemed "little emperors," presumably spoiled by the attention of two parents and four grandparents, free from the challenges of sibling rivalry. According to some, the advantages afforded by the economic reforms of the 1980s and 1990s meant that these children grew up with boundless opportunities and ever-increasing resources. Supposedly, these young princes and princesses are narcissistic and self-involved, unaware of politics and social problems, avid consumers who travel widely, not to discover the world, but to stay on top of fashion trends.[2]

This portrait could not be further from the reality of the artists I met during the research for this book. While a considerable number came from privileged backgrounds, few could be described as spoiled. Yan Xing, for example, was set loose on his own at the age of 12, a direct result of his mother trying to capitalize on economic opportunities newly available in the late 1990s. When I first heard this, I thought it was extreme. But, after listening to countless other stories, I found this to be the case for many of the young artists in China. Though they may not have been abandoned by their parents, in many cases, they had left home by the time they were 14 or 15, to enter the preparatory school of one of the country's prestigious art academies. It was not unusual for them to strudy very far from home, experiencing culture shock and loneliness, to attend the high school of the Central Academy of Fine Arts in Beijing or the China Academy of Art in Hangzhou. Yet they often told me about these experiences matter-of-factly, rarely indulging in self-pity or divulging resentment.

While it may not be obvious how art school applications would be affected by the One Child Policy, in fact they are deeply intertwined. As a result of the One Child Policy, there is enormous pressure on the family's only child to succeed. On the one hand, this is purely an economic calculation, given that that child must be equipped to support his two parents as they age. (The crushing pressure of caring for an aging population was a key factor in the rescinding of the One Child Policy.) On the other hand, it is the measure of the incalculable emotional costs of having only one child that all the family's hopes and dreams are pinned on their sole offspring's advancement. Choosing an art career might seem like a gentler, easier route than, say, becoming a doctor or an engineer. But, in China, where an earlier generation has proven that artists can become millionaires if their careers take off, parents often assume that art can be as much of a career path as medical school or investment banking.

The pressure of being an only child is perfectly captured in the poignant video, *From No.4 Pingyuanli to No. 4 Tianqiaobeili*, 2007, by Ma Qiusha, a young woman artist who now has a daughter of her own. Made when she was just 27 years old, this video presents her talking straight to the camera, recounting her upbringing by parents determined that their only child becomes an artist. It details the abuse she suffered on the road to admission into art school, starting with her childhood drawing classes, reviewed each day by her "tiger mother," who criticized and punished her for every mistake. She describes the decision to become an artist as "the end of my childhood," acknowledging the expense this cost her parents and sharing her guilt over leaving them to study in the USA. At the end of the video, Ma Qiusha removes a razor blade from her bloody mouth, revealing the pain that she literally suffered in sharing this personal story.

"Even though my generation of only children is overly protected, they are always exposed to all kinds of danger, mainly feelings of danger or anxiety that are internal, not something from the outside," Ma Qiusha tells me as we sit in her studio in Beijing in May 2016. I have known her for several years by then,

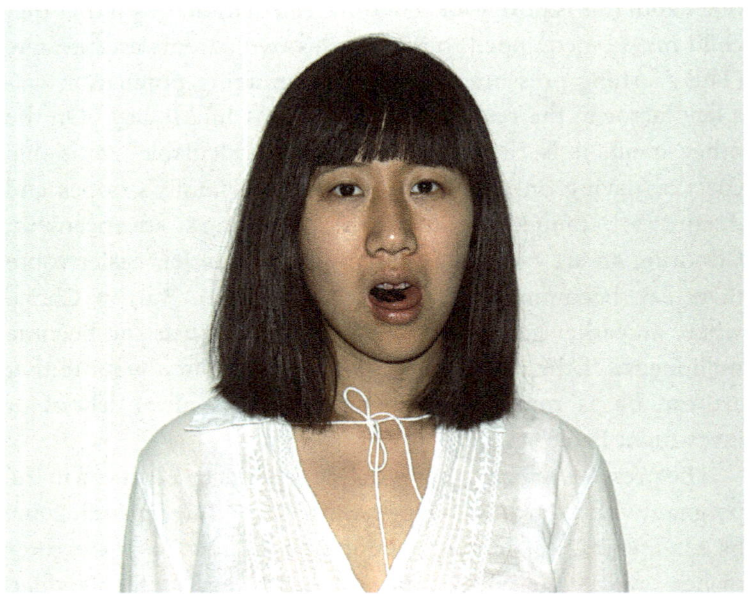

MA QIUSHA, *FROM NO. 4 PINGYUANLI TO NO. 4 TIANQIAOBEILI*, VIDEO STILL, 2007. COURTESY OF BEIJING COMMUNE.

but now that she herself is a mother, she seems particularly self-aware about the downside of the One Child Policy. "It has to do with human relations. Maybe it's because I was always by myself since I was a child whenever a person intervenes, or even engages in a conversation with me, it will induce anxiety in me," she says. "Now that I'm a mother, I realize that I did not receive the stimulus or exercise necessary to form the proper social skills, especially at a time when language skills were in growth. This part is underdeveloped."

"Personally, I am a victim of the One Child Policy," says Chi Peng, an impish digital photographer born in 1981 and living in Beijing. Chi Peng garnered attention while he was still at the Central Academy of Fine Arts for his series *Springing Forward*, 2004, in which he depicts himself streaking through the streets of Beijing. Masterfully created through computer renderings, the photographs sharply convey the sense of freedom and vulnerability embodied by this generation. His studio, where he treats visitors to home-cooked banquets, is filled with vintage toys and children's books from a Peter Pan existence. But underneath, he expresses his profound objection to growing up as a solo child.

"What I want to say is that I really should have had my own brothers and sisters. If I did when I grew up, I would not have to always feel so lonely," Chi Peng tells me, continuing, "As for my parents, nobody should have ever taken away their right to have another child to love." He wants to make sure I understand the depth of this dilemma. "I need to explain this a little bit further," he says.

> The love of Chinese people is quite strong; the emotional connections between Chinese children and their parents are both very strong and intimate. As a result, Chinese parents usually have a high expectation for the emotional return from their own kids. In this case, for the majority of Chinese kids, they feel that it their duty to return their love to their parents. Given this situation, if there is only one kid in every family, the family responsibility and pressure that falls on the child is quite heavy.

Ma Qiusha and Chi Peng—as a woman and as a gay man—are representative of some of the fallout that has happened as a result of the One Child Policy, coming from two sections of society that have been deeply affected by this family planning measure. Gender roles and sexual orientation are highly influenced by the social pressures experienced by this generation, as they begin their own families and must live up to parental expectations to produce a grandchild. One lasting impact of the One Child Policy is that, in a country with a heritage of preference for male children—resulting in abortions, infanticides, and abandonment of female infants—there are now 30 million more bachelors than available brides in the population.[3] Young women may have their pick of husbands, but the corollary of this imbalance is a restoration of traditional gender roles, whereby twenty-somethings are pushed into marrying and having children at an early age, with men working as breadwinners and women as stay-at-home moms. Women who reach the age of 30 and still haven't married are referred to as "left-over women," the Chinese equivalent of old maids.

This pressure is twice as acute in the LGBTQI community, estimated by current government figures at 40 million people, a questionable sum given that homosexuality is still a stigma in China and vastly underreported. Homosexuality has been legal in China since 1997 and has not been ruled a mental illness since 2001, and there are dozens of gay clubs, not only in major cities but throughout the country.[4] Still, in 2017, depictions of homosexuals and transgender people on television and in the movies was once again ruled strictly forbidden by new state policies instigating more restrictive censorship laws.

Many people told me that Chinese mothers and fathers would be devastated to know that their child is gay, since they represent their only hope for a grandchild. As a result, nearly 80 percent of gay men in China choose to marry a woman, rather than come out to their families. Despite a recent case of a couple suing for the right to wed, gay marriage is a long way from becoming a reality in China and it is still not possible for a gay couple to adopt a child.

"This is not just social discrimination. It is happening in every family, so if you want to defend your rights, you have to fight with your family," says Hou Ping, founder of LES GO, a community organizing group based in Suzhou that raises awareness of women's equality and lesbians' rights. A lawyer by training, she is currently pursuing further education at Columbia University. "On the surface, it looks like a family issue, but if you analyze this further, you find out that it is because of government policies—the One Child Policy and all those things—that push pressure onto the family."

Certainly, in talking to young artists in Beijing and Shanghai, the key factor behind discrimination is family pressures, not government policies or the lack of gender equality laws. Artists rarely cite structural discrimination within the art world, despite the severe gender imbalance in most galleries and museum exhibitions. In keeping with a kind of psychological denial of the social problems affecting their lives, Chinese women artists tend to personalize their challenges, blaming their setbacks on the responsibilities of motherhood or poor choice of husband, rather than political causes. And rarely do artists deal with this issue in their artworks, even in those cases in which they acknowledge these challenges.

"Before having a kid, I had never paid attention to the differences between male and female artists. Whether it is energy, creativity, or ability, I was on the same level as my male counterparts," says Ma Qiusha, who was educated in the USA and shows with the prestigious Beijing Commune gallery, telling me that, when people used to ask her about her status as a woman artist, she found the questions to be "annoying." Her artworks do not solely deal with women's issues, though her recent installation, *Wonderland*, 2016, might be interpreted that way. For this work, she covered the gallery floor with a crazy quilt of old-fashioned nylon stockings stretched over a concrete slab.

She tells me that the stockings are reminiscent of the clothing of her mother's generation and are meant to conjure up a time when Beijingers rode bicycles, dabbing clear nail polish on the inevitable runs in their hosiery. While Ma Qiusha may not acknowledge this, the installation reads as a powerful statement on women's lives, reflecting her growing awareness of her own identity. "After I had my child, I noticed clearly that we are not equals: in terms of the time that you allocate towards different activities and the various roles you play in society, all of these have radically changed," she tells me, summarizing with the stark observation that "it is impossible for female artists to be equal to male ones."

Liang Yuanwei, born in 1977, is another woman artist who has found success, yet is questioning the status of women artists. Her labor-intensive canvases are shimmering with beauty, resembling from a distance the floral patterns of embroidered Chinese textiles, echoing the iconography of traditional scroll paintings as well as the kitsch of *Chinoiserie*. "Many people see flowers as a feminist stance, but I am not deliberately using that as an agenda," she explains, sharing with me that she recently became a single mother, deliberately having a child on her own. Liang Yuanwei emphatically states that she did not have any obstacles to an art career, especially since she was always prepared to make sacrifices to become an artist. "The female identity gets more complex as you starting having kids and a family, more responsibilities; you have to be really smart to deal with all this and distribute your time," she says, something she has successfully negotiated with a solo show at Pace London in 2014, just around the time her child was born. According to this artist, things are rapidly improving for female artists. "In the past, women artists rarely worked independently without having husbands who were also artists, but now there are accomplished female artists who are independent. This opens up people's minds and gives them confidence to collect women artists," she says, adding, "Once a few women take center stage, more will follow."

Liang Yuanwei's optimism is hard-earned and rooted in a success that did not come without difficult personal choices. I pointedly ask her about discrimination within the Chinese art scene, the lack of representation of women artists in many of the galleries, and their exclusion from many of the important exhibitions at mainland museums. "For me, I have long accepted that if you want to be respected, you have to be stronger than male artists. It's an irrefutable reality," she tells me, articulating a situation that many other women artists refuse to acknowledge. She goes on to say, "You have to first see yourself as a handicapped person in a patriarchal society, then you will think about how to survive as a less able-bodied person, as well as how you can best utilize your abilities."

Because she used the term, "patriarchy," I ask her if she considers herself a "feminist artist" and, after a few minutes thought, she replies,

> This is difficult to answer. I don't use my work to express my feminist concerns. But I am interested in the feminist movement, and the rise of feminist consciousness in China. It is important, but not important to the point that it eclipses other problems. I pay attention to many issues at the same time.

In my experience interviewing women artists in China, I rarely encountered such a straightforward acceptance of a feminist agenda. More often than not, women artists refused the label "feminist artist," which has as much to do with the stigma attached to the term "feminist" in China as it does with their personal success. Undoubtedly, younger women artists have found more readily available paths to gallery careers than their predecessors, with many exhibiting both in China and abroad. For some, this means that they have not had to consider discrimination as a factor in their development, as the artist Jin Nv told me. Born in 1984, she went straight through high school and college at the Central Academy of Fine Arts and found her anime-inspired sculptures of nubile women collected directly out of her graduation show by Australia's prestigious White Rabbit Collection. With few apparent obstacles to success, she has not had to worry extensively about her status as a woman artist.

Likewise, Ye Funa, born into a family of well-known artists in Kunming in 1986, graduated from the Central Academy of Fine Arts in 2008 and pursued a master's degree in Fine Arts from the Central Saint Martins College of Art in London in 2010. One of her best-known projects turned MOCA Shanghai into a nail salon, inviting audience participation, the results of which she then posted to social media, attracting a huge following. A later exhibition at Space Station gallery in Beijing displayed monumental-sized nails, inspired by the legend of Wuzhi Shan or Five-Finger Mountain in which Buddha turns his hands into a five-pillared mountain. Despite the fact that work like these installations would certainly be interpreted as feminist art in New York or London, Ye Funa denies such a position as her goal, and that she has encountered discrimination. "I think it is mostly female curators who are interested in the Nail Project because maybe men are not interested in this kind of art," she says at first. On further reflection, she explains, "When I did this at MOCA Shanghai, the event was super shiny, pink, and girly. I think the director just came in and quickly ran away. I think he was afraid.

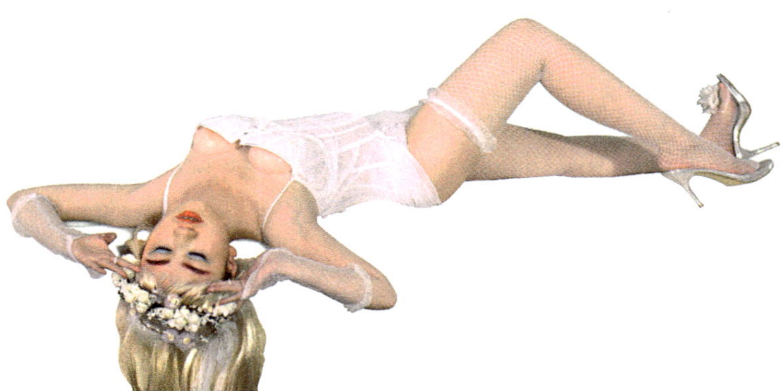

YE FUNA, *CICICOLIA YE*, 2015. COURTESY OF THE ARTIST.

This always happened at my nail events. I think the men felt threatened."

Feminism is a complicated subject in China because, distinct from the history of gender politics in the USA and Europe, women's equality was a state-enforced agenda under the Maoist regime. The All-China Women's Federation was founded by the Communist Party in 1949 to "protect women's rights and interests."[5] Yet women remain scarce in leadership roles. In politics, only two women sit on the powerful 25-member Politburo; in business, only about 2 percent of Chinese women hold managerial roles.[6] The legacy of this for young women artists today is the ever-growing list of female-only, state-sponsored art exhibitions of such poor quality that artists with vibrant gallery careers are wise to avoid. But, in recent years, with the end of the One Child Policy and a decline in the size of the Chinese workforce, the Chinese government has sponsored policies and social campaigns to promote family growth that blatantly urge young women to leave their jobs and marry as soon as possible. In April 2015, the Japanese cosmetics company SK-II released an emotional four-minute commercial that challenged the crushing family pressure that many young Chinese women face to marry. The ad went viral in China, with over 46 million views on YouTube.[7]

In the past two years, a growing number of feminist activists have sought to counteract these policies, primarily by staging impromptu street activities, highly influenced by performance art, which can be accomplished quickly before the police shut them down and which can be photographed and distributed on social media. They have staged sit-ins in men's rooms for Occupy Men's Bathrooms to protest the lack of public facilities for women. To raise awareness of domestic violence, they have stood in public places as brides with blood-spattered wedding gowns. Actions have been taken on subways to highlight groping and sexual harassment. All of these actions would seem mild in the USA, where hundreds of thousands of women can gather to protest the Trump administration. But in China, where mass demonstrations are sharply forbidden, even these modest attempts at protest have come under scrutiny. In March 2015, five leaders of the organization Feminist Voices were arrested when they were attempting to coordinate a multi-city event to coincide with International Women's Day.[8] They were released after a month following an international outcry, but since then, there has been a steady online campaign, probably sponsored by government agencies, to smear the reputation of feminists and link them with more troublesome anti-government forces.

In February 2017, the Feminist Voices account on Weibo, China's equivalent of Facebook, was shut down for mentioning the Women's Strike, an event held in the USA on March 8th, International Women's Day.[9] According to Lu Pin, one of the leaders of Feminist Voices, they have no idea when their privileges will be returned. Lu Pin, born in 1972, is a bit older than the younger generation artists, and attributes her politicization to her experience working as a journalist at a women's newspaper in Beijing in the 1990s. She had just arrived in the USA when her comrades were arrested in 2015. Since then, she has remained in the USA, firstly as a visiting scholar at Columbia and then at the University of Albany, pursuing an advance degree as a way of extending her visa.

"The Chinese government is targeting feminist organizations, not only my organization," Lu Pin acknowledges, citing the wave of internet bloggers who have been paid by the Chinese government to flood social media with anti-feminist accusations. "They said that feminist organizations support Muslims and used as evidence that there was a Muslim woman speaker at the Women's March in Washington, DC," she says, referring to the strongly anti-Muslim rhetoric and policies of the Chinese government since the recent wave of terrorist acts in Xinjiang. "Because we spread information on the Women's March, they consider this proof that we support Muslims," she sighs, adding,

"It is just a trick, but it's effective because so many Chinese people are afraid of Muslims."

Despite Lu Pin's claims that feminism is on the rise in China, it still seems that few women would identify themselves as feminists. "It is not so important that you call yourself a feminist," she says. "If you say you are a feminist, it means you are a loser in society. You cannot find a man. You have no future so you turn to feminism." Underscoring that, in China, most people are naturally afraid of any "isms" and tend to steer clear of politics, Lu Pin nevertheless tells me that more and more young women are participating in feminist actions and sharing pro-feminist postings on social media. "We are the bright line of the struggle with millions and millions of young feminists now," she insists.

Performance artist Gao Ling, born 1980, is a prime example of Lu Pin's army of volunteers. She was initially provoked by a wave of social media comments attacking a scantily dressed young woman on the Shanghai subway, who was accused of looking for trouble. Disturbed by these remarks, Gao Ling took action. "I thought it was not the woman's fault, but rather social expectations," she tells me when we meet in a cafe in Beijing. In response, Gao Ling created a "metro bra" made from metal cake molds bound together by chains. Two women, dressed entirely in black, wearing the bras and holding iPads, played messages such as "I can be sexy, but you cannot harass me" and "I want to be cool, but I don't want sexual harassment." They went to the subway station near People's Square and as crowds gathered, Gao Ling shot photos that she then posted to social media.

Claiming that she is more influenced by Duchamp's spirit of playfulness than by other feminist artists, Gao Ling went on to invent a sleek design object that might alleviate Chinese women's bathroom woes. "I found that women had to wait longer in lines for toilets at concerts or music festivals. So we thought, why not make an outfit for women so they would be able to pee standing up, and thus not wait as long," she says, having exhibited the

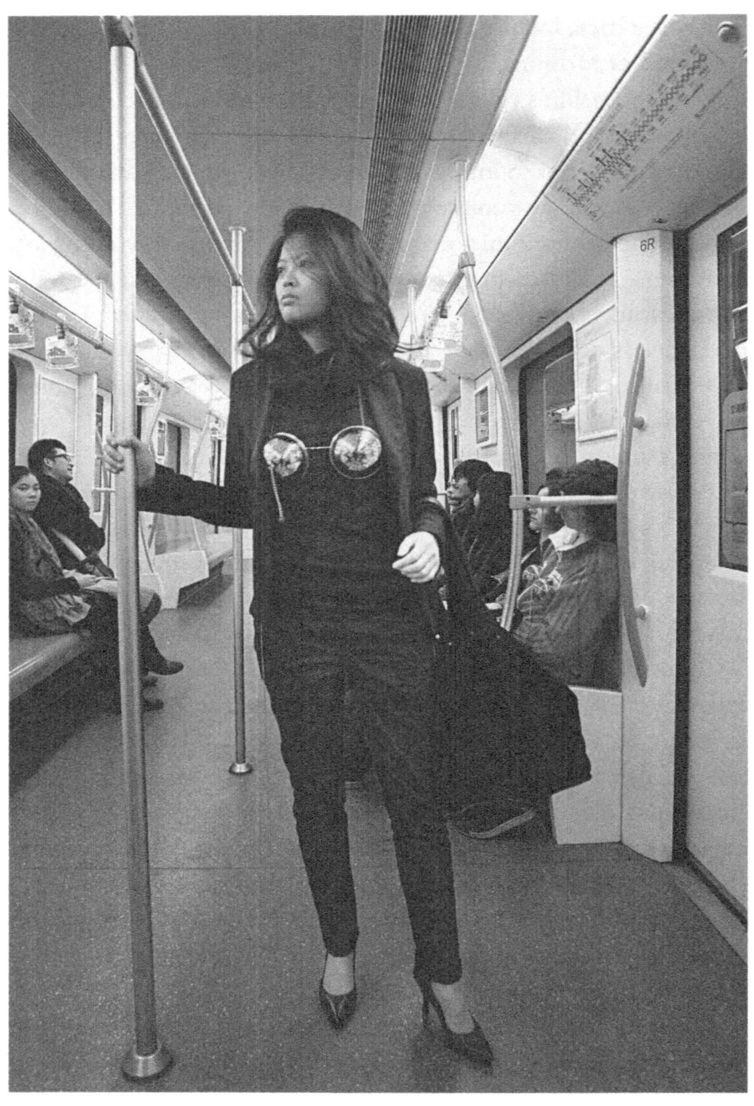

GAO LING, *HEY TOUCH ME*, PERFORMANCE IN SHANGHAI SUBWAY, 2010. COURTESY OF THE ARTIST.

device in galleries in China and abroad. But, despite making such outrageous items as the metro bra and the pee funnel, Gao Ling recoils at the suggestion that she is a feminist artist. "I think conditions have really changed so that women's status has evolved and gained more equality," she says, unaware that her actions contradict this conclusion. Still she insists, "As far as peers go, women already have a high social standing." But when I ask if she thinks artists can make an impact on society and if change is possible, Gao Ling concurs, "As far as the subway performance goes, I feel like I have entered that realm, where things could make an impact."

Even if artists in China were more accepting of the term "feminist," it is doubtful that there would be an insurgence of artworks dealing specifically with the female condition. This is not because of government censorship or social repression, but because few of this generation of artists are interested in identity politics per se, and, just as they avoid associations with "Chineseness" and Chinese identity, they equally eschew references to gender or sexual orientation. In a complex intersection between biographical details and aesthetic considerations, they choose to concentrate on conceptual strategies that complicate the role of the artist and that view the "self" as non-essential and performative. Identity is not a fixed condition but a state subject to interpretation and as such is no longer a fundamental precondition to the creation of an artwork. Whether we discuss Chinese identity or gender identity, Chinese artists view these terms as unnecessary criteria imposed on them by others' expectations. While such identity politics might have been prominent in art in the 1990s, now it is fading from view in an art world entirely suffused in postmodern ideas that challenge authorship and authenticity.

"I think that for a good artist, people should first see your artwork, not your identity. An over-emphasis on identity takes away from the art," answers video artist Tao Hui, born 1987, when I ask him about the role of the narrator in his surrealistic and often violent stories. In his video installations, Tao Hui mimics the look of television dramas and soap operas, placing his films in theatrical environments. But the works often raise the question of who is telling this story and whether they can be trusted with the truth. Rarely, if ever, is the storyteller the artist himself, and rarer still does he reveal in the course of his tales his own identity as a gay man.

For Tao Hui, identity is an imagined state, a fantasy that he can conjure up with his own creativity. "I have always been interested in the Middle East and I even imagine myself as a Mongolian with Islamic beliefs," the young artist tells me, admitting that this is far from the reality of his actual background, growing up in a small village near Chongqing. In this town, the single television set was often tuned into soap operas, which inspired him to want to become a television producer. But he was unable to get into the video production department of the Sichuan Academy of Fine Art that he attended, majoring instead in oil painting. Upon graduating in 2010 and moving to Beijing, he found that he wanted to combine what he had learned about contemporary art with the melodramas of his childhood. These tales, packed with violence and disturbing details, seem a long way from the quiet, almost shy personality of this artist, who has garnered a great deal of attention in a very short time, including a solo project at the Ullens Center for Contemporary Art in Beijing in 2015 and a featured spot as the youngest artist in a 2016 exhibition of Chinese contemporary art at Fondation Louis Vuitton in Paris.

Though I don't know Tao Hui well, I guess from his demeanor that he would not be comfortable posting his personal life on Weibo, like Yan Xing. When I ask him about his gay identity and whether he is in a relationship, he answers in almost a whisper, "It's complicated. My sexuality is fluid, maybe one day, I will fall in love with a girl." This is not out of shame. All of his friends know he is gay and he is certain that his mother will be at ease with this, if and when he finally tells her. Instead it comes from a flexibility about identity evident in his work. "In this time of globalization, you might be able to glean from artists some elements that are particular to local contexts, but what we are trying to express is more universal," he shares with me, while explaining that for his 2014 video, *The Dusk of Teheran*, he went to Iran to film a modest Iranian woman in a taxi recounting the final dialogue of Hong Kong pop singer Anita Mui, uttered on stage a month before her death from cancer in 2003. In *Talk about Body*, 2013, the artist himself performs as a Muslim woman, detailing her anatomy in alternatively clinical and poetic terms. "People may have very similar lives in different areas and cultures. I feel that a lot of human emotions are universal. Other people may see the color of people's skin in your work, or local landscapes, but in fact the emotion or human fate conveyed could be understood by all."

Comparing Yan Xing and Tao Hui in my mind, I am struck by the diversity among this generation of artists. Even though both are gay men, they are clearly individuals in their own right, resistant in their words and their works from being mischaracterized as representative of a demographic or lifestyle. This is the key quality among younger artists, the obstinate "me" of the Me Generation.

Marketing firms and government agencies work diligently to find trends that unite this group of young people, the better to sell them products or develop policies that can control them. But in the art world, it has been almost impossible to come up with a unifying theme or singularized movement that brings them together. This emphasis on individuality may result in feelings of loneliness or alienation at times. But overall, it seems that it has had a very positive influence on art development, encouraging these young artists to speak for themselves, rather than be burdened by social criteria or group thinking. This does not mean that they are free of social pressures, or are oblivious to the broader problems in their society. Yet they interpret these factors in highly personal terms, which should never be confused with apathy or narcissism.

Indeed, this may be the first generation of Chinese artists who are free to do what artists worldwide do every day: think for themselves and create artworks that are individual statements. That they are managing to do this, despite the expectations of family and curators, is reason enough for their widespread international success.

5
POLITICS AND HISTORY

In the USA, it is often said that all art is political, that art by its very nature impacts society; but, in recent years, I have found that only certain kinds of artworks still aim for that modernist ideal. In China, it is even more rare to see artists trying to reach the masses with political slogans and statements; rather, a museum show or gallery exhibition is their ultimate goal.

This prevalent hesitancy to make political art is not a result of censorship, especially in the case of gallery exhibitions, where I have seen many projects that confront social issues with barely a trace of government interference. In museums, this is somewhat more problematic, since the Ministry of Culture previews all of the works of art intended for public view; but, even there, socially conscious artworks can be found. In speaking with artists, few have encountered censorship, and those who have view it as the price of admission to participate in China's art scene. There is rarely outrage, just resigned recognition that this is bound to happen. And while there is rampant censorship of the internet, television, and movies, art has been left relatively untouched for some time, mainly because contemporary art doesn't have a mass audience, and it appeals to just those who support the government, namely, the newly minted millionaires and billionaires in China.

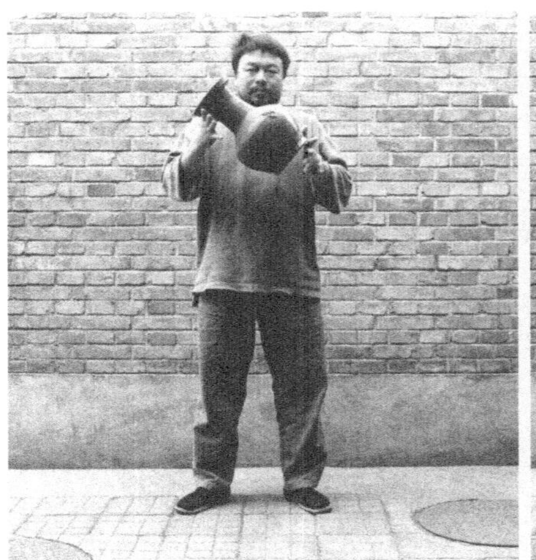
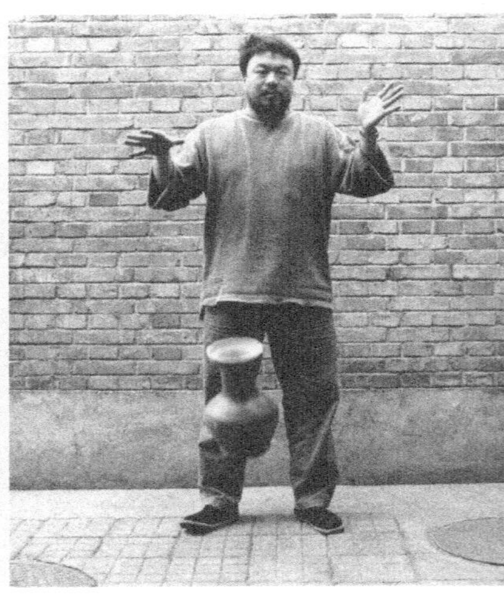

AI WEIWEI, *DROPPING A HAN DYNASTY URN*, 1995. IMAGE COURTESY OF AI WEIWEI STUDIO.

But a deeper form of self-censorship may be at play, brought on not by government censorship but by market forces. Whether we are talking about the USA, Europe, or China, political art is not a money-spinner, and ambitious artists in any of those locales rarely seek to make didactic political statements. Certainly, the young artists in China have learned that if they follow the example of innumerable cultural leaders and skirt outright political confrontations, they can have a successful career, including academic positions and gallery representation. Fewer still will stick their necks out on social media, employing activist tactics as Ai Weiwei has, knowing full well that their posts and blogs will be shut down and that arrest would be imminent.

Renegade, genius, promoter, dissident—Ai Weiwei is all those things, as well as being one of the most famous artists in the world. He had made a name for himself with conceptual art projects from filling the Turbine Hall at Tate Modern with millions of porcelain sunflower seeds in 2010 to turning Jeffrey Deitch Gallery into a showroom for clothing rescued from

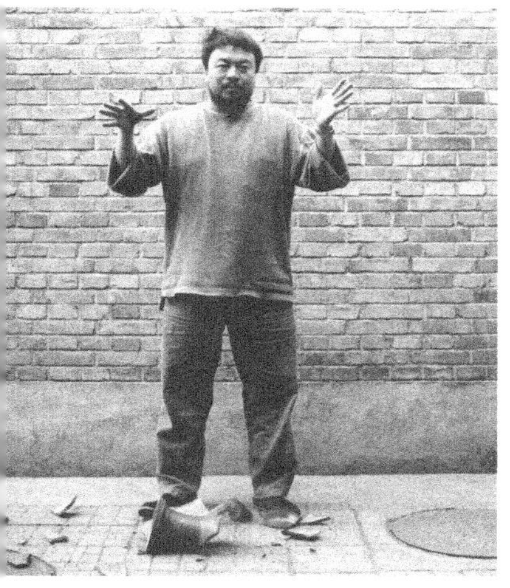

refugees in New York in 2016. But he is better known still as the man who stood up to the Chinese government through online activities and in person, leading to his arrest and detention for 81 days in 2011. Four years after his release, his passport was finally returned to him and he was able to travel to Berlin, where he now maintains a studio and lives.

While he is universally admired in the West, Ai Weiwei remains a controversial figure in the Chinese art world, where few of his peers stood up for him when he was threatened by the Chinese government, and many doubt his sincerity despite his travails. I had hoped that I would find more support for his activism among younger artists, who after all have had far more exposure to Western democracies and have savored the freedoms available in the USA and Europe. While many of them told me that they looked up to Ai Weiwei and regarded him in high esteem, almost none said that they would follow in his footsteps. In part, this is because they know the very real penalties for such activities, especially without a worldwide following of fans who could come to their defense. But actually, their response to politics is far more complicated than mere fear of the Chinese government and reflects a generational shift away from engaging with political issues in general.

By reputation, this younger generation is supposed to be entirely apolitical, unconcerned with social issues and civil rights, and, to a certain extent, this is true. As opposed to their elders who lived through the Cultural Revolution and Tiananmen Square, these younger artists were not framed by political upheaval, nor did they suffer at the hands of the government. Instead, they grew up with upward mobility and economic expansion, beneficiaries of government policies that led to a globalized market economy. So although they grouse about certain government infringements on their rights—censorship of the internet or the family burdens resulting from the One Child Policy—they do not have the life experience to bring political consciousness to bear on their artworks. And yet, I found that beneath the surface, many of the artists I interviewed were deeply concerned with political issues and the future of their country. Though they had doubts that a democratic political system could succeed in a country with 1.3 billion people, they still expressed sadness that they would never have the chance to find out.

Still others object to the very notion that Chinese contemporary art has to be political. They are acutely aware that many of the artists of the 1980s and 1990s were interpreted as making political statements when viewed by Westerners prejudiced by Cold War perceptions of China. Indeed, it seems to be part of their academic training to accuse Americans like myself of looking for evidence of anti-government dissent in the works of Chinese artists. Seeking to redress this situation, they deflect all questions about political views and insist that their art be examined on an entirely different basis, bordering on formalism.

There are a few artists, however, who take on Chinese history and politics in their art. While not quite activists like Ai Weiwei, they are making work that examines the dark side of the Chinese political system and the fallout from a recent history of repression. The artists that most prominently represent this point of view are Zhao Zhao and Sun Xun, two artists with divergent styles and outlooks that nonetheless share a skepticism that sets them apart from many of their peers. While neither would claim credit for being a political artist, eschewing the didacticism that that title often involves, they present artworks that challenge the status quo and provoke others to do the same.

"I don't have big dreams to change the society—there is something more charming to me than that," says Zhao Zhao, sitting in a health food restaurant near the 798 Art District,

Beijing. Despite constant interruptions from people wanting to say hi to him, he continues, "When your goal is to change society, you have to have a certain kind of imagination to make everyone understand what you are doing. But I don't want to make my work too understandable. I don't want to be known by too many people." This is surprising coming from an artist who has built his reputation on making politically charged artworks that have garnered attention from many, including the Beijing police.

Born in 1982, Zhao Zhao grew up in a small city in Xinjiang, an autonomous region in northwest China that is home to the Uyghurs, a Muslim ethnic minority that have watched their rights erode under pressure from the Chinese government. His grandfather, a wealthy landlord and supporter of the Kuomintang, was relocated to this distant region in 1952 during the anti-rightist campaign. Swinging the other way, his father, a university professor, spent his career toeing the Party line and promulgating Communist rhetoric. Zhao Zhao, in turn, was rebellious from birth and recalls numerous instances from as early as his days in elementary school when he stood up to his teachers and was expelled from class. Not many Chinese artists have criminal records, but Zhao Zhao has his share of encounters with the law. In 1999, as a high school student, he proposed a performance to walk naked down the main street of his hometown in the heart of the Muslim community. The date? June 4th, the anniversary of the Tiananmen Square incident. He was brought in for questioning and put under house arrest for a year, delaying his entrance into the Xinjiang Institute of Arts.

In 2004, Zhao Zhao went to Beijing as an exchange student with the Central Academy of Fine Arts but soon switched to the Beijing Film Academy for its curriculum. His uncle had been Ai Weiwei's elementary school teacher, and both families knew each other well because Ai Weiwei's father, Ai Qing, a famous poet, had also been exiled to Xinjiang in the 1950s. Zhao Zhao met up with the elder artist at an art opening and the two hit it off.

"When I told Ai Weiwei that I wanted to be a painter, he said, 'so boring' and suggested I take two years off to make documentaries. We spent the next seven years working together, day in and day out," he recalls.

Their first films together were mind-numbing examples of *cinéma vérité*, such as *Chang'an Boulevard*, 2004, for which Zhao Zhao spent a month recording each block of the famous avenue that runs through Tiananmen Square in a series of over 600 one-minute episodes that were strung together into a ten-hour film. When he was done with this lengthy project, Zhao Zhao was rewarded by having to do the same for the Second Ring Road, then the Third Ring Road. At nearly the same time, Zhao Zhao made his own project, *Walk*, 2007, in which he traversed the length of the narrowest hutong in Beijing, back and forth 52 times, until he reached the distance of 3312.4 meters. The work that records this banal event is a pair of photographs, depicting the artist at each end of the alley. Projects like these combined a sense of performance with a nostalgia for a rapidly disappearing Beijing as urbanization took over.

Zhao Zhao continued to work with Ai Weiwei, filming *Fairytale*, 2007, a project in which 1,001 Chinese citizens were transported to Kassel, Germany on the occasion of Documenta 12. The following year, with the occurrence of the Sichuan earthquake, the duo were led into much more political territory, resulting in a project documenting the deaths of over 5,000 school children as the result of shoddy construction. In 2009, Zhao Zhao assisted in the filming of *Disturbing the Peace*, the story of Chinese dissident Tan Zouren, who was imprisoned for protesting just these conditions. Ai Weiwei was beaten by local police when he came to Sichuan to attend Tan's trial. Similarly, Zhao Zhao was beaten up by a local hood when out filming one night for Ai Weiwei in Beijing, an incident he then turned into a video titled *Happening*, which culminates in a self-portrait showing his bloody face.

All along, the younger artist was making work with a subversive appeal of its own. Encouraged by Ai Weiwei to think of the world as packed with "ready-mades," Marcel Duchamp's invention of using found objects to make art statements, Zhao Zhao turned other artists' artworks into source material for his own inventions. First, he used woodchips fallen from Ai Weiwei's monumental sculpture *Fragments* to fashion a set of 52 toothpicks in *Toothpick*, 2007. Then he went further by making a string of beads from stones he chipped off of Joseph Beuys' famous *7,000 Oaks* installation in Kassel, in *Necklace*, 2007. Finally, in his most audacious move, he stole a bit of lead from Anselm Kiefer's massive artwork *Volkzahlung 1991* when it was exhibited in Berlin's Hamburger Bahnhof, in order to make a set of coins, exhibited in *Euro*, 2008. These acts of vandalism imbue the resulting artworks with a frisson of anti-authoritarianism, as if no cow is sacred, no master untouchable, for this younger artist. Much like Ai Weiwei's own signature work, *Dropping a Han Dynasty Urn*, 1995, in which he announced the onset of his art career through an act of destruction, Zhao Zhao declares his presence as an artist by literally breaking off a piece of the past and incorporating it into his new creations.

Two other works from this period underscore the artist's growing political consciousness, but in subtle, almost repressed ways. In *Cobblestone*, 2007, Zhao Zhao affixed a random piece of stone to the plaza of Tiananmen Square using powerful epoxy glue. The protruding stone is an anomalous counterpoint to the vast expanse of Tiananmen, like a lone protestor standing out from the crowds. In 2008, on the day of the opening of the Beijing Summer Olympics, Zhao Zhao returned to Tiananmen Square, dressed as a police officer, and stood there silently, waiting to be discovered. He went undetected for two hours, a performer without an audience, in the midst of a massive amount of people. Of course, by then, his mentor had totally disavowed his support for the Olympic festivities, even though he was the chief designer of the landmark Bird's Nest stadium.

The year 2011 proved a turning point for Zhao Zhao, most notably as a result of the arrest of Ai Weiwei as he was about to

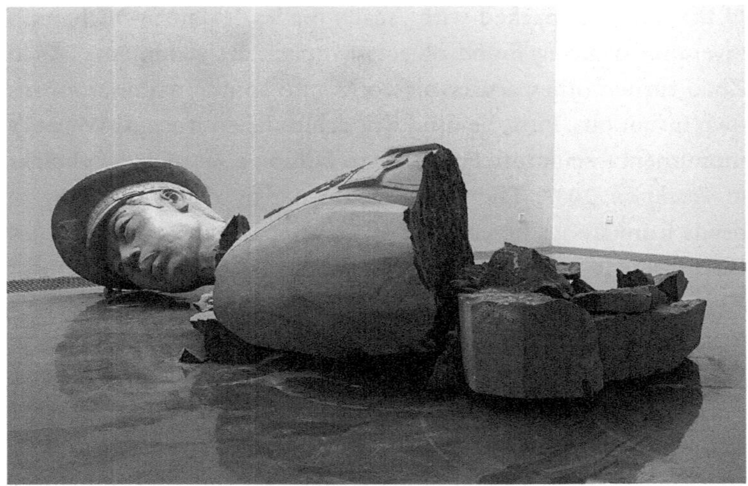

ZHAO ZHAO, *OFFICER*, INSTALLATION VIEW, CHAMBERS FINE ART, 2011.

board an airplane to Hong Kong in early April. Several studio assistants were also rounded up and Zhao Zhao was told in no uncertain terms that his time working for the master was over.

The arrest of Ai Weiwei warranted a response, one that could encompass the range of emotions that Zhao Zhao was feeling at the time. He created *Officer*, 2011, a monumental statue of a policeman, seemingly toppled and shattered across the gallery floor. Zhao Zhao had studied sculpture at his high school in Xinjiang, but to make this work, he hired a craftsman to fashion a life-size replica of himself in a police uniform. He scaled the model up to eight meters tall, rendered in plaster, which he then sent crashing to the floor. The final sculpture was then carved in limestone, carefully replicating the look of a fallen hero. There was one detail that betrayed the true meaning of the work. On the lapel of the officer's uniform was the number 4-3-11, the date of Ai Weiwei's arrest.

Soon after Ai Weiwei's release, Zhao Zhao showed *Officer* at Chambers Fine Art in Beijing. The exhibition went off without incident. But subsequently, Zhao Zhao found that he could no longer show in Beijing. In one instance, the gallery director where he was participating in a group show was called in for questioning and was told quite directly, "Zhao Zhao is not an artist." A second show was also canceled as a result of his participation. A year later, when Chambers Fine Art tried to ship the work from his solo show to New York for what would have been his American debut, the crates were confiscated in the port of Tianjin. Zhao Zhao was fined 300,000 rmb, a price he could not pay, and, even if he could, the works were still earmarked for destruction. To this day, he has no idea what happened to his precious artworks.

"In my opinion, in this country, if you don't accept the reality, what can you do?" he asks rhetorically. "In this country, sometimes problems cannot be solved. Because what you are facing is neither a person nor an organization. There is no door, maybe a wall [. . .] or maybe air."

Zhao Zhao's toppled police officer uses a violent gesture to make a statement. It is a controlled act of aggression that might be interpreted as an anger-filled response to the power of the state, with the artist literally overthrowing an authority figure. But Zhao Zhao complicates such a simplistic interpretation by having the final statue constructed in limestone. By doing so, he concretizes the moment of destruction with an indestructible material, making the gesture perpetually in the present tense, never able to recede into the past. In this way, the actions of the Chinese customs officials in Tianjin virtually completes the work by accomplishing its destruction.

There is also an obvious parallel between Zhao Zhao's fallen policeman and the scores of toppled statues found throughout the globe, often due to changing regimes and deposed dictators. Even if the artist was unaware of the elimination of heroic statues throughout Eastern Europe with the fall of the Soviet Union, for example, he would be entirely knowledgeable about the widespread destruction of Buddhist figures that took place in

China during the Cultural Revolution. Zhao Zhao is a collector of such statues; they punctuate the corners of his studio and have been incorporated into several of his artworks. For the sculpture *Again*, 2012, he gathered a selection of Buddhist statues that he found in antique markets and cut them into featureless bricks. He then assembled them into a single cube, measuring 150 centimeters, looking very much like a minimalist sculpture with no trace of a glorious past. In order to create this and other works in the *Repetition* series, he in fact had to destroy what was left of the damaged sculptures, sheering off any remnants of Buddha's face or torso, completely eradicating its spiritual presence. In this way, he takes the impulse of destruction inflicted during the Cultural Revolution one step further. Yet, by assembling all these fragments into a single cube, he reinvests them with an aesthetic power, an encapsulation of so much that has happened in present-day China, where the past has been eliminated to make way for modernization and globalization.

Similarly, to create his more recent work *How*, 2014, Zhao Zhao bought a 200-year-old wooden Buddha from Shanxi Province and cut it into 258 blocks, which were then covered in gold leaf. In an ironic twist on value, he placed the work for auction at Sotheby's Hong Kong in 2014, where it failed to find a buyer. But his documentation of the process turned the piece into a performative work, raising questions about the nature of creativity, the persistence of influence, the commercialization of the Chinese art market, and the destruction of the past.

Zhao Zhao brought the strain of violence in his work to the forefront when he picked up a gun to create the series later known as *Constellations*, 2013. Guns are not widely available in China, where personal gun ownership is illegal. But Zhao Zhao discovered that he could buy a weapon with relative ease on the internet, completing the purchase of a rifle regularly used for military exercises. He had been examining photographs of the aftermath of the Tiananmen Square incident, noticing that, despite government pronouncements that no massacre had occurred, the evidence of the shootings was clearly visible in the spray of bullet holes on cars and on walls captured in the images. With his rifle, he went about recreating the pattern of destruction, firing bullets into mirrors and glass panels, creating a fascinating pointillism that was reminiscent of stars in the sky. At the same time, these are violent and brutal works, confronting the viewer with acts of destruction.

"*Constellations* turns something specific into something distant," Zhao Zhao explains, noting that "when I made the work, *Officer*, it might have been too specific." As an aesthetic strategy as much as an act of self-preservation, he has gradually moved away from specificity into more conceptual work, he claims, acknowledging that the content is still often influenced by his personal encounters with authority.

In the past three years, Zhao Zhao has engaged in something of a homecoming, returning repeatedly to his birthplace in Xinjiang. He has become fascinated by the vitality and rawness of the Uyghur way of life, which he views as a welcome antidote to the more regulated and sedentary artists' community in Beijing. In many ways, he almost identifies with the Uyghurs, who have staged armed protests and even acts of terrorism, at least according the Chinese government. In *Project Knife*, 2016, he engaged directly with the Uyghur population, gathering knives from over 1,000 individuals and interviewing them about their lives. The knives, archaic and baroque, hold a fascination for Zhao Zhao not only in their potential for violence, but also in their inherent idiosyncratic beauty. They reflect the history of the Uyghur people as well as encapsulating the current eruption of violence in the region. As artifacts used in daily life, each knife becomes a portrait of an individual. He was able to exhibit the installation in Beijing in 2016 despite the fact that these dangerous weapons could be interpreted as supporting the cause of the Uyghurs, in direct conflict with current government policy.

Zhao Zhao has emerged as a global artist in recent years, frequently participating in exhibitions in the USA and Europe.

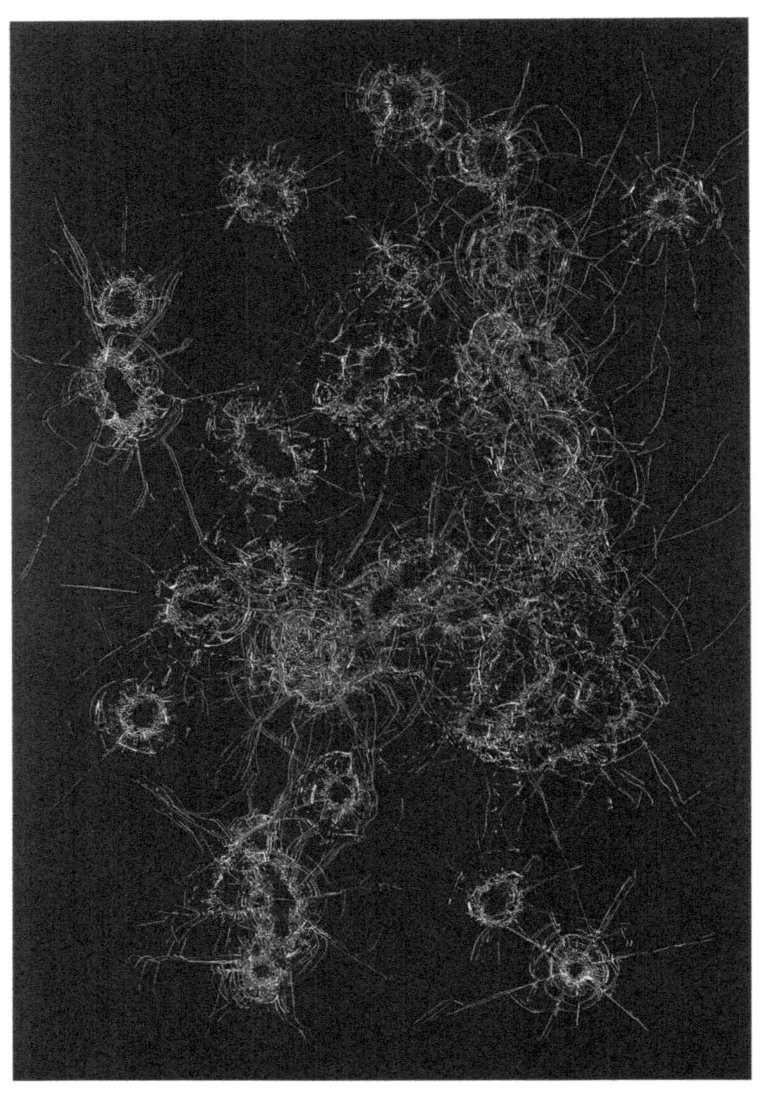

ZHAO ZHAO, *CONSTELLATION NO. 12,* 2015. COURTESY OF TANG CONTEMPORARY.

This is his method of revenge, that is, by demonstrating that he can have a career as an artist even when the odds are against him in China. But even as he has expanded the scope of his audience and the reach of his art projects, he has remained rooted in China, ever attuned to the social issues and political currents that plague his homeland. Zhao Zhao once told me, in an early interview when I was first getting to know him, "When you find a problem, you express it and present the problem to the public, then I think it is already an effective way to make a change."

Sun Xun, on the other hand, is not taking on the Chinese government from the position of activist, but as a philosopher acutely aware that all governments are suspect. He presents his ideas through a wide variety of mediums—woodcuts, charcoal drawings, ink paintings, site-specific installations, and, most of all, hand-drawn animation. His basic concept is to question not only the truth, but all means by which truth is ostensibly delivered in politics, art, cinema, history, and science. To Sun Xun, history is a lie, science is a lie, and art itself is the biggest lie. He believes that even if he wanted to deliver it and was capable of doing so, somewhere in the space between believing and seeing, artist and audience, art world and outside world, the truth would get lost in the telling.

When Sun Xun was growing up in the small city of Fuxin in Liaoning Province near the North Korean border, he already knew that China was a country with at least two histories. First, in school during the day, he studied the Chinese history presented in official accounts, a version remarkably free of such troubling episodes as the Great Leap Forward or the Cultural Revolution. Then, at night, his father would sit him down for a more personal account of the truth, describing what happened to his family during the 1960s and 1970s, when, for example, his grandmother was marched into a public square, forced to wear a dunce cap, and was declaimed as a bourgeois collaborationist for her upper-class background.

Born in 1980, Sun Xun's sense of dual histories was reinforced when he left home at the age of 15 to attend the China Academy of Art's prestigious high school, experiencing severe culture shock as he navigated the differences between a newly modernized city and his provincial hometown. "Everyone where I grew up, including my parents, worked in a factory and thought that people in business were evil capitalists," he tells me. "But in Hangzhou, everyone was doing business." He struggled to reconcile his conflicting experiences: official history vs. family stories; state-controlled factories vs. the new market economy; and past vs. present. It was clear that even in the same country during the same period, two different realities could be found within a span of just a few hours of travel. It was Sun Xun's inheritance to look into this phenomenon.

Much has been made about the fact that Sun Xun's skepticism stems from a specifically Chinese background, as if encounters with duplicitous politicians and historians could only take place in the People's Republic of China. But in fact, this young artist found inspiration in philosophy and novels by Western authors. A key influence was German philosopher Martin Heidegger's 1927 masterpiece *Being and Time*, which challenges traditional methodologies for analyzing existence as inevitably tainting their conclusions through unexamined and inescapable suppositions. Aldous Huxley's *Brave New World* (1932), and George Orwell's *1984* (1949), further advanced his ideas about political agendas manipulating the truth.

"Most people look at history like a performance on a stage. They don't look behind the curtains to see what is really happening," Sun Xun tells me during a visit to New York in 2013 when he was featured in the Metropolitan Museum of Art's Ink Art exhibition. Sun Xun is an artist obsessed with history, as it is recounted in museum exhibits and textbooks, and as it is recalled by its participants. He makes animations from thousands of meticulously drawn frames, often featuring a magician in a tall hat, "the only legal liar," according to the artist. Drawing on political cartoons, instruction manuals, and newsreels, Sun examines how history is recounted, popularized, and manipulated. Yet like many of the artists of his generation in China, he avoids didactic conclusions about his country's political system, preferring to couch his criticisms in surreal metaphors that could apply to any government of any country in the world.

When I ask him if he considers his work to be political, he answers, "To make political art is dangerous." Does he mean he will run into trouble with the Chinese government? He laughs. "No, I can always show my work outside of China, so that is not a problem." Then he turns serious again. "As an artist, to narrow your focus only on the political is dangerous." He then tells me about watching news of the Tiananmen Square uprising on television with his father when he was only nine years old. I ask him if he supports democracy in China. At first, he doesn't understand the word, and checks its meaning in Google Translate. "Ah yes, democracy, yes, of course. But which democracy?" he asks me, ready to debate the differences between the French, British, and American systems of government.

In Beijing, Sun Xun employs up to 30 assistants at his company, π Animation. There in his study, his varied interests are reflected, ranging from many volumes of books in Chinese and English on history and political science to museum-quality prints on the wall by Song Dynasty artists Cui Bai (1050–80) and Fan Kuan (*c.*960–*c.*1030). Tellingly, Sun Xun rejects the influence of such obvious animation enterprises as Japanese anime or Disney studios. Instead, he fuses Eastern and Western influences so thoroughly that several American critics compare his work to artists Raymond Pettibon and R. Crumb while noting that the spirit in his work dates back to the prints of Albrecht Durer, Honoré-Victorin Daumier, and William Hogarth.

But a primary influence that cannot be ignored is South African artist William Kentridge, who also inventively used the tedious process of hand-drawing frame by frame to create evocative and highly romantic animations against a backdrop of political tensions. Sun Xun insists that he did not get the idea to

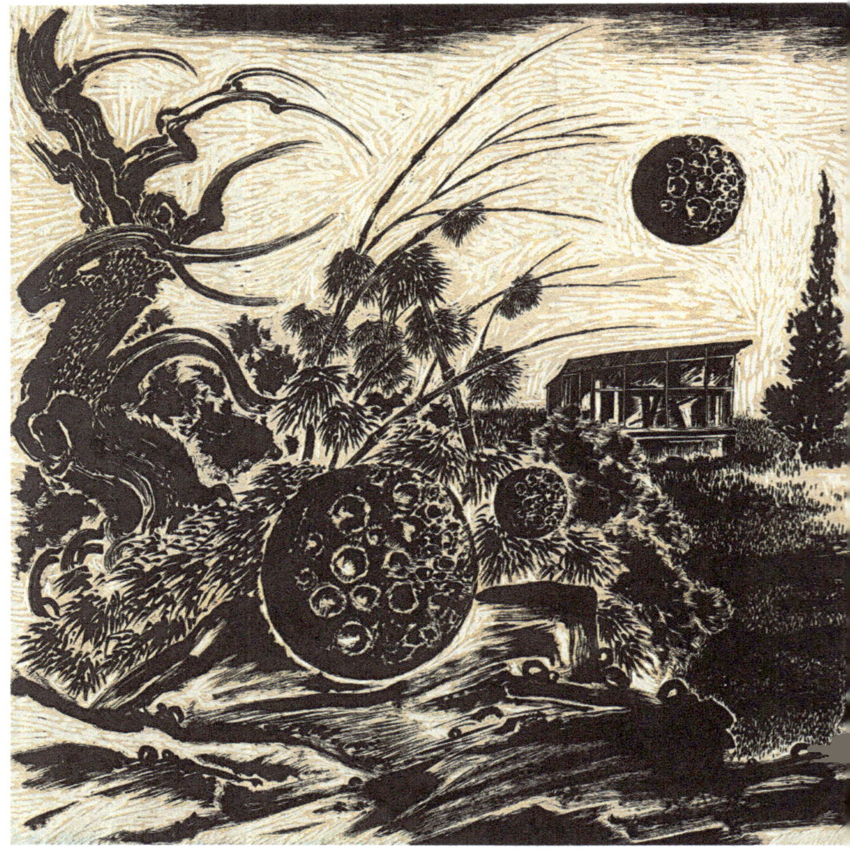

SUN XUN, *TIME SPY*, 2016. COURTESY OF THE ARTIST AND SEAN KELLY GALLERY.

make films using hand-drawn frames from Kentridge, but he does credit the artist with giving him a broader idea of what animation could do, namely, create an entire body of work that amounts to an all-encompassing worldview. From this insight, Sun Xun realized that he was never working on a single individual artwork. Each work was a brick in an overall structure. According to the artist, one thing that makes his

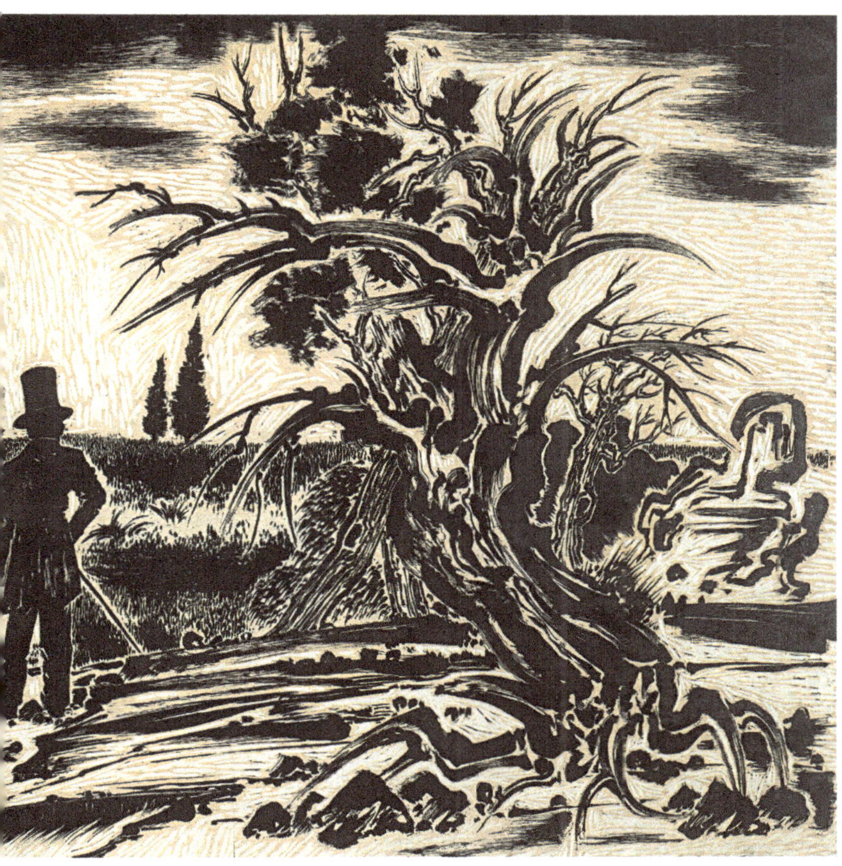

work so difficult to interpret is that, until the structure is complete, no individual work can reveal its meaning. And of course, this structure will never be complete, as long as Sun Xun keeps making more than one film a year, as he has done for the past 12 years.

None of these films provide easy storylines or morals. Instead, Sun Xun appears to be rejecting even the notion of narration, ever wary that any account of history bears evidence of official influence. His concern is not simply political persuasion and government intervention. He is also examining the evolution of historical accounts, from the Dynastic era to contemporary textbooks, noticing the ways that our methods of recounting history have developed over time. Unlike many artists of his generation, he does not adopt a stance of amnesia or an apathy towards the facts. Instead, he searches for "alternative narratives," as once stated by Hou Hanru in describing Sun Xun's work. The alternative he finds is not just a variation on official accounts of political history. It injects doubts into the very notion of objectivity.

"The magician is the only legal liar, though in the seventeenth century, magicians were beheaded like witches, but today they can be superstars," Sun Xun explains. "Now here comes the questions. We know the magician is lying, so why do we pay for the lies? Why does this take place in a theater and why do we buy the ticket? It sound stupid, but it mirrors our world."

This meditation on history culminates in Sun Xun's monumental animation, *21 Grams*, 2010. This film, which runs 27 minutes long, is made from over 30,000 pastel realist drawings depicting 50 scenes in a dystopian landscape. Four years in the making, it was the first work of animation from China included in the Venice International Film Festival. In this film, Sun Xun places the magician in a town filled with colonialist architecture, early twentieth-century technology and World War I flying dirigibles. With ominous music and threatening skies, he establishes a critique of Western capitalist conventions, underscoring his pessimistic view of all political systems.

The title, *21 Grams*, is inspired by the research conducted by one American physician, Dr Duncan MacDougall, in 1907, who claimed to have discovered the weight of the human soul, an experiment that encapsulates the positivist thinking resulting from the capitalist compulsion to quantify and commodify even that thing which is least possible to measure. In *21 Grams*, Sun Xun presents a world where the spiritual has been replaced by demonstrations and monuments, ending with the sorrowful image of a lighthouse beaming out the word "revolution" in Morse code as a lonely man faces the ocean and cries.

For artists of Sun Xun's generation, the primary historical fact they must face is the post-revolutionary transformation of their homeland over the past 40 years. Missing out on the misguided idealism of the Cultural Revolution (1966–76), they must find meaning in a world overrun by capitalist brands. Sun Xun, however, goes farther than any of his peers in evaluating and capturing the psychological mindset induced by this state of affairs. The world he presents in *21 Grams* is not only post-Mao, but also post-Marxist, post-Cold War, post-science, and post-religion. It is an imaginary country filled with plagues of mosquitos, spewing smokestacks, and crowds of magicians.

When Sun Xun chooses ink-and-brush painting, he does not want to evoke a nostalgia for classical traditions or to glorify the past. He often does this to create a juxtaposition between art techniques of the past with present-day conditions and future concerns. In his ink-inspired animation titled *What Happened in Past Dragon Year*, 2014, he startles viewers with a series of quotes from Nikola Tesla and Leon Trotsky, Aldous Huxley and Franz Kafka, posing a sharp and distinctly Western introduction to a film riddled with Chinese allusions. Two dragons in chains wrestle with each other in a sky filled with red clouds, rendered as in a classical scroll painting. But the animation does not remain traditional for long. After an appearance by the magician, now an old man in a wheelchair, the action shifts to a concert hall. The orchestra strains to play a symphony while the ungrateful audience objects, hurling chickens, ducks, and roosters at the stage. The final scenes include images of Presidents Bill Clinton, George W. Bush, and Barack Obama; rallying crowds and ancient erotica; even Tiananmen Square. Instead of the expected loveliness and serenity usually evoked by ink painting, Sun Xun delivers a maelstrom of struggle and discord. According to the artist, his initial inspiration for this work came

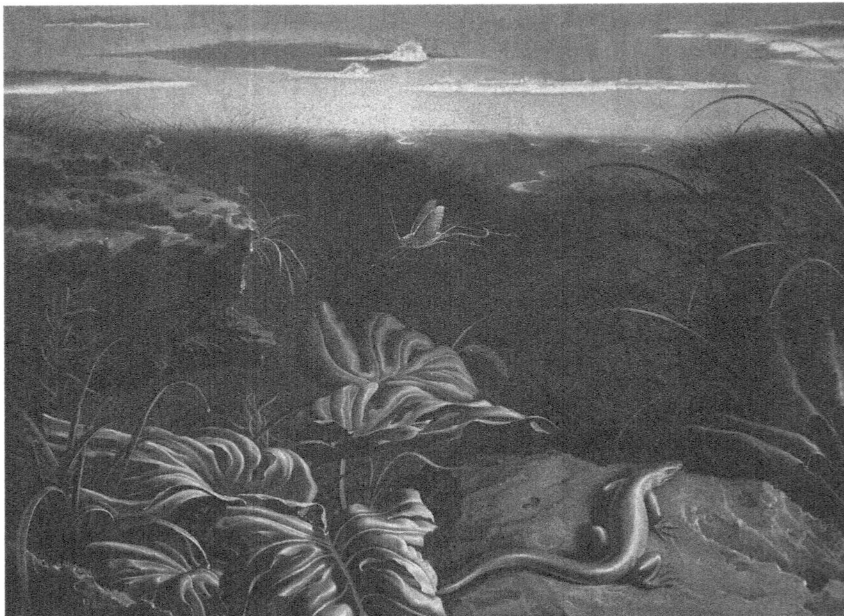

SUN XUN, *21G (21KE)*, DRAWING FOR ANIMATION, 2010. COURTESY OF THE ARTIST.

from a painting by Belgian surrealist René Magritte, *Spontaneous Generation*, 1937, which was in turn inspired by Huxley's *Brave New World*. It is typical of Sun Xun to start in the West, incorporate symbols and techniques from China, and end up with an amalgam that is impossible to tease apart.

Of course, Sun Xun is an artist, not a filmmaker, though many of his animations have been shown in film festivals around the world. As an artist, he is not satisfied to merely have these works projected on blank walls or displayed on monitors and screens. For his installation *New China* at the Hammer Museum in Los Angeles in 2008, he took over the Vault Gallery, incorporating its unique architecture by painting directly on the walls and ceiling to create an environment akin to an old-fashioned history museum. *Beyond-ism* was originally ten three-meter-tall ink paintings displayed at

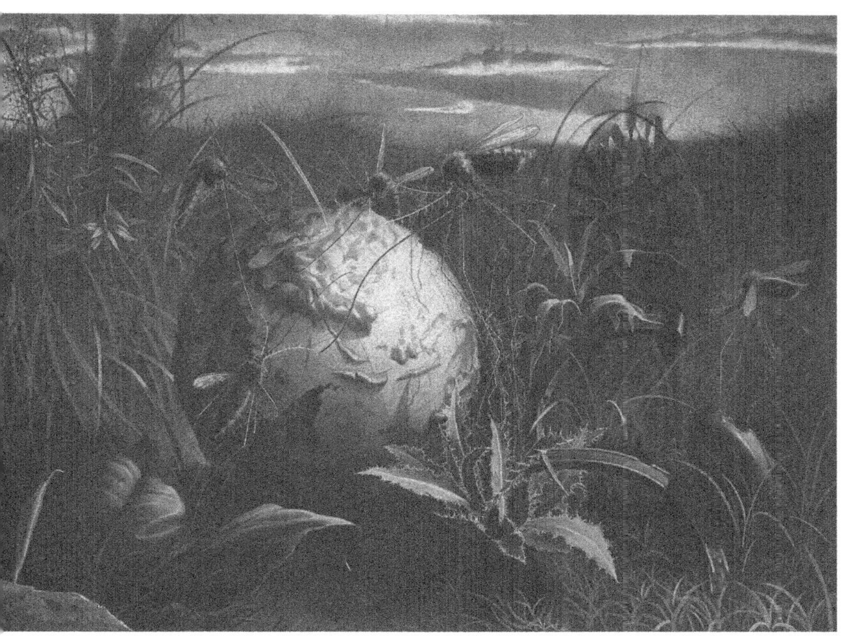

Yokohama City Center in 2010, then the animation produced by π Animation Studio for the Aichi Triennale and finally a major installation at the Rockbund Art Museum in Shanghai in 2010–11, incorporating video, sketches, paintings on paper, and paintings directly on the walls. More recently in 2015, Sun Xun was invited to work his magic on the Zeyi Cinema, a movie theater in Hangzhou. He created *The Script*, a giant immersive environment incorporating murals on the walls and ceilings, paintings hung in hallways, and animations on a mammoth circular screen surrounding the theater's column, while the artist's various films played in four auditoriums. In galleries and museums internationally, Sun Xun has literally moved in, set up shop, and transformed the environment with paintings that would last only as long as the duration of the exhibition.

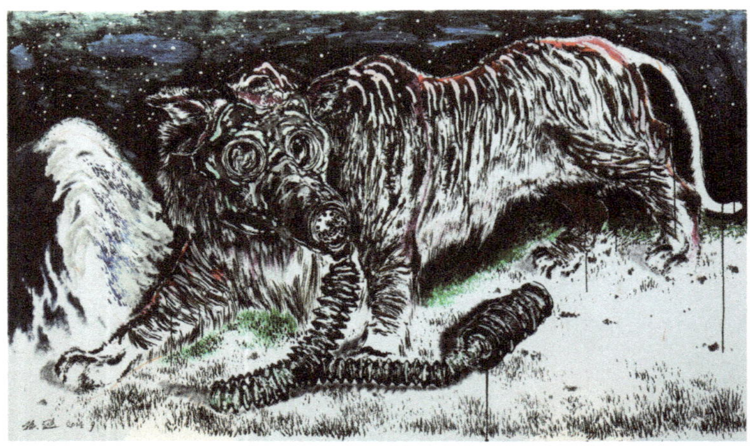

SUN XUN, *TIME VIVARIUM*, 2015. COURTESY OF THE ARTIST AND SEAN KELLY GALLERY.

Sun Xun's latest adventure in mammoth yet temporary installations was his contribution to Art Basel Miami Beach in 2016. Commissioned by the Swiss watch company Audemars Piguet, he created *Reconstruction of the Universe*, a sound-and-light environment built on the boardwalk of Miami Beach. Filling a bamboo structure with scroll paintings, ink drawings, and oversized woodcuts, the space was also punctuated with crystal balls filled with projections of animations. At the end of the exhibition was an outdoor cinema displaying *Time Spy*, a 3D animation film, compiled from thousands of frames of woodcuts made by hundreds of Chinese art students. Spectacular at night, when the film and the exhibition literally glowed in the dark, the installation deconstructed the concept of time, making a watchmaker seem like a magician in his own right.

While Sun Xun's work seems more surrealist than political and Zhao Zhao's installations are more conceptual than populist, both artists are making political statements about the current situation in China, each in their own way. This is not art that comes from reading the headlines, but from a deeply skeptical view of official announcements. Both artists have personally experienced the duplicity of state power, yet they are not merely trying to reveal that hypocrisy. Instead, these artists are trying to shift viewers' perceptions so that the audience can share in their deep-seated disbelief and glimpse the limitations placed on popular thinking, unconsciously and consciously.

It is telling that both Zhao Zhao and Sun Xun enjoy vibrant art careers, with exhibitions in China and throughout the world. They have demonstrated that the use of metaphor may be the most effective way of communicating their viewpoints without the risk that the government will shut down their exhibitions. That does not prevent them from putting their points across, whether it is about the pervasive power of propaganda or the condition of the Uyghurs in western China. It is not government censorship, but the threat of making moralistic, one-dimensional artworks that challenges them and keeps them creating meaningful messages through art.

6
POST-TRUTH

The most pressing issue facing most young artists in China is not censorship or government oppression, but urban redevelopment, which forces them to undergo rapid changes time and again. For every artist in this age range, change is the one constant in their upbringing, often wiping out any remnants of the place where they were born or the neighborhoods they grew up in. Before their eyes, China changed from a primarily rural society where 80 percent of the population lived in the countryside to a nation of megacities with over 50 percent of its populace residing in urban areas. This urbanization, the result of an economic revolution, has had a severe impact on the psyches of many young artists, rupturing any sense of continuity with the past and dislodging them from the assurance of any sense of reality.

For many citizens living in cities like Beijing and Shanghai, they have witnessed a deterioration of their quality of life, as housing costs soar and pollution destroys the environment. Indeed, many young artists have been hit particularly hard, having to pick up and move repeatedly as a result of forced evictions from their studios as one neighborhood after another is slated for redevelopment.

Sun Xun, for example, may have a successful art career with projects taking place throughout the world, but the major project he faced this year was dismantling his studio and moving his practice to a new location. This was a formidable job given that he occupied over 1,000 sq. meters in a two-story building with a succession of rooms for printmaking, draftsmanship, painting, and installation as well as his animation company. The studio was located in Heiqiao, a neighborhood that once was a garbage dump and whose streets were still flooded with debris and stray dogs. Despite its dissolute appearance, Heiqiao had attracted hundreds of artists filling its industrial warehouses, all forced to move when the district was slated for redevelopment. Unfazed, Sun Xun found a new place to work in a storefront in a nearby commercial street, two-thirds the size of the original and almost three times as expensive, raising his rent from $30,000 to over $80,000 annually.

Young Chinese artists like Sun Xun represent a unique generation, in that they have been born into a state of rapid urbanization with little connection to traditional communities that once characterized Chinese society. In this way, they represent the perfect test case for evaluating the long-term impact of these changes on Chinese culture. Will their artworks reflect the economic upheavals they have experienced? How will they interpret widespread cultural transformation? What will happen to their identities as artists? What will be their primary form of expression?

Rather than providing a straightforward response to these questions, young Chinese artists are making works steeped in ambiguity and metaphor. If there is one dominant trend, it is their intent to challenge depictions of reality and to question claims to authenticity. For many artists, sculpture and installation art are the perfect means to convey their sense of alternative realities. They are even creating total environments as a way of interrogating the notion that reality is fixed, permanent, and discernable, in order to convey their life experience, which has been just the opposite.

"I feel that there is a type of formal ambiguity that these artists deal with and that this is a response to realism as an artistic mode," says art historian Lee Ambrozy, who has been a witness-participant to this generation for the past decade. "The use of very realistic, representational or figurative types of art are generally seen to be the work of the state. An artwork that is overtly legible and easy to understand and easy to read is not something this younger generation is interested in at all." According to Ambrozy, this "strategy of ambiguity" is a form of social critique, far more effective than didactic works that might encounter direct government censorship and, at the same time, far more effective as compelling works of art.

Despite this desire to obfuscate or complicate realities, it is impossible for a Chinese artist to escape an engagement with Realism, the dominant art form in China throughout the twentieth century. From 1949 to 1976, Socialist Realism was the only mode of expression tolerated by the political forces in control of the country. Even with the reforms of the 1980s and 1990s, with the attendant experimentation in avant-garde art, forms of realist painting still very much dominated the Chinese art scene. The innovations of those decades were labeled New Realism or Cynical Realism because, instead of depicting the peasants and soldiers of the Cultural Revolution, artists turned their attention to the new conditions in China, such as alienation and the impact of globalization. They employed the techniques of Realism to ironic effect.

All this history leaves its mark on the new generation of Chinese artists, if only because they are rigorously schooled in the techniques and methodology of realist painting and sculpture as part of their academic training. Virtually all of the artists that I interviewed had undergone a lifetime of training in realistic depictions of still lives and plaster casts, starting in early childhood, just to qualify for the entrance exams to the leading art academies. Once enrolled, they would face years of repetitive tasks, copying Old Masters until they had perfected their technique. To them, Realism represents authority, either of the state or of the Academy, leaving many with the desire to reject this as a reactionary form of art-making.

Yet, try as they may, they are still tempted to make use of the formidable skills they acquired and to reintroduce elements of realism in their decidedly postmodern creations. Appropriating and replicating characteristics of Realism is evident during even the most cursory survey of art being made by this younger generation, even though most would say that their work had nothing to do with the lessons that they learned in school.

Given that these artists struggle with their own personal experience of reality and at the same time have to re-evaluate the impact of their training in Realism, their artworks contain a double dose of conflict, both in the issues that they are trying to address and the ways they choose to express themselves. There is a sense that reality is not a fixed, assured state of being, but a negotiation between complex forces, subject to alteration on a whim. While some experience this as a kind of burden of insecurity, others relish the freedom granted by such loosening of the rules. If anything can happen or change, then anything is possible. It is this sense of limitless possibilities that they most relish exploring in their work.

For example, there's Shanghai artist Jin Shan, born 1977, who makes use of his extensive training in realist art to appropriate the look of classical statuary, which he then mutilates and explodes, turning galleries into war zones or funhouses, depending on how you look at it. Ever the provocateur, this is an artist who regularly takes risks, walking the fine line between wicked humor and deadly seriousness. Risks with materials, risks with misinterpretation, even risking his reputation, Jin Shan never shies away from crossing the line, but knows how to stop just short of total chaos. After all, this is an artist who created a spot-on realistic replica of himself, peeing like a fountain in the canal in Venice during the 2007 Biennale. Residents were so convinced by this statue that they called the police to complain.

Trained in oil painting, but now working primarily as a sculptor, Jin Shan blends references from the ancient Greeks and Romans, Renaissance art, Christianity, Daoist temples, and Cultural Revolution iconography. He pours silicon and plastic into molds he creates, adding sticks and wires and other ephemera that bifurcate the resulting forms. Both sensuous and repulsive, his works pull and push his audience in different directions, criss-crossing cultural boundaries. Yet Jin Shan argues that his work is rooted in the current conditions in China, particularly the state of doubt and ambivalence that so many of his peers find themselves in.

"We are living in this kind of shifting period—our society and philosophies are shifting," he says, speaking from his studio on the outskirts of the city, ironically located in the middle of a housing development whose landlord offers space to artists for free to inhabit his half-empty buildings. Speaking of recent Chinese history, he continues, "We tried the right and we tried the left. Now we are not on the right or the left, so we are looking for this new direction for ourselves and I don't know if we can find it."

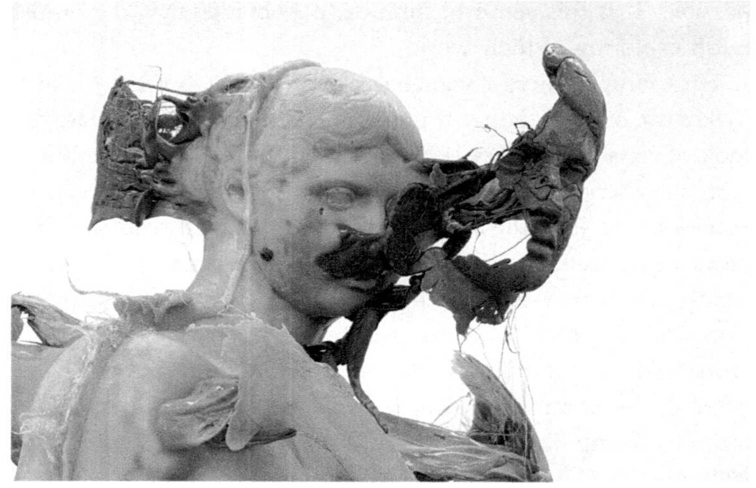

JIN SHAN, *NOWHERE* (DETAIL), 2015. COURTESY OF THE ARTIST.

Instead of the surety of a deliberate path, Jin Shan explores moving in several directions at the same time, intentionally confusing viewers to convey his own fluctuating state of mind.

Likewise, there's the painter Cui Jie, born 1983, who spent years reinventing her approach to realist painting to realize something akin to a kind of cubist rendition of Chinese cities. In works like *Backdoor to Jiayuan Hotel*, 2014, or *Entrance to the Parking Lot*, 2014, she riffs on the patterns of the industrial landscape, while still capturing something of the anonymous architecture that punctuates Chinese cities. Blending the various influences found in these urban settings—European Bauhaus and Futurism, Soviet communist design—Cui Jie conveys the collision of forces impacting the psychological state of its inhabitants, an aesthetic madness born from the era of the Open Door Policy.

Installation artist Zhang Ding goes even further in drawing out the underlying violence of this state of urbanization. Using razor wire and hammers, plywood and tar, he makes works that are dangerous to experience, such as a machine that shatters light bulbs mounted on a conveyer belt as they pass by, or a rickety tower which viewers are invited to climb, only to look down on a bank of prickly cacti. His work is also very noisy, as in the case of one installation in which he mounted monumentally tall audio speakers, blasting so loud that the sound shook the Ullens Center of Contemporary Art in Beijing when shown there in 2013.

Born in 1980 in the remote city of Gansu in the Gobi Desert, Zhang Ding came to Hangzhou to attend the China Academy of Art for graduate school and later relocated to Shanghai where he now maintains his studio. "The city I lived in was quite violent. Everyday you could read news about murders or dead bodies being found in the mountains behind my school," he says, describing the roots of his interest in violence. He talks about gang violence in his high school and one incident when a classmate ran from the police, the officer firing warning shots as he chased him. But when I ask him if he thinks China is a violent country, he answers that it is not possible because "there is too

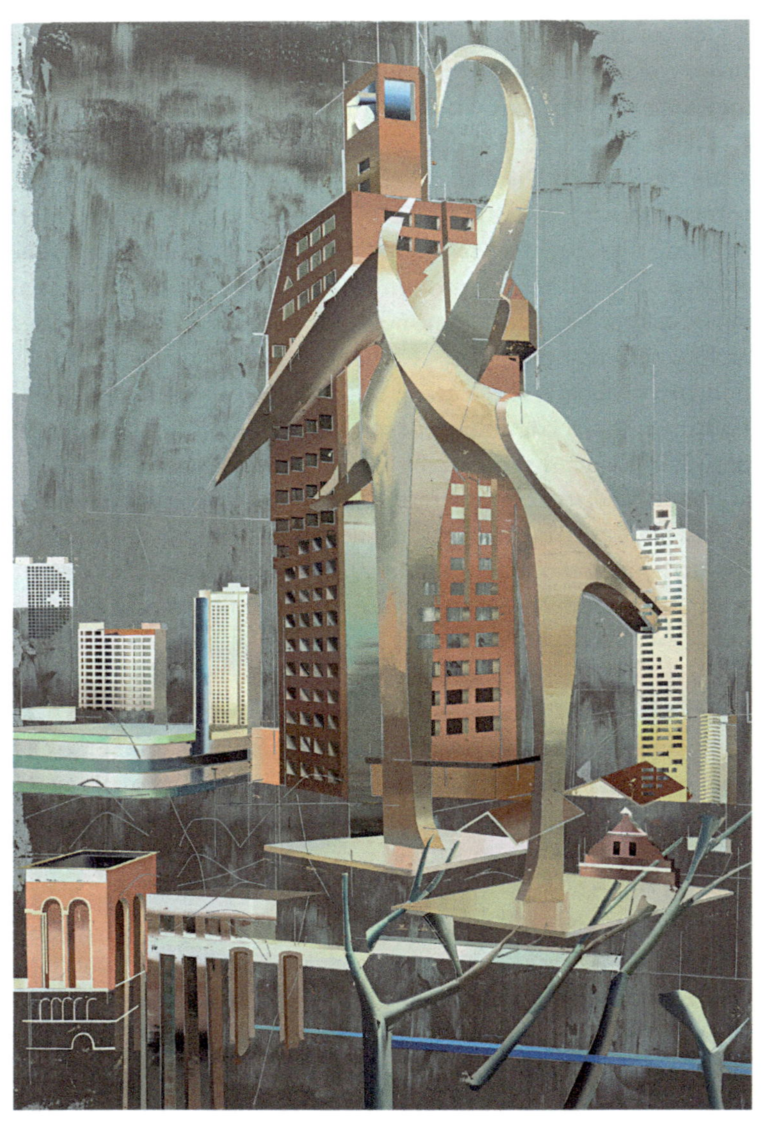

CUI JIE, *SHANGHAI EAST CHINA GRID COMPANY*, 2016. COURTESY OF LEO XU PROJECTS.

much oppression." By this he did not just mean government oppression, but also the oppressive need for survival in a country experiencing increasing material demands alongside very low wages. Perhaps as a reaction to such repressive forces, Zhang Ding has made increasingly explosive works incorporating elements of performance, such as *Opening*, 2011, which converted his opening at ShanghART Gallery into a nightclub complete with go-go dancers, and his more recent *Enter the Dragon*, 2015, at ICA London, where he used his installation as the site of a battle-of-the-bands, with live musicians filling the space with blisteringly loud rock-and-roll music.

It is not coincidental that all three of these artists are based in Shanghai, a city overrun with the cultural collisions brought on by rapid development. In the past two decades, Shanghai has changed beyond recognition, with a population growth rate of 40 percent, resulting in its current population of 23.5 million people. In 2000, Shanghai had just opened its international airport and erected its famous Oriental Pearl TV Tower. Today, the entire skyline resembles something out of science fiction, punctuated by the new 125-story Shanghai Tower, China's tallest building and the world's second-tallest skyscraper. Once considered a cultural wasteland, Shanghai has recently opened almost a dozen new art museums, offering these artists an infrastructure to create and display their work. But beyond the major institutions, Shanghai also offers alternative spaces such as AM Art Space, founded by young artist Yu Ji in 2008.

"I think my generation represents a gap between the local and the international. It has to do with globalization," says Yu Ji, who in addition to running AM Art Space is making an impact with her sculptures and installations, most recently at her solo exhibition *Black Mountain* at Beijing Commune gallery in 2016. In this installation, she created fake boulders from sand and silicon, artificial elements that looked like they came from a natural environment. The sculptural works were accompanied by a video showing the artist dragging one of her boulders up Seven

Star Mountain in Taipei. At her opening, she performed *Improvised Decision*, accompanied by artists Li Bowen and Nunu Kong, leaving residue marks throughout the exhibition space. Yu Ji's physical presence, both in the objects and the video, made palpable the extent to which her work was about labor, finding the spiritual component in banal materials.

In talking about the impact that globalization has had on her generation, Yu Ji explains, "When we were little, we still lived as a collective group. Nobody had a super-individualized identity. Huge economic developments were still yet to come." She herself was born in Shanghai in 1985, a year she believes is a generational turning point. Those born after her represent a still younger generation, totally unattached to a more traditional Chinese upbringing. Those who have grown up with only a landscape of skyscrapers are still more individualistic and self-involved than Yu Ji's generation, according to the artist. But what is certain from her statements is that even an artist who grew up in a major city, remaining in the same place, underwent severe cultural

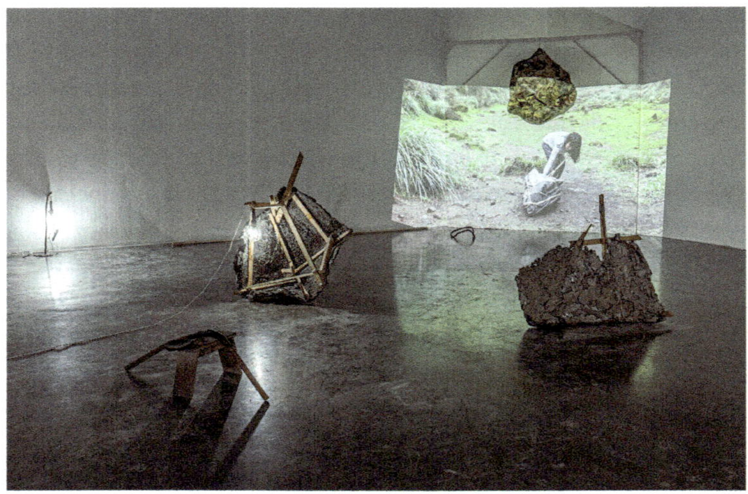

YU JI, *BLACK MOUNTAIN*, INSTALLATION VIEW, BEIJING COMMUNE, 2016. COURTESY OF BEIJING COMMUNE.

upheavals, due to the comprehensive urbanization of their environment over the past 30 years. For artists who grew up in rural areas or came from smaller provincial cities and then migrated to a metropolis to pursue their education and careers, the change would feel even more extreme and disorienting.

Some artists take on the issue of globalization directly, creating depictions of the overgrown cities or polluted skies. Beijing photographer Liu Di, for example, digitally creates pictures of mammoth animals—a panda, a frog, a chimpanzee—towering over and trapped within urban landscapes. Inspired by his rides on crowded buses in the city, these surrealistic photographs perfectly capture the distorted sense of reality experienced in the cramped conditions of a megacity. Rather than merely illustrating a problem, works like Liu Di's complicate meanings and methodologies in ways that may be frustrating to sociologists looking for evidentiary proof. But the results are, in many cases, provocative artworks, even when seemingly serene and quiet on the surface.

Hu Xiaoyuan's practice grows directly out of her training as a realist painter but veers off in its own direction. Born in Harbin in 1977, she came to Beijing to attend the preparatory high school for the Central Academy of Fine Arts and later attended the school for college, where she met her husband Qiu Xiaofei, a semi-abstract painter. But even before she arrived in Beiing, she had undergone training in realist drawing since early childhood. As she recalls:

> According to what I remember, kids went to learn Chinese ink painting only to become amused and cultured, sort of like half-playing half-learning. But, later, when I turned 12 years old, my parents hired a real pro to teach me art. From the beginning, I went to his place every week to learn drawing since he kept many different still life objects and plaster busts there. Anyway, basically my childhood life kind of stopped at 12 years old.
>
> From that time on, all my time is divided between three places. Everyday, I would first go to school in the morning for normal school education. After I finished classes at school at 4 or 5 in the afternoon, I would carry my drawing board with me and go study drawing after

> school. Aside from this class, I still went to my teacher's house for two tutoring sessions each week. I completely lived my life according to my parents' requirements and expectations.

Today, Hu Xiaoyuan creates minimalist works by tracing the grain of wood planks on to silk, drawing stroke after stroke in Chinese ink. She then covers the original wood in white paint and stretches the silk over it, finally arranging the boards into precarious installations. The resulting work is convincingly real—the patterns of woodgrain look natural. Yet it all is a faux reality, manufactured to look original. For Hu Xiaoyuan, like Yu Ji, the work is all about a physical relationship to the materials, evoking a sense of serenity instilled through repetitive labor.

In 2015, Hu Xiaoyuan opened an exhibition, *Ant Bone*, at Beijing Commune. In this installation, Hu took discarded support beams, reclaimed lumber of unknown origin and dismembered guard rails, cut and grinded them, and reassembled them with supporting metal pieces into a brand new structure, highlighting the contrast between the delicate and slender silk and the raw and tough metal and wood. It was a meditation on the symbiotic relationship between the weak and ephemeral and the strong and durable. As the artist herself stated at the time of the show, "During the briefest of moments, the trivial, humble, shallow, and petty characters or animalistic instincts show up ever so faintly, but with a resolve that precludes removal."

But removal, or at least reclamation, did indeed occur after Hu Xiaoyuan's exhibition ended, when the next artist chose to use the remnants of her installation and the refuse of her packing materials to create an installation of his own. *Temple of Candour* by Liang Shuo created a garden landscape from just those cast-off materials, inspired by a Qing Dynasty description of scholars visiting a dilapidated monastery. Over the course of 18 days, using only materials he found on site, he completely reconfigured the gallery to resemble an outdoor space, using packing crates to build columns and sheets of blue foam to form a lake.

The experience was entirely transformative, transporting viewers from beyond the industrial gallery space into a very different time and location.

To create such an evocative work, Liang Shuo (who was born in 1976 and also attended the Central Academy of Fine Arts and is currently working as a professor there) has created his own unique aesthetic system that he calls *Zha*, meaning residue or sediment. By this he means to develop a working practice of finding creativity within the most constricted of realities. According to the artist, he taps the latent energy still present in restricted conditions. In his own words: "If there is no limit, there is no freedom; if there is no condition, there is no expression."

"I don't make a lot of work[s], most of them were improvised on the spot. In fact, I always make site-specific work, which are [*sic*] not replaceable or replicable," Liang explains, sitting in a studio where he is surrounded by crowds of small-scale sculptures made primarily from the kind of plastic goods found in flea markets and knock-off shops. He is an interesting contrast between an almost Zen-like master and a Jeff Koonsian showman.

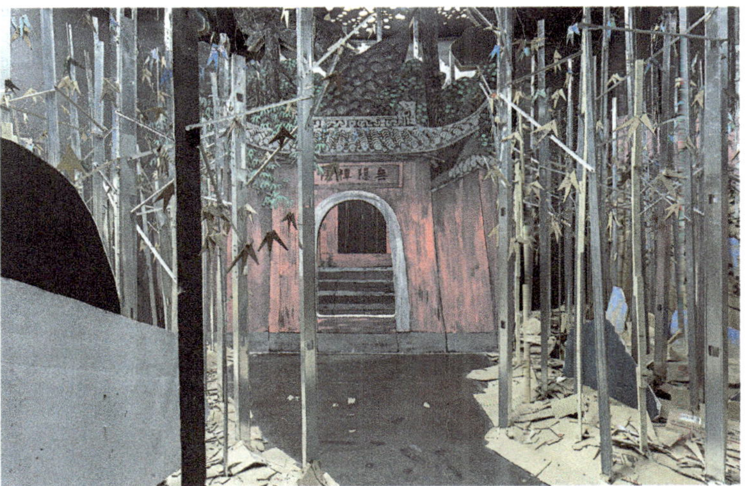

LIANG SHUO, *TEMPLE OF CANDOUR*, INSTALLATION VIEW, BEIJING COMMUNE, 2016. COURTESY OF BEIJING COMMUNE.

He contrasts his current grubby studio space, located next to a dusty parking lot, with the type of landscape valued in classical Chinese literature and painting.

"The present landscape that we see outside the window is not something valued in traditional culture," he explains, continuing, "The scenery that I see is not actually its physical appearance, but rather the physical relationship I have with it as time evolves." He attributes his understanding of materials not to contemporary art but to traditional culture, which brought him to a deeper relationship with reality. Yet nothing could be farther from classical scrolls and Buddhist statuary than the knick-knacks filling his studio. The connection is far from clear. "I live in an environment where many things mix together, a melting pot of a multitude of ideas where ancient thinking may be found. There are some eternal threads and concepts that connect the past and present," he says.

What Liang Shuo so aptly conveys with his words, if not his works, is the palpable collision of cultures evident in every corner of major Chinese cities, due to the dual impact of urbanization and globalization. Urbanization has supplanted traditional community with more atomic and anonymous interactions. Globalization has opened the doors of China to a host of influences from the West. Together, they are eradicating vestiges of traditional culture for which some artists feel a deep nostalgia. As one of the older artists in his generation, now on the verge of turning 40, Liang Shuo retains an allegiance to classical Chinese culture, which he views as a more effective approach to reality than the Socialist Realism of his academic training. Others, younger than him, might not be so keenly aware of this loss of culture, but experience a kind of rootlessness nonetheless.

Installation art is certainly one of the best ways of addressing this state of affairs, given that it challenges reality with an all-encompassing experience in the gallery space. This is one reason why so many of the artists struggling with these issues have turned to installation art as their preferred medium. But to return to Hu Xiaoyuan's use of this strategy, their intention is to create a replica of reality to challenge notions of realism. While this may seem like a Western invention, or at least a reliance on an art form that emerges from a global dialogue, there is something particularly specific about the current conditions in China that might fuel this impulse to create a faux environment. China today is a country filled with replicas, from the knock-off bags at Beijing's Silk Market to The World, a Shenzhen amusement park which contains replicas of the Eiffel Tower, the Statue of Liberty, and other international landmarks. China embodies the postmodern notion of simulacrum, the idea that the replica is ultimately more significant than the original.

"China is super messy, noisy, and full of fake products. It's an extremely restless atmosphere," says Tong Kunniao, born in 1991, one of the youngest artists that I interviewed, who is holding exhibitions of his work in the 798 Art District just a year after graduating from the Central Academy of Fine Arts. With long, dark hair and a handsome face, he could be a rock star. But instead, he is making installations with more than a little resemblance to the American artist Jon Kessler using cast-offs, knock-offs, and plastic products that are mechanized to move and make sounds as viewers approach. Entering one of his exhibitions is like walking into the middle of a three-ring circus, with motion detectors set to animate mannequins as the visitor passes amid various assemblages.

"To a certain extent, I think I am taking the rags of the city—the vicious, the poorly made, and the vulgar—and putting them in my work," he says. "But I've found these can be powerful too." Though Tong would not describe himself as a bad boy, he does admit that he was practically unteachable at the Central Academy of Fine Arts, where he found sculpture classes still based on plaster casts unspeakably boring. Instead, he engaged in performance art, driving his teachers to distraction. He hit upon his method of working when he moved all of his sculptures from class into a single studio and discovered that he liked the cacophony of forms. When I ask him what he would consider his primary influence, he doesn't mention other artists or movements. Instead he says, "I think about releasing something and setting things free."

The concept of freedom resonates particularly strongly for this artist because his father served time in prison for gambling. Even though that happened before he was born, Tong likes to contemplate his father's state of mind. "I've tried talking to my father about his experiences, but he always tells me that the past is past, and there's no point in talking about it," he says. On further reflection he adds, "It's perhaps also a generational thing: my father's generation has gone through the Cultural Revolution—they are more serious, whereas my generation is more open, and don't necessarily hold a strict political, social, or cultural ideal. There's no need to define things as clearly now."

In this, Tong Kunniao embodies the kind of freedom that this younger generation so pursues, a freedom that comes from recognizing the flux and flow of life in a major city in China, where so much is out of your control that you might as well make the most of an opportunity when it is presented. So, for example, this artist made fun of the entire gallery experience by choosing an old dog as the named curator of the exhibition. Also, instead of an elaborate banquet, as is customarily held on opening night, Tong ordered a pile of coconuts, which he served as drinks during the reception. According to him, because there are no definitions or rules to follow, "it leaves more freedom and room to play around." When asked what makes him such a nonconformist, he answers, "I just thought, why not?"

But Tong Kunniao's playful attitude towards exhibitions and galleries is just an extension of a generational awareness of the structure of the art world, a world that has come to replace the preeminence of the immediate urban environment as a bedrock of one's sense of reality. For many of these young artists, while their physical world has been revised and replaced over time, the infrastructure for artistic expression has only expanded, with dozens more galleries, museums, and smaller art spaces opening their doors for exhibitions. The creation of a gallery scene in China is a relatively new phenomenon, starting with the founding of less than a handful of spaces opening in 1997. Today, Beijing and Shanghai boast hundreds of galleries in art districts populated with cafes, boutiques, and tourists. China's recent building boom has seen a concomitant glut of museums, with over 1,200 new institutions opening in the past five years. In many ways, the art scene has become more real for these young artists than other locations.

For this generation, this state of art expansion has meant the opening up of limitless opportunities to exhibit and engage in an art career. At the same time, negotiating this new world and navigating its rules has become the key form of social interaction, overshadowing political action and other forms of civil engagement.

Which is why the strategy of ambiguity is so effective at this moment. In a society where direct political action would certainly be met with repercussions, but public engagement can take place in the more elitist realm of art institutions, making work that raises more questions than answers is an effective path towards a productive art career.

Several artists have capitalized on this contradiction, exploiting it with works that challenge the authority of the art world, rather than confronting social issues. In many ways, this is the target for an artist like Xu Zhen, a role model for many young artists in the way he blends references to East and West and pokes fun at the art market. His influence is widespread, extending to the opening of a gallery of his own, both to promote the work of younger artists and to underscore the commercial success of his own art production. His strategies are evident in the work of a number of younger artists who look up to him, along with Damien Hirst and Jeff

Koons, as models of success who manage to manipulate the art world to their advantage.

One such artist is Yang Dongxue, who creates installations and drawings that deliver a satirical punch. Born in 1984 in Shenyang, he dropped out of the Guangzhou Academy of Fine Arts in 2003 to start a heavy metal rock band. Since then, he alternated between rock-and-roll and fine art, with a somewhat more cynical view of the art world than the music industry. "I always feel that the Chinese people are collectively committing suicide because if a man loses his consciousness and goes numb, that means a spiritual suicide," Yang Dongxue tells me, proudly showing off his tattoos as a kind of proof that he would never meet such a fate. In recent years, he has increasingly made art about being an artist, emphasizing the conception or "prelude" to art production over the actual making of works themselves.

Yang Dongxue's attitude to the Beijing art world is highly critical. "Chinese contemporary art is getting more and more bourgeois. No matter the concept of the work, the quality is getting lower and lower." This has not prevented him from exhibiting his artwork widely, including shows with titles such as *Got Used to Consume Today's Achievement with Achievement Habitually* or *Romance in a Humble Moment* at galleries in Beijing and elsewhere. When this contradiction is pointed out to him, he replies a little defensively, "Actually, I don't think there's a concept called art that exists. Art could be defined as a way of a practice. It's a method to extend the boundaries of your consciousness."

This stance is the ultimate rebellion against a product-driven mode of art-making—both that which is taught at Chinese art academies and that which is rewarded by the gallery system. But it is also an expression of personal consciousness, a sense of playful space, that has been so encroached upon by the pressures of life in Chinese cities. Young Chinese artists, such as Tong Kunniao and Yang Dongxue, feel the need to push back against the pressure to conform in the tight living conditions of urban environments, even the pressure to conform to the vagaries of an art career. As such, they are truly representative of a new stage in Chinese contemporary art, in which challenging reality is an expressed intentional goal. For artists like these, it is not necessary for their works to appeal to a broader public or reach wide audiences. It is enough for them to express their own personal meanings, making sense of the world for themselves alone.

7
POST-INTERNET ART

Nothing refutes traditional notions of Chinese identity more than Lu Yang's provocative superhero, Uterus Man. Fueled on blood and estrogen, clothed in a bright pink jumpsuit, Uterus Man is the protagonist of a 3D animation and a fully operational video game, which has attracted thousands of online players as well as support from curators worldwide. While ostensibly appearing to be male, the character derives superpowers from various aspects of the female reproductive organ, including the cervix, the vagina, the placenta, and an umbilical cord. He rides around in a pelvis-shaped chariot, conquers enemies by altering their DNA, even unleashes streams of blood that set off atomic explosions. Part science, part science fiction, the concept of identity in this work goes well beyond more conventional notions of gender roles or transgender personae to posit a state of being that powerfully defies stereotypes.

Like a twenty-first-century Leonardo Da Vinci, Lu Yang herself resists easy categorization. Born in 1984 in Shanghai, she attended the China Academy of Art in Hangzhou, whose new media department, headed by artist Zhang Peili, is renowned, both in China and abroad.[1] Upon graduating in 2007, she began making disturbing videos that involved experiments on dead frogs or capturing the twitches of patients with Parkinson's disease, with action taking place against a throbbing techno soundtrack. Her breakthrough work was *Wrathful King Kong Core*, 2011, an animation in which a Tibetan god of rage is scientifically analyzed for its neurobiology, pinpointing the source of its anger in the amygdala, the part of the brain that controls responses to emotions. Lu contrasted the beauty of a traditional Tibetan mandala with the precision of laboratory techniques, such as brain scans and X-rays. Her point? To question whether consciousness as posed by religion is in fact merely the result of brain chemistry, better studied by neuroscientists than monks.

"A hundred years ago, people used brushes to make art; today we have science and technology," Lu Yang once told me during our series of conversations that have taken place over a number of years, since her first visit to New York in 2012. In person, she does not come off as a geek, but more of a precocious and hip androgyne, with a preference for Japanese fashion and *manga* cartoons. Whereas in global cities like Tokyo or London such types can be found in hoards, here in China, where her look is entirely unique, she undoubtedly stands out in a crowd.

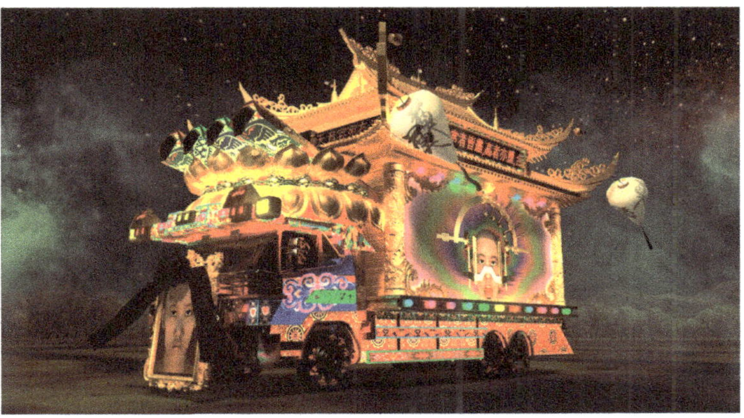

LU YANG, *DELUSIONAL MANDALA*, VIDEO STILL, 2016. COURTESY OF BEIJING COMMUNE.

Nothing about Lu Yang—not her artworks or her fashion sense—would be possible without the internet, which for Lu is both a tool for research and a world she inhabits. When asked about her identity, she immediately responds, "I don't live in Shanghai or Beijing. I live on the internet." As such, she joins China's 731 million netizens, which may be only 51 percent of the country's population but still represents the largest group of internet users in the world.[2] Of course, the Chinese government goes to great lengths to surveil and curtail these online users' activities through outright censorship, often referred to as the Great Firewall. But through proxy servers, known as VPNs, many young Chinese circumvent government restrictions and access the widest range of websites. As such, the internet has revolutionized this generation of young Chinese citizens, not only the artists, drawing them out of isolation and enabling them to cross all sorts of cultural boundaries.

"The internet has had a huge impact on all of us and everything that we do," says Philip Tinari, the director of the Ullens Center of Contemporary Art in Beijing, who witnessed the growth of its power as editor of *Artforum*'s Chinese language website. "When we started the Artforum website, it was still possible that a curator could be named to a Western biennial and people would not have the accurate information for weeks. Most people didn't know who these people were," he recalls, adding, "There was a moment in the mid-2000s when the floodgates really opened and suddenly all information was accessible and available and you were expected to engage with it." This moment so influenced the generation of Chinese artists emerging at that time that when the UCCA opened a survey show of their work, it was titled *ON | OFF*, a reference to switching on VPNs and gaining access to the web.[3] Tinari still refers to this young generation of Chinese artists as the *ON | OFF* generation.

It could be argued that the internet has affected the careers of every Chinese artist across all generations, insofar as it has brought the world closer to them, fueling their aspirations to exhibit internationally and participate in a global dialogue. But for an artist like Lu Yang, the internet has been particularly influential, exposing her to Japanese anime that has inspired her aesthetics and allowing her to access chat rooms with scientists to formulate her research. In return, she posts her videos on YouTube, reaching much wider audiences than she could through gallery exhibitions in China. For Lu and her peers, the internet is the source of inspiration on a number of levels, challenging their belief in an inherently Chinese culture, transcending nationalism and history.

For better or worse, Chinese artists working in this manner are often grouped together under the banner of "post-internet art." The term is highly contentious among Western critics, with some arguing that it is so vague that it could include virtually any form of art practiced today whole others take the view that the movement constituted no more than a short-lived phenomenon between 2008 and 2014 the relevance of which has already passed. Robin Peckham, who co-curated the landmark show *Art Post-Internet* at the Ullens Center for Contemporary Art in 2014,[4] described his criteria as "a historically and geographically defined community of artists who were interested in how network thinking had infected all forms of production, circulation of art and culture while also using the same techniques in the work." Surprisingly, given that the show took place in Beijing, none of the artists were Chinese, which Peckham explains was due to the curators' view that "even though there were Chinese artists who were working with internet ideas, aesthetics and modalities, we never found them trying to absorb how this network thinking had effected the production and distribution of their work." In other words, he found many artists in New York and Berlin who were not only making work about the internet but were using the internet and digital platforms for the distribution and circulation of their artworks. Chinese artists, according to Peckham, remained surprisingly close to the gallery system as their primary means for promoting their projects.

But in the past year, the idea of Chinese artists engaged in post-internet art has seen a revival, with two shows addressing this issue, specifically *.com/.cn*, co-curated by Klaus Biesenbach and Peter Eeley of MoMA PS1, held in Hong Kong, and *After Us*, curated by Lauren Cornell of New York's New Museum, taking place in Shanghai. Both exhibitions were sponsored by the K11 Art Foundation.[5]

"Post-internet is a slippery term, but I think what it has come to mean is art which includes installation, painting, sculpture and every medium, that reflects a culture that has been effected by the internet," says Lauren Cornell. According to Cornell, there are many Chinese artists who are interested in how access to the internet has internationalized their lives in China. But, there are apps for smart phones and websites particular to China, that differentiate the Chinese online experience. Indeed, while Facebook, Twitter, Google, and YouTube are censored and unavailable in China, there are smartphone apps, like WeChat, or online communities, like Weibo, that have their own unique characteristics.

A pioneer in this field is Cao Fei, born in 1978, who was nominated for the prestigious Hugo Boss award given by the Guggenheim Museum for her 2007 artwork *RMB City: A Second Life City Planning*. Existing primarily online, the project is conceived for Second Life, a website comprising virtual worlds where people interact as avatars. Cao Fei is often described as the embodiment of new China, capturing the problems and opportunities of the booming market economy. Young as she is, she has been on the scene internationally for nearly 20 years, including a retrospective at MoMA PS1 in 2016.[6] "Cao Fei visualizes the tension that a person of her age has to face in China on a daily level," says Klaus Biesenbach, director of MoMA PS1, who has championed her work throughout her career.

The story of Cao Fei is a story of contrasts between two generations of Chinese artists. Her father, Cao Chong'en, is an accomplished Socialist Realist sculptor whose statues of leaders

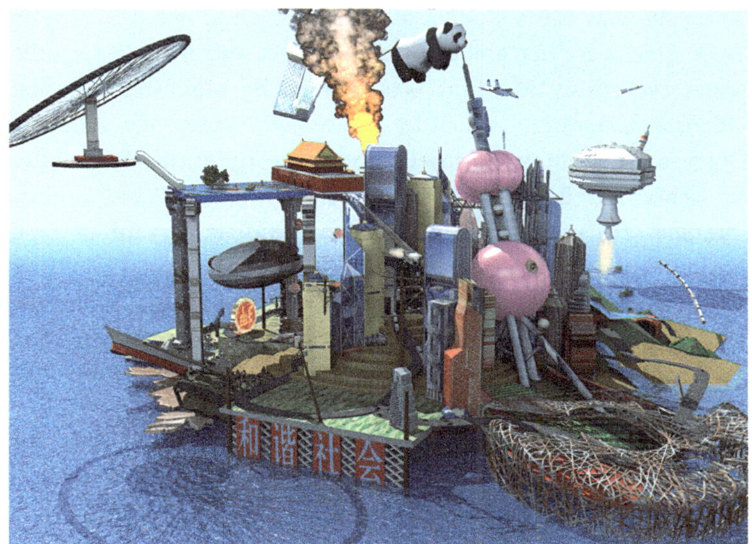

CAO FEI (SL AVATAR: CHINA TRACY), *RMB CITY: A SECOND LIFE CITY PLANNING*, 2007. COURTESY OF THE ARTIST AND VITAMIN CREATIVE SPACE.

from Mao to Deng Xiaoping appear in cities throughout China. He is perhaps best known for his mammoth statue of Bruce Lee gracing Victoria Harbor in Hong Kong. In terms of materials, Cao Fei rebelled entirely, pursuing video art and photography from the beginning of her career. But she has admiration for her father's skill at remaining relevant throughout political upheavals. Growing up in Guangzhou, the center of China's economic reforms, she witnessed her share of change due to urbanization and globalization, and continually sought for ways to make her work reflect those changes.

"She was really fresh and really young but you could feel her potential to be an incredibly unique artist in that she approached the youth culture in a very contemporary way," says Hou Hanru, the renowned curator who is now artistic director of MAXXI, National Museum of the 21st Century Arts, in Rome. He met Cao when she was still a student at the Guangzhou Art Academy in 1999. Struck by her ability to both reflect and interpret a time when everything in China was in flux, he requested her first video, *Imbalance 257*, which loosely tells the story of a group of Chinese art students confused about what the future holds after art school. It is a combination of documentary and drama, interspersed with Communist revolutionary graphics and Japanese animation. "When I got the phone call from him asking for my CV, I was so excited," Cao Fei recalled. "It was the first time I received an international call. I had no internet, I had no email, I did not speak English and I didn't have a resume. I had to ask my classmates for help with translation."

But Cao Fei rapidly got online and on the international art circuit, leading to her breakthrough work, *RMB City*. In 2007, Cao entered a true fantasy world when she engaged with Second Life. Donning the guise of China Tracy, she spent eight to ten hours a day on her computer, even developing an ill-fated romance with an aging Marxist in the USA, captured in her film, *i.Mirror*. In Second Life, she went on to create a virtual city, *RMB City*, where Shanghai's Pearl TV Tower abuts the Forbidden City and skyscrapers overshadow statues of Mao. This city sold genuine real estate, attracting the Swiss collector Uli Sigg and the Ullens Center for Contemporary Art in Beijing as buyers. *RMB City* is now in the collection of the M + Museum in Hong Kong. "I do not see the impact of globalization in black and white terms," says Cao Fei. "I observe from different angles."

The explosion of the internet in China occurred so rapidly (especially with the introduction of the smart phone in 2007) that Cao Fei's experience and Lu Yang's capabilities represent two different generations, even though there is only a six-year age difference between them. As a student in Guangzhou, Cao Fei did not even have access to the internet, whereas Lu Yang majored in new media, thoroughly familiar with the latest online developments. For artists of Lu Yang's age or younger, the internet is taken as an essential part of one's artistic development, a way of accessing information about global art movements and a means by which to open dialogues with international curators. Virtually every artist I encountered through my research had their own website, in English and Chinese, and many employed assistants who were fluent in English to conduct business with Western galleries and institutions through email. This is not even to mention their extensive networks through social media sites, where applications like WeChat offer access to 850 million users worldwide.[7]

There have always been new media artists in China, going back to Zhang Peili and Wang Gongxin, pioneers in video art. More recently, Shanghai artist Xu Wenkai, who goes by the handle aaajiao, has explored installations with sculptural elements generated by digital algorithms. Trained in computer science, his initial contribution to the art scene was as a programmer and founder of such websites as cornersound.com and the artblog "We Need Money Not Art." But lately, he has been actively pursuing a gallery career, showing internationally as China's leading new media artist. In 2016, he presented *Remnants of an Electronic Past*, at the Centre for Chinese Contemporary Art in Manchester, UK, in which obsolete operating systems were displayed as if in a computer graveyard. In the exhibition, *Alias: aaajiao* at Leo Xu Projects in Shanghai, data was translated into form, with stone-like protrusions covering the gallery's floor and walls.

Xu Wenkai's experiments tell us more about the omnipresence of screens and software's domination of the imagination than about the impact of the internet on the creative process. Lin Ke represents the other end of the spectrum, creating short videos using screenshots that documents his various ramblings online. In these works, the artist films his face staring at the screen, capturing his interaction with the computer, his only studio. Though Lin Ke attended the China Academy of Art's new media department, and knows better than to fall prey to seductive software like Photoshop, he presents himself as an average user, relying on websites and digital techniques that are formulaic and commonplace. In his videos, he is seen drawing lines between the constellations of a starry night sky or making up a rap song to go with music he found at a sound website, random acts with little consequence or meaning. But his work has been championed by curators who see in it a new conception of self, generated by interaction with a screen and the endless resources of the internet.

Of far greater relevance to a discussion of "post-internet art" is an artist who, at first glance, has nothing to do with new media at all. Guan Xiao is a sculptor and installation artist who uses the internet as artists from earlier times perused museum archives. Finding serendipitous connections between ancient artifacts, Maori statuary, African textiles, camera equipment, and modern design, she creates amalgamations that are both ironic and well-composed. Mimicking the look of museum installations and

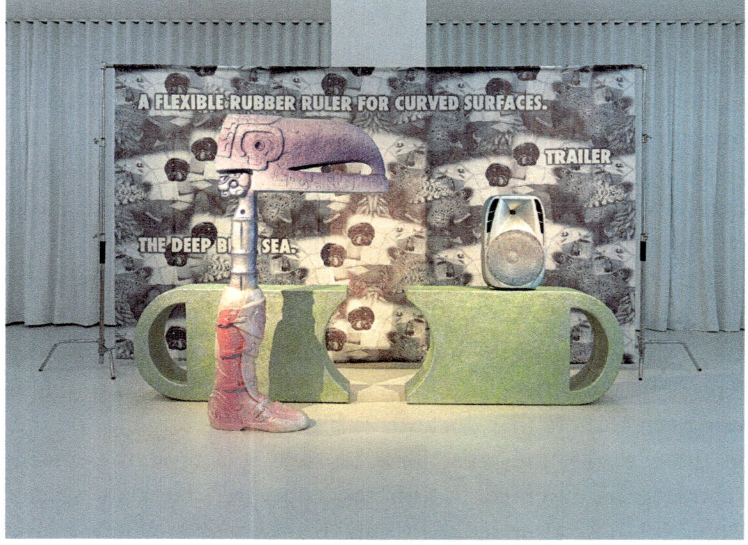

GUAN XIAO, *AMAZON GOLD, JAGUARS AND ELECTRIC EELS*, JSC COLLECTION, 2016. COURTESY OF ANTENNA SPACE.

furniture showrooms, these works remix visual culture, offering a contemporary spin on the notion of the ready-made.

Born in 1983, Guan has been working in Beijing since 2006, when she finished a BA in film directing at the Communication University of China. I met her shortly afterwards, when she was barely yet an artist, much more interested in going out to clubs and following her favorite bands. I immediately felt that she represented a new spirit in the Beijing art scene, freed from the necessity to address social or political issues and much more concerned with addressing the significance of various social trends. Since then she has matured considerably, through an exhibition history that includes projects at the Zabludowicz Collection in Berlin, the ICA in London, the Jeu de Paume and the New Museum in New York.

Still, Guan Xiao is skeptical of the term "post-internet," or of any label that reduces art to a technological innovation. "I learned some things from the internet. The best thing it provides you is that it makes you realize how many kind of combinations are possible," she says, quickly adding, "But you do need to go to the real world, where you can have real feelings about artworks. You can realize whether the work has a body, or if it's a spirit." To explain, she describes the experience of visiting an exhibition by the Swiss duo Fischli and Weiss, which consisted of copies of the entire contents of their studio. "When you see it on the internet, it seems like just copies of real objects. But when you see it in a museum, you can understand their point and see how amazing they are," she says. "They know how to intrigue your heart and your eyes. It's like a big adventure ten thousand times better than Disney Land."

Having exhibited widely abroad, Guan Xiao is also skeptical of any labels, such as "Chinese artist," that have been used to circumscribe her work. "I never think about identity. I don't care about it at all," she says, sitting with me this past year at a fashionable health food restaurant in Beijing. "Everyone's identity is transformed all the time. You can be a bus driver, or a nurse.

Or you can change your nationality. Basically you are growing up and getting old every day, and your identity is always changing," she explains. Transformation, not fixity, is the key concept in her work, not just the way materials are transformed by her zany juxtapositions, but how ideas and concepts are transformed through the experience of engaging with her work. "What would it be to compare a stone to a cell phone, or to a rabbit or carrot? I believe that as long as you can find an equivalence, you can effect a transformation between anything you want," she says.

This conception of identity as expressed by Guan Xiao is shared by many young artists in China, who proclaim a preference for terms like "human" or "universal" to any of the more geographically determined notions of self. What they have gained from their interactions with the internet is a notion that their identity can be altered to match the needs and demands of a particular website or social network. For many, this is tantamount to freedom, a utopian belief in the possibility of escape from societal limitations through transformative experiences that appear to be boundary-less. In this optimistic outlook, there is little room to critique the internet or question whether its offer of freedom is more than an illusion.

Perhaps this is the case for internet users around the world, who regularly escape into fantasy realms or post alternative user profiles on dating sites, guided by a belief in the unregulated nature of the web. In China, this aspiration to assume control of self-identity is all the more poignant given the challenges of an online environment so heavily controlled by the government. To demand consideration first and foremost as merely "human" may be banal in one country, but an outright declaration of human rights in another. Few of the artists I spoke to took into account the politics of this position when they asserted their more generalized identity, instead focusing on the idea that "online, nobody has to know I'm Chinese." This position is not held out of shame or embarrassment for their cultural identity. Not at all. But the fact is that the way they even conceive of framing identity has been shaped by the online experience, which appears to defy cultural or geographic distinctions.

In contrast to this position, there are a few young artists who are now questioning the internationalized promise of the web and are examining the specifics of the Chinese online experience. It would seem obvious for such artists to challenge the limitations of the Great Firewall. But instead, they are taking a more neutral position on government censorship and documenting the enormous creativity that internet users in China demonstrate to navigate around the obstacles of censorship. At the minimum, their artworks and projects demonstrate that the web is not a universal experience but one that is diversified depending on location.

"I think the internet provides common ground and common concerns and common materials," says Cornell. Among those issues of commonality, she includes "common concerns around social media, how one represents oneself online, how one represents oneself through social media, issues of commodification, how everything is marketable on the internet, the increased presence of games, the increased presence of artificial intelligence." To Cornell, these are all things that cut across national boundaries. But she is quick to emphasize that while concerns may be shared, the way artists use the internet is very different in different places. "The internet is very variegated," she says.

For at least one artist, Miao Ying, the Great Firewall is not the end of an experience but the beginning of a journey into a territory brimming with innovation. Claiming she lives on the "Chinternet," her favored term for the Chinese internet, this young artist actually shuttles between New York and Shanghai. She has made work that not only comments on censorship, but also which incorporates the various unique responses to censorship employed by Chinese netizens, from GIFs and memes that are difficult for government censors to control to outright parodies of online government promotional tactics.

Born in 1985 in Shanghai, Miao was a high-school classmate of Lu Yang, with whom she attended the China Academy of Art in Hangzhou, where they both majored in new media. They had no idea what that education would entail, but it turned out to be an introduction to the latest in contemporary art as well as training in the newest technology, under the tutelage of Zhang Peili and Geng Jianye. During this time, she began to surf the net through the only means available, a dial-up connection, making the process painfully slow and expensive. She visited US news websites like Boingboing.net and Reddit.com, discovering for the first time that China censored the web.

With little understanding of what she was getting herself into, she created a dictionary of terms censored on the Chinese internet, titled *Blind Spot*, for her senior project in 2007. It took her three months to go through an actual dictionary, feeding words into google.cn and discovering countless blocked web pages. This was the beginning of her awareness of the vagaries of the Chinese internet at a time when Google, Facebook, and Twitter were not yet blocked in China.

"I remember that Zhang Peili told us that most of us would not think that our final projects were that important, but that these artworks would influence the rest of our lives," Miao tells me, as we meet in New York, hovering around her laptop, her portable studio. She goes on to explain, "Back then, I was feeling like everybody should know about censorship. I could have become a designer, but I chose to be an artist to let people know through my work that censorship exists." Shortly after, she moved to upstate New York where she earned a Master of Fine Arts degree in Electronic Integrated Arts from Alfred University in 2009. She relished the seemingly unlimited access to the web that she had in the USA, but upon graduating, she immediately relocated back to Shanghai. By then, Google, Facebook, and other social networking sites were permanently shut down in China.

"I feel like my feelings towards the Chinese internet has changed over the years," says Miao. "At first I resisted it a lot because I felt that it was very limited. But then it really blew my mind when it entered a different age where everybody started to contribute to the [Chinese] internet, until I felt that it was more powerful than the Western internet." She is referring to the point in 2009 when iPhones and iPhone clones became regularly available in China, allowing huge numbers of Chinese citizens who previously had not owned computers to get online. Coinciding with this influx, people began inventing new words and images to circumvent the Chinese censors, spawning a unique vocabulary and form of self-expression.

In 2009, for example, came the rise of the "Grass Mud Horse" phenomena. A grass mud horse, or *caonima*, is an actual animal residing near the Gobi Desert. Its name, however, is a homophone for the expression *Cao ni ma*, or "fuck your mother," a particularly vile slur. In that year, a YouTube children's song about a grass mud horse drew 1.4 million viewers and a grass mud horse cartoon logged 250,000 more hits, all interpreted as a defiant response to the Chinese government's patrol of the internet. Likewise, the term *hexie*, meaning river crab, is a homophone for the term for harmony, the government's favorite excuse for censoring websites and maintaining stability in society. The story of the grass mud horse's struggle against the evil river crab flooded the Chinese online community. Government censors, who scan cyberspace continuously for sensitive topics and have developed algorithms to block seditious content, were unable to stem the tide of this outright rebellion and looked ridiculous for even trying.[8]

Miao Ying's artworks are inspired by just this form of expression, which she considers examples of self-censorship. According to the artist, her relationship with the Chinese internet has all the hallmarks of Stockholm syndrome. By this she means she has a deeply codependent relationship, falling in love with that which she knows is her oppressor. "I really think self-censorship is the creativity of the Chinese internet. It's more interesting when you know you have this limitation, because then you have to find a way around it," she says. "It's not black-and-white but rather multi-layered. The more I used the Chinese internet, the more rich and fulfilling I found it to be."

Since then, Miao Ying's projects have taken many forms, from self-designed GIFs of the kind frequently employed on WeChat to fully formed installations making use of inexpensive stock images and designs that she spotted on Baidu, China's equivalent to Google. In *LAN Love Poem.gif*, she makes use of webpages announcing a site is inaccessible (censored), then runs text across this background, using corny phrases and poetic usernames found on web comments. In 2016, she created *Chinternet Plus*, an online project sponsored by the New Museum, in which she appropriated a 2015 government initiative, *Internet Plus*, and created a satiric take on the idea of using the internet to promote a political cause. For example, at one point, there is a GIF of celebrities applauding an image of Chairman Mao, which falters

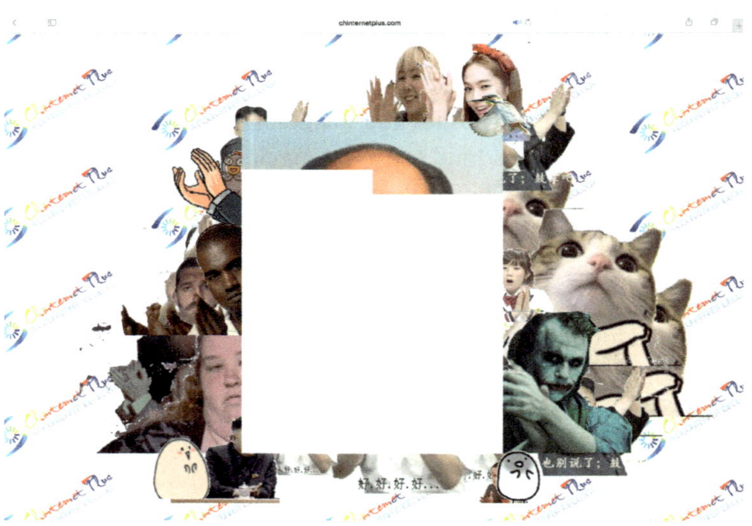

MIAO YING, *CHINTERNET PLUS*, 2016. COURTESY OF THE ARTIST.

as it begins to load. All that viewers can see is his famous forehead, while the rest of his face is stalled on a white screen, never fully appearing. This, however, was enough for local authorities to ask the work to be withdrawn when it was later shown at the Ullens Center for Contemporary Art in Beijing. Instead, Miao Ying adjusted the work, pixilating the image further, using self-censorship to avoid the official censors, which is precisely her point.

While Miao Ying has received worldwide attention in trendy publications for her audacious defense of the Chinese internet, the politics of her work has not been thoroughly examined. For American audiences, her projects may be a fun-filled introduction to the quirky aspects of China's online culture, which may prove popular enough to attract a following in the West, just as Japanese anime has become an international sensation. But for Chinese audiences already familiar with these strategies, however cute and clever, her creations may be a misguided celebration of a troubling situation. After all, every year, dozens of activist netizens in China are jailed for testing the limits of the Great Firewall, a reality overlooked in Miao Ying's analysis.

"For my generation, the education and culture that surrounded us when we grew up was not as limiting," says Chen Zhou, a video and installation artist who was born in 1987 and studied with Wang Gongxin at the Central Academy of Fine Arts in Beijing. Like Miao Ying, he has found the internet to be a source of creative inspiration. "In this case, my generation enjoys much more freedom in what we think and what we want to get from the internet; contrary to the previous generations, there is less limitation on our ideologies," he says.

With long hair and tattoos, Chen Zhou is a bit of a bad boy, who claims to have been rebellious by nature since kindergarten. His views are tinged with conspiracy theories that might be an indication of a demented psyche in the West, but make perfect sense when applied to China. For the Shanghai exhibition,

After Us, he offered his video work, *Life Imitation*, 2016, which "interweaves intimate portraits of daily life in Shanghai with winding WeChat dialogues and scenes captured from a video game," according to curator Lauren Cornell in her exhibition essay. The female protagonist of the video is emotionally repressed as she communicates with friends through texts and chats. Only when she enters the game does she become ultra-violent and vengeful. Like many of Chen's works, there is a subtext here about power relationships, including manipulation of the viewers' emotions.

In works like *Life Imitation*, Chen Zhou is openly negative about Chinese society and the role the government plays in creating it. "I don't believe that young artists don't think about politics," he says. He points to Weibo, the Chinese equivalent of Twitter, where people post opinions and news all day, until sensitive posts are taken down by censors. "Everyday we get on Weibo and the majority of the information and news we have encountered is not optional to us at all. Before we know something, we cannot choose what we want to know and what we want to ignore, thus we are almost forced to confront all this information, this reality," Chen Zhou explains, adding, "When we open the webpage, it is all there and nobody can escape from the reality."

Another artist who is taking a hard look at some of the realities of internet culture in China is performance artist Li Liao, who directly challenged Apple with his project *Consumption* in 2012. For this work, Li Liao got himself hired at the much-criticized Foxconn factory in Shenzhen, where he worked on the assembly line 12 hours a day making iPads for 45 days. It was just enough time for him to make enough money to buy one for himself. In *Consumption*, the artist then displayed his uniform, identification badge, his contract and his precious iPad—that's all. It was a muted protest on behalf of all the thousands of workers in factories in China making the devices that make the internet accessible for popular use.

In many ways, Li Liao's *Consumption* is the most Chinese of any of the works under the rubric of post-internet art, demonstrating precisely how life in China has been altered by the introduction of this innovation. For many other artists, the internet and attendant invasion of global influences has had a liberating effect. But for Li, the reality of globalization is the empowerment of multinational corporations and their impact on the daily lives of Chinese workers in the form of mind-numbing work and back-breaking schedules. Yet, even for him, identity is transformational, not fixed, as he reinvents himself from artist to worker and back to artist again. As he said in an interview in the *New Yorker* in 2013, "I will never go back to the factory again."[9]

"Recognizing that there are localized networks and regional fragmentation to the internet is a very exciting space," says Peckham, who sees differences in internet culture not only between the USA and China, but between China and other Asian countries. "Artists working with internet material in the West can't pretend to have access to global culture; they are dealing with an American digital culture or a European digital culture." Chinese artists are already at the cutting edge of this approach, recognizing the opportunities for creativity that lie in indigenous idiosyncrasies and localized concerns. They have learned to process the particular obstacles of their own online experience to achieve their desired goals.

Whether we are communicating through WeChat or posting comments on Weibo, a cursory use of Chinese apps and websites demonstrate that innovations in China are soaring ahead of their counterparts in the West. This has empowered a generation of Chinese artists who have grown up with the rise of the internet and who have had little access to or use for Facebook or Twitter. The "Chinternet," with all its shortcomings, has still operated as a bridge to a wider world and broader cultures. More importantly, with the introduction of avatars and user profiles, the internet has offered access to alternative personae and presentations of identity. This innovation, perhaps more than any other, has encouraged Chinese artists to reconfigure their definition of themselves, wearing "Chinese-ness" as a loose garment that can easily be exchanged for another costume on a whim. In this way, all Chinese artists of this younger generation can be described as "post-internet," better equipped to navigate a global art world than any generation that has come before them.

8
MOVERS AND SHAKERS

Whether we are communicating on WeChat or surveying the latest Shanghai Biennial, it is undeniable that we will see the impact that this young generation is having on Chinese culture. But no study of this phenomenon can be complete without considering the young curators, collectors, and gallerists emerging in the Chinese art scene and the extensive role they are playing in reforming their country's approach to contemporary art. Like the artists of this age group, these young movers and shakers are often educated in the West and travel extensively. Their taste in art is likewise international, frequently visiting art fairs in the USA and Europe and bringing home their discoveries of foreign artists. The institutions they support—and many are starting their own museums and galleries—reflect this international outlook with exhibitions of global art movements that would be equally at home in New York, London, or Berlin.

This outlook sets them apart from an older generation whose tastes for collecting often exclusively favored Chinese art. Just five years ago, Chinese collectors for the most part began their acquisitions with purchases of works of classical Chinese art, only later moving in to test the waters of contemporary art. In that field, they pursued works by the generation of artists that emerged in the 1990s, primarily painters such as Zhang Xiaogang and Zeng Fanzhi, who by 2008 had become household names with record-breaking auction prices. Rarely did they frequent foreign galleries and the only foreign artists that they knew well were Andy Warhol, Damien Hirst, and Jeff Koons. To a large extent, museums in China merely mirrored these preferences, offering little to change collectors' minds or further their tastes.

All of this began to change in 2013 with the inaugural edition of Art Basel Hong Kong, not the first art fair in Asia, but the first to demonstrate the highest international standards. This fair attracted well over 200 galleries, over 100 of which were from Europe or the USA. Dealers from New York of the likes of Gagosian, Pace, Lehmann Maupin, and Sean Kelly were all lured over by the prospect of hordes of Chinese millionaires. What they discovered was that it would take time to cultivate mainland collectors, a process that they deemed well worth the effort. Not long after, several major galleries, including Pace and Gagosian, opened outposts in Hong Kong (Pace already had a gallery in Beijing). This way, Chinese collectors began to have access to a steady diet of Western contemporary art, enough to become familiar with the names of a broader spectrum of artists.

While the older generation may have had to go through a process of several years to acclimatize to a more international approach to contemporary art, the younger generation leapt right in, pursuing works by artists of their own generation, both Chinese and Western, without too much concern for the differences. After all, by then, *Artforum*, the leading art magazine in the West, had founded a Chinese-language website. In the global environment in which they lived, it was just as easy to know about Western artists as it was for Westerners to know about Chinese artists—if not even easier. The information flowed both ways.

"Most of the young collectors that I've met are educated in more than one continent; they are accustomed to frequent overseas travel and they are not intimidated to walk into a gallery in any major art center in the world," says Meg Maggio of Pékin Fine Arts in Hong Kong and Beijing. She points out that many of these clients are building museums in China. "They are very civic-minded, bringing their knowledge home to benefit the domestic art scene," she says.

Hong Kong business leader Adrian Cheng is a case in point. Born in 1979, he is one of the world's youngest billionaires, as chairman of the $16 billion New World Development real estate and retail empire, founded by his grandfather Cheng Yu-Tung. He spent ten years in the USA—at Taft, a boarding school in Connecticut, at Harvard, and later at Goldman Sachs and UBS—studying the humanities and soaking up culture. Now, he has returned home to Hong Kong, launching his K11 brand, which includes a series of shopping malls that feature art exhibition spaces, a foundation that supports exhibitions in Europe and the USA, promoting the works of young Chinese artists and an extensive artist-in-residency program allowing young Chinese artists to cultivate their careers. Positing his endeavors as a "new museum model," Cheng has brought major shows to his malls, such as *Master of Impressionism—Claude Monet*, the first show of the artist's works in mainland China, to the 3,500 sq. ft art gallery located in the basement of his K11 shopping development in Shanghai.

"In China, you really need art education because even though everyone in China studies the history of China, they do not learn how to appreciate contemporary art," says Cheng, who has placed works by leading international artists such as Nara and Olafur Eliason between stores in his malls. His business ventures underwrite his cultural activities, creating what he terms "a sustainable model." By fueling profits from the retail business back into the art foundation, he is able to produce 50 shows a year, attracting over 1,000 visitors a day. In a country where audience development is a profound problem, the K11 Foundation has found a particularly effective solution: a VIP club with now over 10,000 members.

But bringing art to China is only half of his goal. A major aim of the K11 Art Foundation is to promote works of Chinese art throughout the world, and for this, Cheng has been extremely busy. In the past three years, the foundation has collaborated on exhibitions with the Serpentine Galleries and Institute of Contemporary Arts in London; Centre Pompidou, Palais de Tokyo and Musée Marmottan Monet in Paris; The Metropolitan Museum of Art, The Armory Show, New Museum, The Museum of Modern Art, and MoMA PS1 in New York.

To appreciate Cheng's accomplishment, look no further than the two shows of post-internet art that he sponsored during Art Basel Hong Kong in 2017. In Shanghai, he hosted *After Us*, curated by the New Museum's Lauren Cornell and in Hong Kong, there was *.com/.cn*, curated by MoMA PS1 director Klaus Biesenbach and curator Peter Eeley. The shows brought together a combination of young Chinese artists and international names, generating widespread discussion about the impact of the

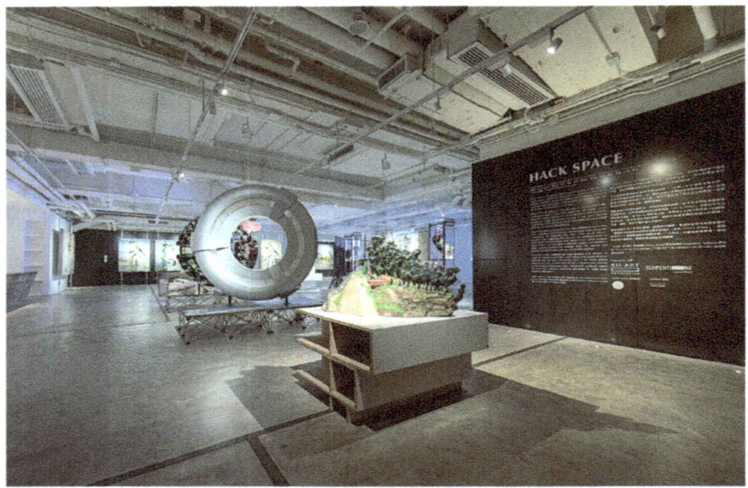

HACK SPACE, CO-ORGANIZED BY SERPENTINE GALLERIES AND K11 ART FOUNDATION, INSTALLATION VIEW, HONG KONG, 2016. COURTESY OF THE K11 ART FOUNDATION.

internet on a younger generation of artists, both in China and abroad. "I think the new contemporary Chinese art is reinventing Chinese cultural identity and building up a new Chinese culture," he says. "I am only an entrepreneur and business person, a collector and art pioneer, but I try to help to bring this discussion to a different platform."

"The internet and technology are really my passion," says Michael Xufu Huang, a young collector who is already making a name for himself. He explains that his generation of Chinese collectors are more internationally minded, not only because many have been educated in the USA or United Kingdom, and travel widely like himself, but also because of an interconnectedness, a universal language, enabled by the internet. It also provides the focus of his collection, which is populated by post-internet artists from New York, Berlin, and London as well as Beijing. "I think that every generation has something that is really prominent—for the Renaissance, there's religion and for Impressionism, there's the invention of the camera—but nowadays, everything is technology and the internet."

In addition to his evident enthusiasm, on first meeting Huang, one is struck by his impeccable fashion sense and his youth. At 23, he has just completed his undergraduate degree at the University of Pennsylvania. School work did not slow him down at all; he could be spotted at museum galas and art fairs all over the place, bringing a touch of glamour with him wherever he went. Earning a degree might be the greatest accomplishment of many people of his age, but Huang has already surpassed that goal. In 2014, when he was just 20, he co-founded M WOODS, an ambitious Kunsthalle in Beijing. The museum is already garnering critical praise for its exhibitions of international artists, including a knock-out Warhol show, organized in cooperation with the Andy Warhol Museum in Pittsburg.

M WOODS is a new brand of Chinese art museum, a not-for-profit private museum, run by three individuals, including Huang. The other two partners in this venture are Beijing collecting couple Wanwan Lei and Lin Han, both born in 1987, who have become celebrities in the past three years since founding the museum, appearing on the covers of fashion magazines and attracting over 100,000 social media users. As beautiful as a fashion model—and in fact a model for famed Chinese artist Liu Ye when she was still a teenager—Wanwan Lei met Huang in New York, just after she graduated from her master's degree at Columbia University, during which she interned at David Zwirner Gallery. After staging a series of pop-up shows in New York, she returned to Beijing in 2013, already dating Lin Han, who runs a successful public relations firm for luxury brand companies, such as BMW, Mini Cooper, and TAG Heuer Watches. By then, Lin Han had already established his profile as a collector by famously buying a $5 million painting by Zeng Fanzhi, the most expensive living Chinese artist, at a Hong Kong auction when he was just 27. Since then, he has assembled a collection of an estimated 500 works, including such leading contemporary artists as Tracey Emin and Kader Attia.

"We all thought it would be interesting, and beneficial, to have three founders—they say the triangle is the most stable structure," says Lei, who is currently planning upcoming shows for young post-internet artist Lu Yang as well as contemporary art master Paul McCarthy, whose scatological installations will be something of a shock in Beijing. Commenting on her younger partner, she says, "Michael's ideas are different to ours, but they are never in opposition. I think we learn a lot from each other. And it's been very helpful for us to have a set of eyes in New York, to report back from other museums or galleries and in turn to promote M WOODS."

Huang has been doing his part to do just that, promoting M WOODS and researching other institutions based on his solid belief that museums represent the future of the Chinese art ecosystem. Most recently, he was appointed to the board of the New Museum after serving for two years on their International Council. He himself caught the art bug as a teenager attending boarding school in London and visiting the Tate regularly. "The Tate is really where everything started because they have such great retrospective exhibitions for artists," he says, recalling that one exhibition in particular, an Alex Katz show of beach paintings presented at Tate St Ives, made a searing impression on him. "You could see the sea through the windows and I really felt connected with the work," he recalls. "That is where I really grew my passion for art."

Ironically, it was in London that he also got a chance to appreciate developments in Chinese contemporary art, by visiting *Art of Change: New Directions from China* at the Hayward Gallery in 2012. While he was already aware of such Chinese painters as Zhang Xiaogang and Zeng Fanzhi, this was his first exposure to contemporary installation and performance artists including Chen Zhen, Yingmei Duan, Gu Dexin, Liang Shaoji, Sun Yuan and Peng Yu, Wang Jianwei, Xu Zhen, and MadeIn Company.

"We decided to do the museum because we felt there is such a need in China," says Huang. "I wouldn't be where I am right now without the museums in London." Emphasizing that galleries have their place, but museums fulfill an educational function lacking in the marketplace, Huang states that a primary goal of M WOODS is to educate its audience. "And 80 percent of our audience are really young people, which is amazing because they are the future of the Chinese art world."

When it comes to collecting, Lin Han sees a big difference between his peers and his parents' generation. "Our attitude toward nationality is the key difference," he told me in an interview just before the museum opened. "The older generation buys mostly Chinese art, but for our generation, nationality doesn't mean a thing."

"We want to bring an international spirit to our site," says Lu Xun, who co-founded with his father, real estate developer Lu Jun, the Sifang Art Museum in Nanjing, opened in 2013. Born in 1983, Lu Xun studied nanotechnology at Cambridge, but left school in 2007 to run the museum project. Designed by American architect Steven Holl, the 7,000-sq. meter museum is the centerpiece of a collection of 24 buildings, including a conference center by Arata Isozaki, a recreation center by Ettore Sottsass, a hotel by Liu Jiakun and leisure homes by David Adjaye, Alberto Kalach, and Ai Weiwei, among others. The entire project is called "Contemporary International Practical Exhibition of Architecture," or CIPEA, and cost the Lu family over $164 million. They hope the entire complex will generate 20 million yuan a year and be able to sustain itself by the fourth year of operation. The inaugural show, curated by Belgian historian Philippe Pirotte, featured works on loan and from the museum's permanent collection by artists including Olafur Eliasson, Danh Vo, Marlene Dumas, Anselm Kiefer, Luc Tuymans, Yang Fudong, Zhang Enli, Zhou Chunya, and Zhang Peili.

Projects like M WOODS and CIPEA stand out, even in a country like China that is undergoing its current museum-building boom. According to the latest government statistics, China is building approximately 100 museums a year, increasing from fewer than 2,500 in 2001 to over 3,500 a decade later, with a peak of 400 museums opening in 2011 alone.[1] But most of these museums have little to do with contemporary art and fewer still have international programs. The focus on international collections of M WOODS and CIPEA is unique among Chinese museums, as is the passion and dedication of their young founders. Since China still lacks a model to ensure the sustainability of art museums, with little state-funding and no tax laws that would encourage donations and contributions by either corporate sponsors or individuals, these new private museums are primarily funded by the wealth of the founders alone. CIPEA has the potential to survive long-term if the architectural projects, such as leisure homes and hotels, fuel profits back into the museum side of the project. M WOODS, a registered not-for-profit, has been relying on ticket and gift shop sales as well as attracting some corporate sponsorship, especially for their high-profile events.

This situation requires that collectors apply the same entrepreneurial skills to their museum-building projects as they do to their business ventures. But, despite the challenges, they are driven to create these institutions to increase the health and vitality of the Chinese art scene. These new museums rarely have full curatorial staffs and research facilities, as one would find in art museums in the West. But they do serve as a counterbalance to the overheated art market in China, which too often values profits and record auction prices above other ways of appreciating contemporary art.

Even those involved with the art market can agree that new institutions are necessary to create a more stable art environment. David Chau and his wife Kelly Ying have tried to bolster the scene in Shanghai while keeping their fingers in almost every aspect of the art market. Chau helped launch two of Shanghai's best galleries, the former Leo Xu Projects and Antenna Space, both run by young Chinese curators. At the same time, he has been building his own collection under the name of C.C. Foundation. He is also the financial backbone of Shanghai's newest art fair, Art 021, which attracted White Cube and Galerie Perrotin in 2013, its first year of operation. The fair's official organizers are Ying, a former director of Aether Gallery in Beijing, and Bao Yifeng, general manager of Activation Liquid, a public relations firm.

Born in 1984, Chau studied art history at the University of British Columbia in Vancouver, where he assisted with exhibitions by Xu Bing and Huang Yong Ping at the Vancouver Art Gallery. Back in Shanghai, he worked with Hwa Gallery, but spent most of his time at auctions, making his first fortune in coin collecting and then assembling a cache of mid-century Chinese modernists. He got in early before the Chinese art market had peaked and did well with his investments. In recent years, he has shifted his focus to younger contemporary artists, such as Xu Zhen, Liu Wei, and Yang Fudong, who he collects in depth.

In New York or London, people would be critical of a collector who backs galleries while simultaneously starting an art fair, viewing such relationships as representative of a sizeable conflict of interest. But in Shanghai, Chau fills an important role. "I'm the kind of guy who doesn't quite play along with the system. I just do what I think needs to be done," he says. He insists that he makes his living from his company, Metropolis International Leasing, which manages over $200 million worth of assets and over 2,000 cars and trucks, not from his art ventures, on which he estimates he has spent more than $1.5 million. Still, Art 021 has been highly successful, growing from 29 participating galleries to 90 in 2016, with attendance reaching 60,000 visitors.

Art 021 was not intended to compete with Art Basel Hong Kong, but a comparison demonstrates how challenging it is to launch an art fair in mainland China at all. Hong Kong's main advantage over Shanghai or Beijing is its status as a tax-free zone, as opposed to the 34 percent VAT attached to sales of luxury goods in mainland China. Foreign dealers bringing in valuable artworks to a mainland fair, therefore, have to face a steep penalty for selling there, or else charge clients a formidable increase in price. For this reason alone, mainland fairs have had trouble staying afloat. Prior to the establishment of Art 021, there was another fair in Shanghai titled ShContemporary. It had been organized by an Italian art fair company, BolognaFiere, and ran from 2007 to 2014, but was continuously dogged by customs problems and government censorship, losing over $2 million in its last five years in operation.[2] Today, Art 021's main competitor is the West Bund Art and Design, a more select government initiative, with 40 galleries including David Zwirner, White Cube, and Barbara Gladstone galleries, organized by the West Bund Art District.

"Shanghai needed a good art fair for those big collectors, but at the same time, we want to bring in new collectors, those people who have the spending power but also taste," says Art 021 organizer Bao Yifeng. "My PR company has a database of all those people who love to buy Hermès bags; for them to buy a painting for 100,000 or 200,000 rmb is very easy." One section of society that unfailingly attends the fair, according to Bao, is the second generation of Chinese millionaires who are now returning to the mainland after their studies abroad. They know the benefits of a rich cultural scene, and it is up to people like Bao and Chao to provide them with such a milieu back home.

David Chau is confident that China has enough museums in the works, but worries that that standards need to rise for galleries and art fairs. "If I lived in the United States or Europe, my main focus could be collecting," says Chau. "But here in China, if I'm not helping out galleries and supporting an art fair, who would do it? There's no one." In any case, he believes that the benefits to China are worth the risk to his reputation. "China doesn't need more art museums. China needs a mature art system and guys like me help form that system," he says.

From Adrien Cheng to David Chau, these individuals are making contributions to the Chinese cultural landscape, each in their own way. To fully understand how significant these efforts are, it is important to have some knowledge of the state of China's art scene prior to their entry. In the last 15 years, China has gone from being a country with a handful of galleries and no contemporary art museums to one of the world's largest art markets, second only to the USA.[3] In the past five years, China's galleries and museums have gained international stature, with quality exhibitions and growing professionalism. This gain has occurred in no small part as a result of the efforts of this group of young Chinese professionals and millionaires.

First of all, there is a significantly different landscape in Beijing and Shanghai as each city competes to be deemed China's cultural capital. Beijing is home to thousands of the country's leading artists and it has two vibrant art districts—798 and Caochangdi—with several hundred galleries, including Pace Beijing, Beijing Commune, Long March Space, Boers Li Gallery, Pékin Fine Arts, Chambers Fine Art, Tang Contemporary,

Galerie Continua, and Platform China. On any given day, these districts are packed with young people and tourists openly enjoying the art on view as they pass time in the cafes and boutiques that line the streets.

But Beijing is lacking a robust museum culture. It is true that the city boasts the country's oldest art museum, now called the National Art Museum of China, but this institution's contemporary art program is antiquated and dominated by rental shows that local artists can obtain for a fee. The leading private contemporary art museum in the city is the Ullens Center for Contemporary Art, founded by Belgian collectors Guy and Myriam Ullens in 2007, which has hosted such significant shows as *'85 New Wave: The Birth of Chinese Contemporary Art*, *ON | OFF: China's Young Artists in Concept and Practice*, and *Xu Zhen: a MadeIn Company Production*. Most recently, UCCA has been sold to a group of private investors and is in the process of becoming a fully public institution with a board of directors. Another private museum, the Today Art Museum, founded by real estate developer Zhang Baoquan in 2002, lags behind UCCA in quality and ambition.

In this environment, projects like M WOODS can have a major impact, filling a vacuum left by the absence of more major institutions.

In addition to M WOODS, another private museum worth mentioning is the Sishang Art Museum, whose executive director Linyao Kiki Liu is the daughter of Liu Fengzhou, chairman of Hengchangxiang Investment Management Limited. Kiki Liu is known throughout the art world as a contributor to New York's Museum of Modern Art, hosting a party in Shanghai during Art 021 with MoMA PS1's Klaus Biesenbach. Located on the 6th Ring Road of Beijing, this 400,000 sq. ft art museum in a former food-canning factory has been making important acquisitions and staging exhibitions of international contemporary artists including Anri Sala, Ed Atkins, Frances Stark, Lizzie Fitch/Ryan Trecartin, Mark Leckey, and Mika Rottenberg, artists that have had limited exposure in China.

In contrast to Beijing, Shanghai has a surplus of art museums, opening in large part with the encouragement of the local government. Just ten years ago, when art-interested visitors came to Shanghai, their choices were limited to two museums: the Shanghai Museum, a 40,000 sq. meter institution built in 1996 as a home for Chinese antiquities; and the Shanghai Art Museum, a much smaller facility housed in the colonialist architecture of the clubhouse of the city's former racetrack, devoted to exhibitions of modern and contemporary Chinese art. Today, Shanghai tourists have the choice of no fewer than ten contemporary art museums, most private ventures supported by individual investors.

Shanghai's impulse to build so many museums is the direct result of a government policy that initiated a municipal five-year plan dedicated to establish its profile as a cultural capital on par with London, Paris, and New York.[4] In 2012, the city opened the Power Station of Art, China's first state-run contemporary art museum, an expansive facility situated in a former electric plant that was converted to a museum at the cost of $64 million, provided solely by the Shanghai government. It also opened the China Art Palace, housed in the former China Pavilion of the 2010 Shanghai Expo site, a 160,000 sq. meter, bright-red edifice that is one of the city's most identifiable landmarks. Three months later in December 2012, the Long Museum opened in the suburbs of the Pudong district of Shanghai. Costing $43 million, it is the personal project of Wang Wei and her husband Liu Yiqian, China's biggest collectors. Designed by architect Zhong Song, the 10,000 sq. meter brutalist structure houses the couple's collection of contemporary realist painting on the first floor, their Cultural Revolutionary "classics" on the second floor and their treasure trove of Chinese antiquities on the third floor. In one trip, you can find *Mao's Visit to Guangdong Countryside* by Chen Yanning, 1958, acquired from the Uli Sigg collection, or an eleventh-century throne of Emperor Song Huizong, purchased at auction for $9.9 million in 2009.

China Art Palace, the Power Station of Art, and the Long Museum joined a roster of art museums already open in Shanghai, including MOCA Shanghai, founded in 2005 by Hong Kong jewelry designer Samuel Kung in 2005; the Minsheng Art Museum, established in 2008 by China Minsheng Banking Corporation, China's largest bank; the Rockbund Museum, a Kunsthalle situated in the renovated 1932 former headquarters of the Royal Asiatic Society that opened in 2010; and the Zendai Himalayas Art Museum, designed by Japanese architect Arata Isozaki, completed in 2011. Both the Rockbund and the Himalayas Museum are typical of many museum projects in China in that they are part of real estate development plans. The Rockbund Museum was founded by Thomas Ou, chairman of Sinolink Worldwide Holdings, a real estate company listed on the Hong Kong Stock Exchange, as the centerpiece of a luxury redevelopment plan of Shanghai's prestigious Bund district. The Himalayas Art Museum was created by local real estate developer Dai Zhikang in 2011 as one facet of his $480-million media city in the Pudong district.

Not satisfied with this abundance of museums already in existence, the Shanghai government has now decided to develop a section of the Huangpu River under the banner of the West Bund Cultural Corridor. This city-sponsored development stretches more than 8 kilometers and features two museums, namely the Long Museum, Puxi Branch, and the Yuz Museum Shanghai. Both opened in 2014. The Yuz Museum Shanghai is the brainchild of Chinese-Indonesian collector Budi Tek, who has already opened the Yuz Museum as the first contemporary art museum in Jakarta in 2008. Shanghai Tanks, a museum and recreation facility sponsored by local collector Qiao Zhibing, will open in late 2017 in a series of renovated oil tanks running along the river. The complex, designed by Beijing-based OPEN Architecture, measures some 640,000 sq. ft, with about 100,000 sq. ft of exhibition space, costing approximately $15 million.

So when David Chau bemoans the lack of infrastructure beyond museums, his comments must be put in the specific context of Shanghai, with its overabundance of private institutions. But, in contrast to Beijing, Shanghai lacks a major gallery scene. Its sole art district, M50, has nothing like the hundreds of galleries of Beijing's 798 Art District and nowhere near the quality of exhibition spaces. For many years, Shanghai's gallery scene was dominated solely by one space, ShanghART, run by Swiss dealer Lorenz Helbling. ShanghART has accomplished a formidable job of putting Chinese artists on the international map, being the first Chinese gallery to exhibit at Art Basel in Switzerland. But the city has been lacking in worthy competitors, a situation that is changing as a result of the efforts of a few younger gallerists.

Leo Xu is one of these emerging art dealers, having opened his gallery, Leo Xu Projects, in 2011 at the age of 29. Located down a quiet lane in the French Concession, the three-story gallery hosted exhibitions of an international array of artists, ranging from Cheng Ran and Cui Jie to Gabriel Lester and Michael Lin. But most importantly, Xu made significant inroads in the international art market on behalf of his artists, participating in events like the Frieze Art Fair in New York and collaborating with galleries such as Metro Pictures and David Kordansky to bring exhibitions to the USA. Now Xu is moving on, taking the position as gallery director for David Zwirner's new space in Hong Kong.

When asked why he became an art dealer, Xu answers, "I didn't have any other choice." Hoping to become a curator after completing his degree at Shanghai International Studies University, his optimism was dashed by his experience working in the short-lived Duolon Art Museum in Shanghai. He then went on to work as a gallery director at Chambers Fine Art in Beijing and the Shanghai branch of New York's James Cohan Gallery. Xu recalls that, in early 2011, he was reading *A Short Life of Trouble*, the memoir of New Museum founder Marcia Tucker, when a light bulb went off. "I had worked with Chen Wei and Cheng Ran and Guo Hongwei, artists who were then unknown and off the radar, and I thought that nobody was really working with them, helping them, developing them," he recalls. "I thought to myself, I know curating and I have experience as an art dealer. All I need to do is open a space."

"This may sound a bit cocky, but I think we were one of the game changers," says Xu, who was able to get financial backing from David Chau for his first year of operation. According to the young dealer, everyone thought he was crazy when he decided to open in Shanghai, where little was happening in 2011, especially in a side street in the French Concession where few art galleries survived. He raised the stakes further by concentrating on younger artists in video and photography instead of established painters. "But I had my theories, and I had things I was willing to fight for," Xu told me, explaining that he chose the French Concession for its convenience and ambience. "I wanted people who go to theater, who go to concerts, who want to have a beautiful contemporary lifestyle to want to spend an afternoon with us, and those people are not going to M50 because that's out in the middle of nowhere." Indeed, since Xu opened his space, several other galleries have moved into the district, including BANK and Capsule, both run by expats.

For Xu, a proud moment came when one of his artists, Cheng Ran, was given a solo show at the New Museum in New York City. Cheng, an experimental video artist, had several early shows at Leo Xu Projects by which he came to the attention of Adrian Cheng, who in turn established a residency for the artist at the New York museum. For the exhibition, titled *Diary of a Madman*, the artist shot a series of 15 short videos in a month, creating a kind of surrealistic account of his first trip to the city. This was the first time the museum had exhibited a solo show by a Chinese artist since the 1990s.

"The only reason I wanted to work in art is because I wanted to be someone riding the wave of contemporary art today, not

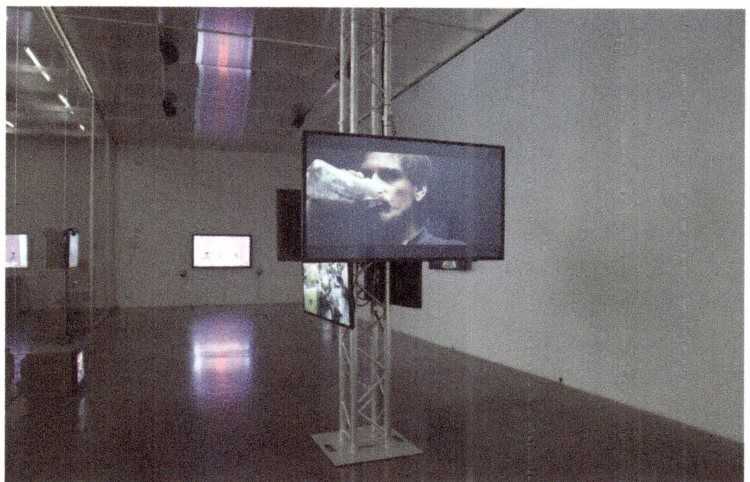

CHENG RAN, *DIARY OF A MADMAN*, INSTALLATION VIEW, NEW MUSEUM, 2016. COURTESY OF THE K11 ART FOUNDATION.

someone representing China today," says Xu, explaining the thinking behind his international program. "It does not have to be an American artist. It could be a Dutch artist or a Latin American artist. It can be an African artist. I have this eagerness to engage with people from all over the world ever since I was student."

Another gallery which benefitted from David Chau's support is Antenna Space, founded by Simon Wang. Wang is as plugged into the international art scene as Leo Xu, participating regularly at Frieze and Art Basel Hong Kong and the Shanghai art fairs. The remarkable success of one of his artists, Guan Xiao, is proof of his global reach. Guan Xiao is best known for her quirky sculptures and installations that combine references from a wide range of cultures, gathered together from internet research. In the past year, Guan Xiao was featured at the 57th Venice Biennale, Antwerp's MHKA Museum of Contemporary Art, New York's High Line, Shanghai's chi K11 Art Museum, the Moscow Museum of Modern Art, and CAPC Musée d'Art Contemporain de Bordeaux.

Young art dealers like Leo Xu and Simon Wang are making inroads into the international art market, a formidable achievement given the art world's reluctance to embrace Chinese contemporary artists as equal peers to their counterparts in Europe and the USA. It is true that there was a kind of fad in Chinese contemporary art in the 1990s, followed by an auction boom in prices in the early 2000s. But since the market contraction in 2008, collectors in the West have been wary of the high prices for these artists, and Western curators, especially American curators, have been slow to focus their research on the new generation of artists emerging in China. With the help of Adrian Cheng and his K11 Art Foundation, the situation in museums is slowly being remedied. But dealers in Chinese contemporary art, especially of young emerging artists, are laying the groundwork for a sustainable market internationally that can support these artists into the future.

But global reach is not the goal for every young professional in China. For some, it is just as important to have an impact at home, introducing new ideas and art movements to a domestic scene that is still dominated by formally trained painters. There is a group of curators emerging, though few of them are affiliated with any of the new museums, owing to the lack of infrastructure in these institutions. One curator who is making an impact both in China and abroad is Carol Yinghua Lu, born in 1977, who served as the artistic director and chief curator of OCAT Shenzhen, a privately funded Kunsthalle known for its experimental exhibitions, from 2012 to 2015. Graduating from the critical studies program of Malmö Art Academy at Sweden's Lund University in 2005, Lu has also worked as co-artistic director of 2012 Gwangju Biennale in South Korea and co-curator of the 7th Shenzhen Sculpture Biennale in 2012. Lu was the first visiting fellow of Asia-Pacific at Tate Research Centre in 2013. Together with her husband Liu Ding, she has initiated a series of shows that have traveled internationally.

It is challenging enough to be an independent curator anywhere in the world, but especially in China. Despite the fact that dozens of new art museums are opening each year, few are willing to support curatorial expertise. Which is why so many young professionals, aspiring to be curators, wind up working in galleries. Sammi Yiyuan Liu opened Tabula Rasa Gallery in the 798 Art District in 2015 with the help of a sales partner and a Chinese backer. The gallery promotes emerging Chinese artists such as London-educated Xiao Hanqiu and rising star Yuan Yuan. But Liu's passion is Outsider Art—self-taught artists, street artists, and designers of graphic novels and comics—a category of art unheard of in China. With great enthusiasm, she launched Almost Art Project (AAP), an annual alternative art festival in July 2015. It attracted 3,000 visitors to the event, which featured more than 300 works by more than 40 outsider and comic-book artists.

In the West, Outsider Art is an established term, going back to Jean Dubuffet's study of art brut, the work made by mental patients. In New York, the Outsider Art fair has taken place every year since 1993. In fact, the notion of Outsider Art is so established that it is almost passé, with many critics arguing that outsider masters like Henry Darger or Martin Ramirez should be considered peers of leading modern artists René Magritte or Cy Twombly. In China, with its extreme emphasis on training at one of the leading art academies, these artists have been largely overlooked, yet there is an Outsider Art Center in Nanjing that caters to people with disabilities. It has helped several artists gain attention, such as Wang Jun, who makes drawings of wacky vehicles in magic marker, or Ba Zi, who creates dystopic scenes with finely drawn lines.

Sammi Liu traces her interest in Outsider Art back to a visit to the Museum of Everything in London in 2009 while studying at the Sotheby's Institute. There she became enthralled with art that was not intended for the art market and that often fell outside of the mainstream. Born in 1986, Liu herself fell outside of the Chinese education system, doing poorly in an environment characterized by its incessant stream of examinations. Instead of pursuing a degree in China, she went to Carleton University in Ottawa, Canada, a country she considers her second home. She completed her graduate degree in London in 2010 before moving back to Beijing, where she took up a position as a senior editor at the Chinese-language edition of the *Art Newspaper*. This experience—with its brutal deadlines and endless demands of censorship—left her disillusioned. Upon leaving that job in 2015, she was offered the opportunity to open her own gallery, leading to the establishment of Tabula Rasa.

I know Liu very well, having employed her as my Beijing assistant from 2011 to 2014. She is bright and earnest, rather than hip and jaded, despite the disappointments she has experienced since returning to China. She once told me that the most influential text she read during her education was Hou Hanru's *On the Mid-Ground*, the book that so aptly describes the aesthetics and condition of artists living in Paris in the 1990s, making work about their dual identities as Chinese and as immigrants. Likewise, Liu feels divided between her place of birth and the more open world she encountered when she went abroad to study. Despite living in China, she feels much like that earlier generation of artists, living in a middle-ground between cultures.

"Chinese contemporary art is boring," she tells me, admitting that such opinions would prove a liability for most art dealers. "Everybody is just imitating anybody else and everybody wants their market success," she says. This point of view has fueled her desire to find artists outside the mainstream. But there is something deeper at play: a search for an underground culture in China. She has invested in a music venue, termed a Live House, where underground bands can perform. She supports underground comic artists whose publications elude government censors. She even investigated the possibility of holding a street art festival in the 798 Art District, but found that it was impossible to get permission to have artists graffiti the stone walls of the art district. "Just the gesture is an act of rebellion which interests me," says Liu, explaining that, while these groups rarely develop into a single movement, they all have the potential to constitute the foundations of an underground culture in Beijing. "I feel they are looking to rebel, and at least getting to know they exist make me feel there's hope."

Sitting in Sammi Liu's modest apartment, crammed with her various art finds, I too experience a glimmer of hope. I have hope that the future of the Chinese art market will not solely rely on the beneficence of millionaires, though they play an important part. I have hope that, with the assistance of these individuals, Chinese art will find a place in the global art world. But, most importantly, I have hope that, through young professionals like Liu, the Chinese art scene will do more than generate sales, do more than penetrate international art fairs. Liu demonstrates that there is the potential to encourage a Chinese cultural underground that can emerge and inspire this country's younger generation. There are, of course, formidable obstacles to such a movement emerging in this country of restrictions, but it is something that I feel many young Chinese artists are looking for, even as they participate in a more conventional art market system.

9
TRANSNATIONALS IN NEW YORK

When the Solomon R. Guggenheim Museum opened the exhibition *Tales of Our Time* in November 2016, crowds turned out for the celebration, excited to see new works by younger Chinese artists shown for the first time in New York. With an entrance decorated with Sun Xun's fantastic wall paintings and an animatronics machine sweeping blood-like pools of red liquid by the duo Sun Yuan and Peng Yu, the exhibition made a distinct impression, even though it did not claim to represent the entirety of the new generation of artists from China. But of equal import was the make-up of its audience. Scores of young Chinese twenty-somethings, all living and working in New York, filled the rotunda to bask in pride at the accomplishments of their peers from across the world.

Anyone who attended this opening could not help but notice this growing community that is making its presence felt in the New York art world. Key among this group is the curator of the show, Xiaoyu Weng, who was born in 1985 in Beijing and came to the USA in 2007 to attend graduate school at California College of the Arts in San Francisco. After a series of significant curatorial positions—at the CCA Wattis Institute and as head of Asia programs for the Kadist Foundation—she landed the position as Robert H. N. Ho Family Foundation curator at the Guggenheim, remaining in the USA for ten years, much to her surprise.

"I've never felt like an immigrant. I believe in thinking about a global citizen in a more cosmopolitan way," she says in a recent interview, expressing a position shared by many of her compatriots, born in China but now living in New York. She has no regrets about relocating, but feels little pressure to assimilate into American culture, nor defensiveness about maintaining a Chinese identity. In fact, she admits that she probably could not have achieved as much if she had remained in China. "I don't think I would have been exposed to all the intellectual work being done here—philosophy, theory, and intellectual discourses. I have always wanted to be a curator, but I wouldn't be able to do things in such an intellectually rigorous way, or participate on an international level," she says. She is probably right. Despite the burgeoning number of museums opening in China, there still is not an intellectual community of curators challenging and supporting each other, as Weng has found in the USA.

In many ways, Weng's situation parallels that of the many young Chinese artists who are now living in the Chinese diaspora. Most have come to the USA to complete their education, based on the belief that American art schools provide more exposure to art theory and more freedom to experiment with new art forms. They then remain, working when their visa permits as artists' assistants or gallery directors, trying to find opportunities to show their work somewhere in Chelsea, but more likely in Bushwick. Though many would admit that they might have more chances to succeed in Beijing and Shanghai, amid the growing legions of galleries in mainland China, they find something in New York that they consider irreplaceable, though they have a hard time articulating just what that may be. In some ways, they are a most optimistic group of young artists, earnest in their ambitions to expand their horizons and reach larger audiences than they might find back home.

Since gaining residence in the USA is not a straightforward process, we can assume that this is also a highly motivated and ambitious group of artists. Almost all originally entered the USA with a student visa, allowing them to complete their education through the graduate and postgraduate levels. They then applied for an OPT visa—Optional Practical Training—which permitted an additional year of residence to pursue employment related to their chosen field. But beyond that period of time, these artists had to gain an O-1 visa, granted to creative individuals demonstrating extraordinary ability and achievement, better known as the "artist's visa." This visa requires proof of national or international status as an artist and can cost up to $8,000 in legal fees to obtain. Virtually all of the artists that I interviewed were pursuing an O-1 visa, though the odds are stacked against being granted one, given that as young, emerging artists, few had the credentials necessary for this status. Without this visa, the only other option would be to apply for permanent resident status in the USA, an even more challenging process given government limitations on the number of visas granted each year to Chinese foreign nationals.

Brooklyn-based filmmaker Bo Wang is in the process of applying for a green card, the piece of paper that would grant him permanent resident status in the USA, where he has lived for the past ten years. Born in Chongqing in 1982 and trained as a physicist at Tsinghua University, he originally came to the States in 2007 to pursue a PhD in Physics from the University of Maryland. But on a whim, he also applied to art schools, submitting a portfolio of photographs he had taken as a hobby during his time as a student. The School of Visual Arts in New York City accepted him, much to his delight. After one month in Maryland, feeling claustrophobic in the school's suburban surroundings, he chose to leave for New York. His biggest challenge at the time was to explain to his parents why he gave up a full fellowship in physics for the much more risky and expensive course of an art degree.

Since graduating, he has made a series of photographs and a film that brought him back to his hometown of Chongqing, a sprawling municipality of 30 million people, which has experienced the seismic changes of urbanization and political upheavals. In his photographic series *Heteroscapes*, he captures the collisions of traditional culture, commercial development, and Communist propaganda found in the streets and construction sites of the city. In 2012, he finished a feature-length film, *China Concerto*, which documents the rise of Chongqing mayor Bo Xilai and his "red culture" campaign, a revival of Mao-inspired spectacle, before the mayor's dramatic downfall following corruption charges later that year. The film had its US premiere at the Museum of Modern Art in 2013.

So although Bo Wang now bases himself in New York, his projects bring him back to China for months at a time. When asked if he views himself like an immigrant to the USA,

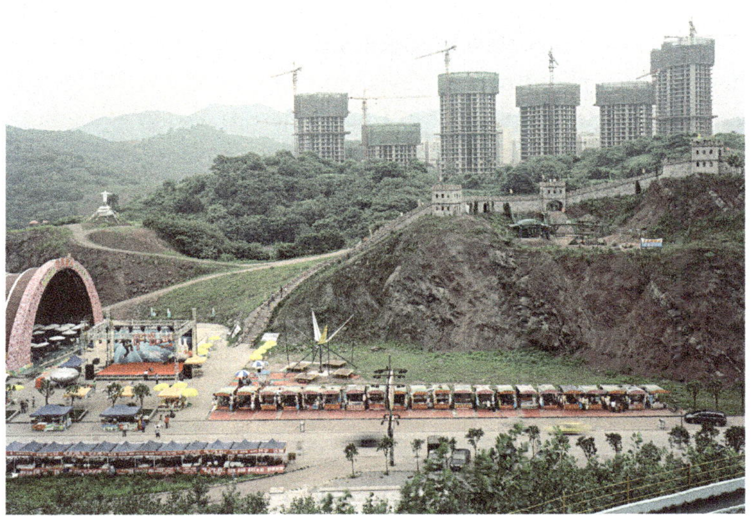

BO WANG, *HETEROSCAPES NO. 02*, 2009. COURTESY OF THE ARTIST.

he answers, "That's a very important question, but I never really thought about it. Before I came to the States, I never saw myself as a minority. In China, you're always in the majority. So, in that sense, the feeling of being immigrant is true, but I feel more like a global citizen. Even when I'm not traveling, I see myself going back and forth." This was especially true when Wang was in the process of filming *Traces of an Invisible City: Three Notes on Hong Kong*, a *cinéma vérité* approach to the city of Hong Kong, completed in 2016. For this extended film, he spent five months of the year filming in Hong Kong, including a week at Art Basel Hong Kong, a particular highlight of the footage. *Traces of an Invisible City* was featured in the film program accompanying the exhibition, *Tales of Our Time*, at the Guggenheim.

I'm curious why Bo Wang, who seems totally at home in New York, finds himself returning to China over and over again. "Why don't you make a movie in New York?" I ask him. He admits this seems like a contradiction. "I don't think there's an obvious or intentional decision made about focusing on China. I think it's more a matter of when something happens in China, the issue is so attractive, I cannot avoid looking at it and dealing with it," he answers. "I feel that New York is more of a base for me. So I come here to think about myself, research, study, and have intellectual exchanges with people. But in China, there is always something going on, so many changes happening that I have to start paying attention and try to figure out what's going on."

For Wang, China is subject matter, not an identity. Predisposed to analyzing societies based on their political structure and architectural landscape, he finds the cities in China to be rich with material for his documentary-style films. Like many of the Chinese artists that I have met in New York, he returns to China not with a sense of a homecoming, but with a fresh perspective gained from time spent in the West. As such, he is producing a new form of Chinese contemporary art, framed by academic theory learned in Western art schools, but located in the issues raised by life in contemporary China.

"When artists in New York say that they are Chinese, it doesn't mean that they have to use symbolism and languages that reinforce their identity in their artwork," says Xiaoyu Weng, explaining that she herself does not dismiss her cultural background but incorporates it into her work. "I don't see myself as a global curator per se; my cultural background and position make me think things in a certain way. It's important to bring in these different perspectives," she says. "But that doesn't mean that Chinese artists always have to talk about things with Chinese elements, calligraphy or landscape painting. They can talk about the contemporary social-political reality of China, and that reality is hardly Chinese in the way we project it to be because that reality is often influenced and shaped by different cultural contacts."

To a curator as sophisticated as Weng, the concept of Chinese identity has transformed over time because it no longer carries a fixed, predetermined meaning. Through education and travel and even exposure to other cultures from the internet, young Chinese artists not only have a different perspective on their homeland, they have a different attitude towards themselves. They self-present and self-reflect differently than the generation before them, particularly those artists based outside of China. Rather than setting themselves up as some equivalent to Chinatown, carrying with them the weight of nostalgia for their homeland, they are using their unique perspective to perform identity in new and complicated ways. Sometimes, they come off as brashly confident in the notion of a global identity. More often, though, they can be confused by their situation, struggling to process layers of influence to create their art.

Jennifer Wen Ma is an important artist to consider in this discussion about global identity. Born in Beijing in 1973, she moved to Oklahoma with her mother when she was a teenager. She comes from a different generation of artists to those born after 1976, most of whom moved to the USA much later, in the mid-2000s. But Ma is a transitional figure in other ways as well.

Upon graduating with her MFA from Pratt Institute in 1999, she went to work for Cai Guo-Qiang, the artist who so commandeered the field of Chinese contemporary art from his perch in New York in the 1990s. For Cai's generation, the first to bring China into a global dialogue, there was a burden to share their cultural background with an international audience, and a sense of "Chinese-ness" was palpable in their work. For Ma, who had left China at an early age, the experience of working for Cai for eight years was a refresher course in her cultural heritage.

According to Ma, her initial encounter with the USA was a typical immigrant experience, in that her mother was determined to integrate into mainstream American culture, and set about eliminating their Chinese accent in order to do so. "I have to say, during high school and college, I really tried to assimilate as much as possible. With that, I didn't stay connected with Chinese culture," she recalls. She views Cai Guo-Qiang and the older generation of Chinese artist who came to the USA in the 1990s as "staking a claim for a larger cultural identity" in contrast to her experience. "It's less so for my generation and even less so for those who grew up in the 1980s and 1990s. For us, it's more about speaking for oneself and having an individual identity."

A turning point for Ma came in 2008 when she served as one of seven members of the core creative team for the opening and closing ceremonies of the Summer Olympic Games in Beijing. Working alongside Cai, who designed the fireworks for the ceremonies, and Zhang Yimou, the famed Chinese filmmaker, Ma found that they had to work hard to create a vision of a new China that did not rely on stereotypes of Chinese culture. "It's quite clichéd now to say, but I really wanted to share with the world a more modern vision of China that's not all dragons, ribbon-dancing, and lanterns," she says. According to Ma, the team spent ten months—ten hours a day, seven days a week—trying to figure out how to represent 5,000 years of Chinese history in 15 minutes. They brought in experts on a variety of subjects—from warfare to drumming—an equivalent of a graduate program in Chinese identity. "Even though I don't think of the Olympics as my personal work—it belongs to the nation, it was collective, and the director was Zhang Yimou—but I took pride in the fact that if Cai and I weren't there, it would have ended up being very different," she says, pointing to the image at the finale of an LED rendition of an unfolding scroll painting as proof of their success.

Since then, Ma has emerged as an artist in her own right, often incorporating elements of Chinese culture in her work, despite living and working in New York. While she was never trained in traditional calligraphy, Ma's experimental use of ink painting is a hallmark of her work, which ranges from installation, public art and theatrical performances. In 2012, Ma covered 1,500 live plants with ink in her installation *Hanging Garden in Ink* at Ullens Center for Contemporary Art, Beijing, referencing the Hanging Gardens of Babylon to meditate on the contrast between nature and myth, among other broader themes.

Her explorations of gardens and of ink continued with *Paradise Interrupted*, an "installation opera" that premiered at the Spoleto Festival USA in 2015, Charleston, SC, and was performed at both Lincoln Center Festival and Singapore International Festival of the Arts in 2016. Treating the set design as a three-dimensional ink painting, Ma reinvigorated the Chinese *kunqu* opera *The Peony Pavilion* with a score by composer Huang Ruo that blended influences from Eastern and Western opera practices. The star of the performance was Quan Yi, noted Chinese opera singer who has been banned from performing in China since her appearance without official permission from the Ministry of Culture in the 19-hour Lincoln Center production of *The Peony Pavilion* in 1998. But the set design played an equal starring role, with the garden fabricated from hundreds of sheets of Tyvek that unfolded, like an origami creature, into a black exotic landscape during the course of the 80-minute opera.

Despite the fact that Ma makes ample use of Chinese cultural references in her work—a practice that superficially aligns her with the older generation of Cai Guo-Qiang—she does not view

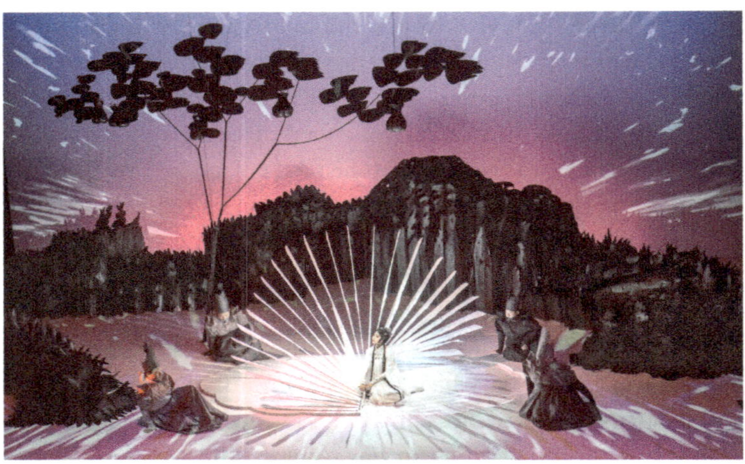

PARADISE INTERRUPTED, DIRECTED AND DESIGNED BY JENNIFER WEN MA; PRESENTED AT GERALD W. LYNCH THEATER AT JOHN JAY COLLEGE, LINCOLN CENTER FESTIVAL 2016.

herself as under an obligation to present a version of "Chineseness." Instead, she views herself as, first and foremost, an artist making use of appropriation from a wide range of cultures. "I only think about culture as far as it's a part of my thinking as an artist, Chinese or not. It's not something I consciously worry about, though I do recognize the question as important," she says. To underscore her way of thinking about these issues, she points to a recent commission to redesign the information kiosk in New York's Chinatown, which up to now has been cast in the style of a stereotypical pagoda. "I told the architectural team that we have to look at what the community needs, rather than the stereotype. You really have to do the research with an open mind, with no preconceived notion," she recalls. Likewise, with her own work, she believes that she is not merely representing a preconceived notion of Chinese culture, but a reconfiguration of cultural elements as works of contemporary art.

Still, Ma's engagement with Chinese elements differentiates her from the new younger generation of Chinese artists in New

York who Ma herself describes as "more transnational and fluid." Transnational is the new buzz word in curatorial circles, aimed at artists whose cultural identity is a hybrid of the many countries where they have lived, studied, and now make work. Prime examples of such transnational identity are Cici Wu, Ho King Man, and Wang Xu, three artists who were born in China, studied in the USA, and now call New York their home. In 2015, they turned their shared studio in Chinatown into an ad hoc alternative space and impromptu residency program called Practice. Run on a shoe-string budget covered by the artists' income from part-time jobs, Practice has attracted a following among young international artists in the city who, like the founders themselves, live nomadic lives.

"I think what we are trying to do is to find a new alternative to identity politics, to put our Chinese identity on a lower level and open ourselves to something more focused on the relationship between the three of us," says Cici Wu, a recent master's of Fine Art graduate of the Maryland Institute College of Art who charmingly works artspeak into heartfelt statements about their mission. Wu was born in Beijing in 1989 and moved to Hong Kong with her family where she attended college before coming to the USA in 2011. She met her two partners in Practice just when she was graduating from MICA in 2014 and was considering moving to New York. Since then, they have hosted a dozen artists—from Cao Fei and Zheng Yuan to João Vasco Paiva and Casey Robbins—in their fifth-floor walk-up, holding opening receptions and performances by invitation only, while keeping their presence low-key so as not to attract the attention of their landlord.

"I think of myself as an immigrant only in the sense that immigrant means moving around a lot," Wu tells me, communicating by WeChat from a residency in Taiwan where she spent three months in 2017. I ask her if her goal is to integrate herself into American society, to which she replies, "I want to intervene in American society."

Her own art projects combine film, sculpture, and installation, using technology to conjure up a romantic atmosphere. In her 2017 installation *Closer, Closer, Says Love*, she projected an almost blank video onto one wall across from a contraption used to open automatic doors, stripped of its function and reequipped with a pair of torn sleeves that broke apart and then approached each other, activated by motion sensors. The video, a foggy haze of clouds of color, was made by filming the ambient light in movie theaters as romantic dramas, such as *Moonlight* or *In the Mood for Love*, played on the big screen. In another installation, Wu used a similar practice to capture the ambient light of the underground film *White Dust from Mongolia*, by the late Korean-American artist Theresa Hak Kyung Cha, who died at the age of 31 in 1982. Based on the study of Cha's writings, storyboards, and raw footage, she transformed the unfinished film shot by shot into interconnected objects scattered on the floor, and again, responsive to the audience as they navigated the space, through the operation of motion sensors.

Wang Xu, another Practice founder, was well on his way to being a leading realist sculptor in China when he chose to pursue a different path and study contemporary art through graduate school in the USA. Born in Dalian in 1987, he attended the sculpture program at the Central Academy of Fine Arts in Beijing, a five-year course that prepared students to fill the hotel lobbies and public squares of China's new megacities. But during his time at the Academy, Wang spent a year as an exchange student at Rhode Island School of Design, where his interest was awoken in more experimental notions about sculpture. When he returned to China, he applied to attend graduate school at his alma mater but was rejected, a decision that fueled his determination to continue his education abroad. For that, he would need to improve his English, so he took a three-month intensive course that was well beyond his means. Unable to afford to heat his studio in Heiqiao, he spent the winter months relying on Wi-Fi at the local McDonald's and sleeping nights in a cheap bathhouse. When he received his acceptance letters, he felt as if they were magical messages from a far-off wonderland. He chose Columbia University because he had fallen in love with the museums in New York during his earlier stay in the USA.

While many of the artists I met in New York came from undoubtedly privileged backgrounds, Wang Xu's father was a taxi cab driver who could ill afford grad school tuition. Instead, Wang picked up a series of teaching assistant positions and lived secretly in his studio space at Columbia, using the school's gymnasium to shower. He continued to work for one of his professors after he graduated. Since then, he has pursued residencies, including the Lower Manhattan Cultural Council, Pioneer Works, and Storm King's Shandaken Project.

But a turning point came for Wang in 2015 when he was selected for a group show at Sculpture Center in Long Island City. He proposed a work called *David and Eve*, appropriating two figures he found at Quyang, a center in China known for the mass production of classical statuary, mainly Greek, Roman, and Renaissance. Using two local workers as models, Wang recast the faces of Michelangelo's David and a version of Eve to look like ordinary people and then shipped the final works back to New York. Participation in this exhibition confirmed his decision to remain in New York.

"I wouldn't say I'm a Chinese artist, but rather an artist from China," he tells me when I ask about how he prefers to be identified. Wang explains,

> I think the two phrases mean different things. With the latter, the "Chinese" prefix sometimes would give an extra layer of meaning in terms of who I am, or the kind of work that I'm supposed to make. But just an artist is better. Like you would say so-and-so is an artist from Israel, or an artist from the UK, so "artist from China" paints a better image. You can work in the UK and not have grown up or been born there. So identity is complicated.

"Personally, I don't really want to identify as anything. Not artist, not Chinese. I am just a normal human being making things. I don't want to bring nationality into it," says Bill He, who exhibits with his Chinese name, Ho King Man. Of all the partners in Practice, he is the most comfortable in the USA, having studied here, on and off, since high school. Born in 1988 in Xuwen in the south of China, He holds a law degree from Fordham University but chose to become an artist after practicing at an international law firm in Washington, DC. "People would ask, are you a Chinese artist? But how can I answer this?," he asks me rhetorically.

> Yes, I am Chinese, and yes, I make art. But does that make me a Chinese artist? I've never made things in China, nor did I go to school for art in China. So I don't know how these labels could be interpreted and defined. If you insist on this question, I would say that I am a New York artist, because I live here.

Interestingly, He is making work rooted in the experience of another Chinese artist, the photographer Ren Hang, who

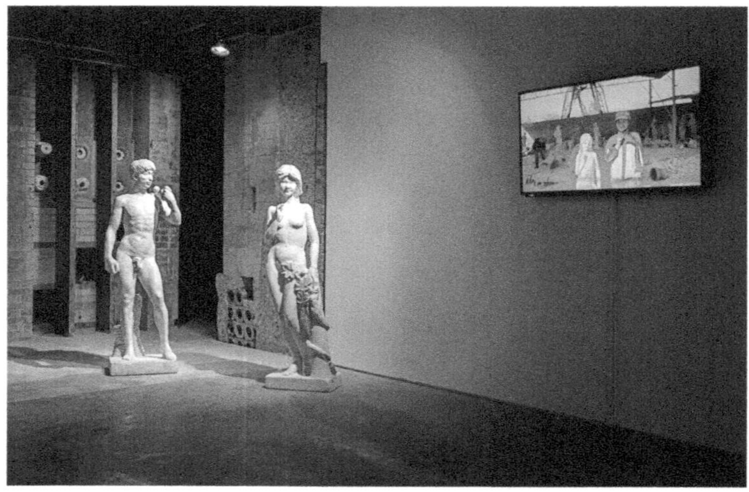

WANG XU, *DAVID AND EVE*, INSTALLATION VIEW, SCULPTURE CENTER, 2015. COURTESY OF THE ARTIST.

committed suicide in early 2017. Ren Hang, an openly gay artist, made striking, highly erotic pictures of young people, posed in an almost surrealistic manner, full of humor and wit. Before his death at the age of 29, Ren Hang was arrested many times in China, yet he had found a following worldwide with solo exhibitions in Antwerp, Athens, Bangkok, Copenhagen, Frankfurt, Hong Kong, Marseille, New York, Paris, and Vienna, as well as a hugely passionate following on Instagram. In addition to his photography, he was known for his poetry, which he posted on his website, often referencing his struggle with depression in these works.

"I think what Ren Hang's work represents is what's lacking in voice in China," says Bill He, who met the photographer in New York in 2015, when they became close friends. He took it upon himself to translate Ren's poems into English, which he assembled in an artist's book that he exhibited as an installation, positioned in a carefully designed box on a small wooden table under a spotlight. He showed this work at a New York gallery only two months before Ren's death. "For me, because of cultural differences, the key issue is translation and mistranslation," says He.

Even though Bill He self-identifies as a "New York artist," it is clear that his source material is drawn from China, which is an interesting dichotomy not easily explained simply by geographical location. Though he is now based in New York, his life trajectory has not severed all his ties to China. He clearly identifies with Ren Hang, an artist who managed to have an international following in spite of his challenges back home. As such, He tips his hand and reveals his own ambitions, which are at this moment more aspirational than actualized, yet by establishing a platform such as Practice, he is able to gather a community of like-minded young artists around him, normalizing a shared sense of identity crisis.

For other artists, perhaps a bit less familiar with operating in the New York art world, a state of identity crisis presents more confusing challenges, expressed at times in the artworks themselves. For example, one recent graduate, Hua Shuangyu, created an installation for her master's in Fine Art thesis project that is riddled with nostalgia. For her final project at Maryland Institute College of Art she created *Room 502*, a homage to her family home back in Zhejiang, where she was born in 1990. For *Room 502*, she asked each member of her family to draw a blueprint of the apartment that they had left some years before, revealing five different layouts of the home, a consequence of the divergent memories of each family member. She displayed the drawings and scale models that she built based on them, as well as a pair of videos.

In one of the videos, she focuses on a single object, a plaster cast of a Greek philosopher, that had come into the house through a relative who was training as an artist. Shuang herself had attended Fudan University in Shanghai, majoring in new media art, thereby bypassing the type of training required in Chinese art academies that would require copying such a cast over and over again. Yet, for her, the object held the key to her development, an early exposure to Western thought that was slightly out of place in her family home. When I asked her about the strong sense of displacement in the video, she acknowledged that, now that she was herself displaced, a Chinese student living in the USA, she identified even more strongly with the bust.

"In China, everything was about technology and media, but at school in the US, I found that I needed to think about content," Hua tells me, adding, "Being here allowed me the distance to reflect on my past and my connections to my culture. I started thinking about my identity as a result." She refers back to the image of the Greek philosopher, how it originates in the West but has become a part of the Chinese education system, a fact that might be lost on Western audiences. She also explains that, because her educational training was so loaded with Western influences, she did not anticipate the culture shock she experienced when coming to the USA. "Things were more different than I expected them to be," she says. "Being here, I realize that my background and knowledge is grounded in

China, and that ultimately it is related to identity. The difference is more obvious here." Yet, when exploring that identity, she does not fall back on using traditional Chinese elements or stereotypes about China. Instead, as she has learned in graduate school, she uses conceptual strategies that translate well in a global vocabulary. "I don't want to emphasize the fact that I'm Chinese—I just want to be a normal artist, like other artists here," she says.

Mo Kong defines himself as a political artist, making artworks based on research into the coal mining industry in his hometown in Shanxi Province. Born in 1990, Mo Kong trained at Jilin University to be a journalist, taking a job as a fashion editor at GQ Magazine after graduating. But after just one year on the job, he decided to pursue a different path as an artist, precisely because he felt that this would allow him to speak about things that were regularly censored in the press in China. In 2013, he entered the Rhode Island School of Design, and since graduating in 2016, followed by a prestigious fellowship at the Skowhegan School of Painting and Sculpture, he has been regularly creating conceptual art projects that deal with issues of censorship and pollution in subtle, almost abstract ways.

For example, in his 2016 video, *See Sun, and Think the Shadow*, Mo Kong conveyed the emotional anxiety provoked by strip mining, using Google Maps renditions of mining sites juxtaposed with images of sinkholes, black holes, and other types of voids. According to the artist, the video "projects the land abuse, corruption, government censorship and environment pollution to my personal life." In the installation, *The West of the Mountain*, 2016, Mo Kong combines elements such as bars of soap and piles of coal dust positioned on a series of precarious shelves with texts taken from interviews and the internet. The work evokes the way that, in China, discussions of topics such as pollution are truncated and disjointed as a result of government intervention.

For now, Mo Kong is based in Brooklyn and relishes the freedom he has to address these issues while in the USA. Like many of the artists in New York, he can stay here with an O1 artist's visa for another three years, even longer with permitted renewals. But he has no intention of immigrating or becoming a US citizen. "I like being Chinese. If I try to emigrate to America, I would lose a lot of my voice and my history," he tells me.

Still, he credits his time abroad with giving him a different perspective on the situation in China. "When I was a kid, I believed every single thing the government told me in the mainstream news. But when I came here, I saw a lot of protests, and people believing in different things; people have their own voice and they go out on to the streets voicing their own interests," he says. "In China, we are talking about more harmony, but that slogan only makes you forget what you really want, especially when we put a lot of trust into the government." When challenged about why he is making work about China from the safety of the USA, he gets defensive, insisting that if artists like Glenn Ligon or Kara Walker can make work about race or gender, then he should be able to make work about his Chinese nationality. "That's another reason why I don't want to emigrate here. I'm a Chinese artist. If I change my nationality, my identity can't stay the same. Then who and what would I represent, what would I make work for?," he says.

In the case of Mo Kong and several of the other artists discussed here, it is difficult to determine which is the best audience for their artworks: American or Chinese? While all of these artists are working toward having their work shown in New York, they are also exploring the possibilities of showing in Beijing and Shanghai. This raises the issue of translation, or more accurately, mistranslation, as there is always some slippage in meaning between the two cultures. Some artists feel that their work is best understood in the West, where audiences have the necessary background in conceptual art to appreciate their experimental efforts. They believe that Chinese audiences are still too rooted in more traditional art forms, such as realist painting. Others, however, are finding that their work is more readily appreciated in China, where their references are familiar and without need of elaborate explanation.

Photographer Pixy Yijun Liao has had success in both the USA and more recently in China with an exhibition at Leo Xu Projects. Born in Shanghai in 1979, she is best known for her series *Experimental Relationship*, in which she captures the role reversal between herself and her much younger, Japanese husband, Takahiro Moroka, whom she calls "Moro." This description barely conveys the humor and sexiness of these images. In one, *The King Under Me*, Liao wearing a bright pink bra sits on the shoulders of Moro who wears an equally vivid pink pair of boxer shorts. In *Homemade Sushi*, Moro lies prone over a roll of mattresses with a dark green shawl draped over him, like a piece of nori. Deadpan and subversive, these works completely reverse the male gaze, allowing the woman to be entirely in control of the artistic process.

Liao came to the USA in 2005 to pursue her MFA in photography at the University of Memphis, meeting Moro, one of the few other Asian students on campus. They remain in the USA through a preference for English as a shared language, since neither one of them feels able to adjust to life in Shanghai or Tokyo because the language barrier would be too great. Now, equipped with a green card, Liao is able to travel freely between the USA and China, where her parents still reside.

"The reason why I can make this work is because I left China and met Moro," says Liao, insisting that, back in Shanghai, she was raised to believe that a husband should be the older and more dominant partner; the wife submissive. "Living here made me more independent, as my family and my friends are not here. I could just do things without being judged and pressured," she says. She also acknowledges that in the USA, there is a context to address issues of gender equality and roleplay, something she never thought about while in China. "It's kind of socially taboo," says Liao, always smiling.

Yet, at the same time as she credits the USA with giving her a certain kind of freedom, she still views her identity as resolutely Chinese. She recognizes that some artists, especially artists in China, might reject the Chinese label because they don't want to be associated with an older generation of artists, whether its Zhang Xiaogang or Ai Weiwei. But once she arrived in Memphis, she was confronted with a lack of social diversity for the first time, making her realize just how Chinese she really was.

"I think it definitely adds more layers to my work," says Liao, referring to her Chinese identity, adding quickly, "At the same time, it also limits people's understanding of my work." She explains that those who didn't grow up with the social pressures she experienced in China don't fully understand her work, which she insists has its biggest following among young women in China. "When they see my work, they respond to it personally," she says, explaining that they understand that she is portraying

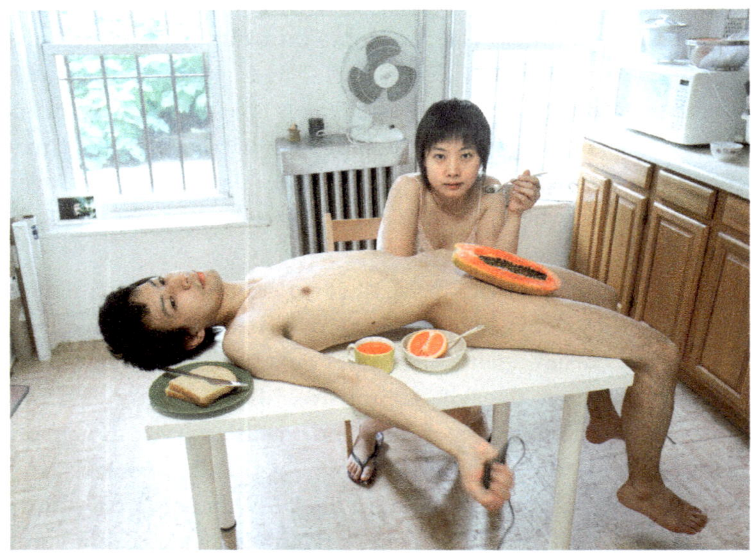

PIXY LIAO, *START YOUR DAY WITH A GOOD BREAKFAST*, 2009. COURTESY OF LEO XU PROJECTS.

the exact opposite of their norm. But, she explains, when she shows her work in Western countries where equality is more presumed, the response is more cerebral and less spontaneous. In fact, the biggest misunderstanding of her work, according to Liao, is when people associate it with feminism. "I didn't even know about feminism when I first started this project," she says.

Despite this ostensible misunderstanding, Liao's work has proven to be vastly popular in a wide range of museums and galleries. In the past two years, she has participated in exhibitions at Galleri Vasli Souza (Sweden), First Draft Gallery (Australia), Metro Pictures (New York), Museum of Sex (New York), Museum of Modern Art in Bologna (Italy), chi K11 Art Museum (Shanghai), Asia Society Texas Center (Houston), OPEN ART Biennial (Sweden), and FORMAT Festival (United Kingdom). Additionally, Liao and Moroaka have been performing as a band called PIMO, playing charming duets at alternative music venues. When asked if she believes that her background has given her a more global perspective than her American counterparts, Liao answers affirmatively. "Yes, I do. My first impression when I came to the USA was that people are simple-minded compared to people I knew in China, because they stay in their comfort zones and don't really see the complexity of the rest of the world, and how dark that can be," she says. But, she admits that coming to the USA has added a layer of complexity to her own life that she greatly appreciates. "If I stayed in China and never met Moro, I would never think that I could be a different person," she muses. "After meeting him, I found a different me, which I think fits me much better than before."

Whether it is by choice or by circumstance, young Chinese artists living in the USA have undergone an experience that has turned them into global citizens, though not necessarily more cosmopolitan than their peers in China. Most of the artists I encountered in Beijing and Shanghai insisted on being evaluated as individual practitioners, not predefined by Chinese culture, and wholeheartedly embrace the term, "global artist." But in New York, I found greater ambivalence about this label, with more than a few reverting back to "Chinese artist" as the proper frame for their identity. This may be a sign of resistance, a reluctance to capitulate to a homogenized global environment that eliminates important cultural differences. At the very least, it is an indication of the levels of discomfort, alienation and displacement that are an inherent part of the immigrant experience.

I gained some insight into this situation from talking to Bingqin Cao, a gallery assistant in New York whom I've known since she was my translator back in Shanghai in 2010. Born in 1990, Cao came to the USA in 2011 to get a master's degree in arts administration at New York University. She met and married a young Chinese-American doctor, a US citizen, in 2013 and worked for two years at the Sean Kelly Gallery, which represents Chinese artists Sun Xun and the older painter Liu Wei. After that, she worked briefly at Hauser & Wirth, where she was part of their growing Asian team, preparing for the gallery's participation in fairs such as Art Basel Hong Kong and Art 021.

"When I was in China, every day we received information on how to be more international and global, to move away from Chinese cultural stereotypes," Cao explains, adding, "Being able to speak an international language and be considered on equal grounds with other global artists was a primary concern for Chinese artists." But, even with this preparation, she was shocked when she relocated to New York and for the first time encountered ethnic differences. She found that people made assumptions about her because she was Chinese, that even in the ostensibly tolerant New York art world, stereotypes persisted. "I think I now have two brains operating at the same time," Cao explains. "On the Chinese side, I'm more aware of why I think the way I do, and I use that to monitor myself when making decisions. At the same time, I have a second brain that is very Westernized, and I view myself as an international citizen."

This sense of bifurcation—a dual identity—is what many artists are fighting when they embrace the label "global artist." For them, there is a sense of a new identity emerging, one that transcends East–West divisions and more perfectly captures the transnational experience. But as Cao points out, the success of a merger is partially dependent on perception and reception by the mainstream. To that extent, transnationalism will remain only an optimistic goal as long as cultural stereotypes dog the Chinese artists' experience in the USA.

"If there's such a thing as a global artist that could erase and blur people's identities, then I accept it," says Bill He, sitting in the front room of Practice's tenement space in Chinatown. "In that case, everybody is a global artist. I think that's a good approach." He would like to reject all labels: artist, Chinese and global. But he concedes that society insists on labels, that categories are one way that we comprehend each other and reach a level of understanding each other. "In a sense, if you have labels, it's easier for people to talk to you, to understand you. I get that," he says. But for now, he will continue to make art that is difficult to categorize, even if it leaves him open to misinterpretation. Perhaps, with time, and with the continued success of these Chinese artists penetrating the global art dialogue, misunderstandings will become but a new way to consider contemporary art and our presumptions about Chinese contemporary art will diminish, until we stop using the term all together.

CONCLUSION

In June 2015, Parisian audiences had something of a shock when they attended a performance-happening staged by Beijing artist Chen Tianzhou at the Palais de Tokyo. Celebrating hedonism as a new brand of religion, the show stole references from South Park and Japanese Butoh dance, drug-filled raves and hip hop rants, masturbation and Buddhist meditation, gender-bending costumes and underground subcultures. Meanwhile, videos played on the walls, floors, and ceiling, blaring out commandments, such as "Jerk Off in Peace" and "Ordo Ab Chao," or order out of chaos, the Freemason's motto.

This is a prime example of "post-passport" art. Every sense was assaulted by this work of art; all sense of a world order that established certain expectations from a Chinese artist was upended. Because in this performance, titled *ADAHA II* as a reference to a Buddhist deity, the East–West dichotomy, so often explored by other Chinese artists, was entirely exploded. Instead of engaging with a simulation of Chinese culture, viewers were delivered into a brave new world where religion and popular culture collided together in nuclear fission. Under Chen Tianzhou's direction, we are all inductees into a cult determined to drag us away from more mundane forms of brainwashing.

"Art transcends borders—we can't talk about Chinese art and foreign art," Chen told an interviewer at the time of his opening in Paris. He went on to explain, "As a young artist, I choose my palette from a globalized world—elements from everyday life I share with artists of my age all around the world." Born in 1985 in Beijing, Chen is every bit a global citizen, having graduated with a BA in Graphic Design from London's Central St Martins College of Art and Design in 2009 and an MA in Fine Art from Chelsea College of Art and Design, UK in 2010. Since then, he has been staging events at galleries in China that often devolve into drug-filled rave parties, most explicitly when he presented *PICNIC PARADI$E BITCH* at Bank Gallery in Shanghai in 2014 and *Tianzhuo Acid Club* at Star Gallery in Beijing in 2013. These evenings underscored the existence of a vital underground scene in China, one that operated beneath the radar of both the authorities and of outsiders unfamiliar with this aspect of Chinese culture.

Because of his unrepressed outrageousness and his unarguable talent as an artist, Chen Tianzhou came to the attention of Adrian Cheng, the Hong Kong billionaire behind the K11 Art Foundation, who is not much older than his protégé. Cheng first presented Chen at his K11 museum in his shopping mall in Shanghai, before sponsoring the Palais de Tokyo exhibition. This is a prime example of the new Chinese power, the power of a younger generation, making its mark on world culture. For some, especially in China, it may be surprising that a young artist has departed to such a degree from Chinese traditions, flaunting global mass culture rather than cherishing more homegrown elements in art. But outside of China, it may be equally startling to find a Chinese artist who knows so much about alternative subcultures, both popular and more obscure, from a wide range of places throughout the world.

Perhaps we should not be surprised that Chen Tianzhou should find a partner in Lu Yang, the young woman artist who

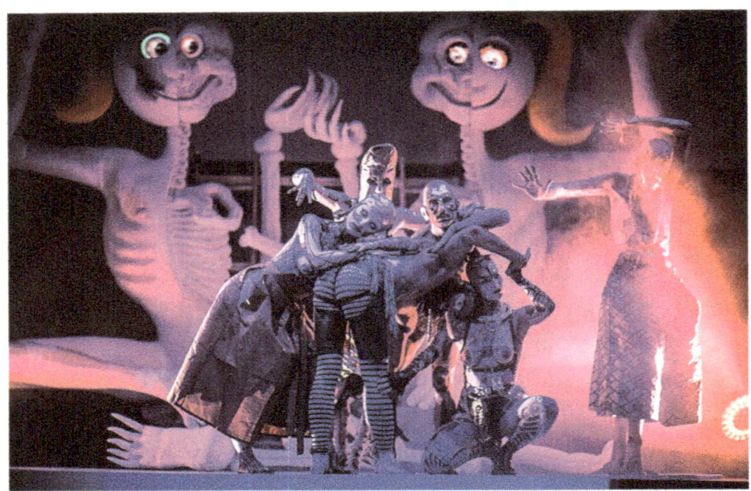

TIANZHOU CHEN, *ADAHA II*, PERFORMANCE VIEW, 2015, PALAIS DE TOKYO, PARIS, FRANCE. COURTESY OF LONG MARCH SPACE.

created *Uterus Man*. The married couple make quite an impression, each having dabbled in fashion lines, and frequently spotted sporting their self-designed outfits, more appropriate for Shibuya district of Tokyo than the more casual art enclaves of Beijing and Shanghai. Both are highly attuned to LGBTQI trends and carry themselves with a distinctly androgynous style. Most importantly, both are denizens of the internet, finding cultural influences from across the globe and recycling them into Vimeo clips, a primary means of broadcast for their creations. Together these two—while remaining individuals in their own right—embody the iconoclasm and creativity of this new generation of Chinese artists, demonstrating how far mainland artists have come in just the past 30 years.

"This generation are like the baby boomers in the USA, in that it is a generation that has written the play book and has always been the protagonist of its own historical drama, coming out of a moment of stability and prosperity at the end of a long period of uncertainty and upheaval," says Phil Tinari, director of the Ullens Center for Contemporary Art. Indeed, as opposed to the hardships and political upheavals experienced by the previous generation of Chinese artists, this younger generation inherited a period of rapid expansion and relative security, granting them a kind of self-confidence and blatant ambition. At the same time, as products of the One Child Policy, their state of isolation was ameliorated by a sense of privilege and unbridled access to opportunity. "This is a lucky generation," Tinari says.

We can see these qualities—assured self-confidence and exploration of limitless possibilities—in the works of young "post-passport" Chinese artists. Xu Zhen, the bad boy of Shanghai, takes risks with his audience, willingly confusing them with his mash-ups of Asian and Western iconography. Liu Wei exudes confidence with the scale of his installations, towering abstract sculptures made from the cast-off materials from demolished housing projects. Cao Fei offers viewers a spectrum of choices to enjoy and investigate in her internet sensation, *RMB City*. And Miao Ying boldly asserts the supremacy of the Chinese internet, or Chinternet, with her digital experiments. Engaging with the works of these and other artists, one is struck by the self-assurance and audacity in evidence.

Still, this is not a generation free from all anxiety or insecurities. Under the existence of the One Child Policy—a policy that has recently ended and will not apply to future generations—the burden of social responsibilities fall squarely on their shoulders. Many of the artists I interviewed were put under undue pressure to become artists and succeed professionally, starting their training as young children in order to enter one of the country's prestigious art academies. Now as adults, the pressure continues: to be self-supporting through sales of their work, to take care of their family, to marry and produce children of their own. All of this takes place in the context of a society that refers to unmarried women over 30 years of age as "left-over women" and forces almost 80 percent of gay men into heterosexual marriages.

This state of social anxiety counterbalances the more positive aspects of life for this generation, as reflected in several of these young artist's works. Ma Qiusha, for example, proffers a confessional video describing her training as an artist from an early age under the watchful eye of her "tiger mom." Chi Peng creates digital photographs that superimpose his image, naked and alone, in the streets of Beijing, capturing the vulnerability of life as a single child on his own in the city. Other artists—from Liu Di to Bo Wang—respond to the rapid urbanization of the landscape, life in an alienating environment that is wiping out traditional values and family life. There is a mournful undercurrent to these works that betray the optimistic outlook that is this generation's supposed birthright.

But, the most lasting impact of the One Child Policy and the fortuitous circumstances of this generation's life choices is the unbridled individuality found in the works of young Chinese artists. As opposed to the previous generation, who would have their works grouped as movements, such as Political Pop or Cynical Realism, this younger generation must be viewed as individual artists making singular statements through artworks covering a wide variety of styles. Their differences are obvious to grasp in a single glance; their similarities more subtle to discover. But, by and large, they are unwilling to adopt labels for their work—not even "Chinese art"—preferring to be viewed as individual creators.

"These artists are looking at the world from where they are, instead of them trying to tell the world who they are," says Guggenheim curator Xiaoyu Weng. She explains that the older generation of Chinese artists were attempting to counteract Eurocentrism, the belief that European and American culture is superior, forcing them to prove that they and their culture were worthy of attention. "Now, younger artists don't need to carry that burden on their shoulder anymore. It gives them more freedom to work on whatever they want, instead of carrying out a certain mission," says Weng. "That's part of the reason that younger artists don't feel that it's necessary to carry that kind of Chinese identity."

Instead, according to Weng, this younger generation of Chinese artists are able to maintain a connection to China as a matter of perspective, offering them a unique point of view on world events. They do not deny that growing up in China has given them a particular outlook, but this is rooted in the social and political circumstances they experienced, rather than 5,000 years of Chinese culture. For the most part, these young artists are more closely influenced by international pop culture, discovered via the internet, than they are by calligraphy or Cultural Revolution iconography. They do not hesitate to address issues unique to the Chinese scene, but they often adopt more global conceptual strategies in their approach to art-making.

So, for example, there are a wide range of artists addressing issues of realism, or Post-Truth, responding to their training in realist painting and sculpture to confront the compromised state of reality in contemporary Chinese society. We see Jin Shan exploding classical Greek statuary as an act of rebellion against his strict training in Socialist Realism, and Cui Jie reinventing cubism to capture the extreme juxtaposition of new and old on Shanghai's streetscapes. Hu Xiaoyuan meticulously creates simulations of wood panels in ink as a comment on the fabrication of fake products in China, from knock-off bags to bootleg DVDs. Meanwhile, artists like Yu Ji and Liang Shuo use decidedly low-tech materials to create environmental installations that mimic the look of natural landscapes. These artists are taking on a condition of life in China, that is, its perpetual state of simulacrum, without falling back on the crutch of Chinese characteristics.

In so doing, these younger artists are using China as a launch pad to confront issues relevant to cultures and societies across the world in a postmodern age. In many ways, they are "post-passport" pioneers in exploring the impact of mass production, digital innovation, and urban alienation in their artworks. These are issues that now effect cultural production in virtually every society. Yet, in China, due to the unique circumstances of globalization and urbanization of the past 30 years, these artists are particularly attuned to these conditions and can offer fresh insights for artists throughout the world.

Nowhere is this more evident than in Chinese artists' embrace of internet culture and digital media. In many ways, the internet has impacted the careers of every Chinese artist—young and old—by bringing the world closer to them, making it possible to exhibit internationally and participate in a global dialogue. But, for some young artists, the internet is also a source of inspiration, whether or not their works are digitally based. We have seen how an artist like Lu Yang surfs the internet to communicate with scientists and graphic designers who can help her to further her research in neurobiology for her 3D animations. Likewise, Guan Xiao, a sculptor who works offline, gathers images and iconography from a broad range of cultures for her installations, pairing weird, quirky sculptures with textile-like backdrops.

For some observers, this reliance on the internet and the exploitation of its possibilities may be surprising, given the Chinese government's strict control of the web. But without Facebook, Twitter, Instagram, or Google, Chinese netizens have had to come up with their own alternatives that in many cases are more advanced than those of the West. This is the position of Miao Ying, an artist who explores the glories of the Chinese internet, from mobile app WeChat to microblogging site Weibo. According to Ying, China may lead the way in digital culture, given its population's self-imposed creativity in circumventing government censors.

More importantly, the internet, with its promulgation of avatars and user profiles, offers access to alternative identities and personae. This innovation has encouraged Chinese artists to reconfigure their definition of themselves, allowing them to view "Chinese-ness" as just one of a number of options. Some, like Lu Yang, eschew Chinese identity entirely, claiming the internet as her country of origin. Others, like Miao Ying, embrace cultural identity, but update its meaning by transferring this sense of self to a digital age. In either case, it is clear that the internet has equipped this young generation of Chinese artists with a passport to world culture, allowing them to fully participate in the global art world.

All of this activity and innovation would have limited impact if it remained within the confines of China. But, this young generation is operating on a global scale, participating in gallery exhibitions, art fairs, and biennials around the world. Sun Xun, for example, is now represented not only by ShanghART in Beijing and Shanghai, but by the Edouard Malingue in Hong Kong and Sean Kelly Gallery in New York. In July 2017, he had the opportunity to present his animation *Time Spy*, 2016, on 78 screens surrounding Times Square, running for three minutes every night for a month at midnight. As the streets came alive with mammoth images of his drawings, Sun Xun commented that "this is a dream come true." Tourists in the area, unaware that such a presentation was planned, were mesmerized by the dramatic scenes playing out over electronic billboards throughout the streets.

Like this event, young Chinese artists are taking over more and more venues in the West, embracing the opportunities that are coming to them. While the older generation of Chinese artists were most often introduced through group exhibitions, such as *Magiciens de la Terre* at the Pompidou Center in 1989 or *Inside Out: New Chinese Art* at Asia Society and PS1 in 1998, this new generation of artists are most often presented in solo exhibitions, claiming their right to be viewed as individual artists. In the past year alone, two young Chinese artists were given solo shows at New York galleries: Liu Wei at Lehmann Maupin and Xu Zhen at James Cohan Gallery. It is telling that these exhibitions did not take place in Sinocentric venues, such as Asia Society, but at mainstream galleries with a global stable of artists.

To some extent, this is happening because of the transformation of Western art museums and galleries, which

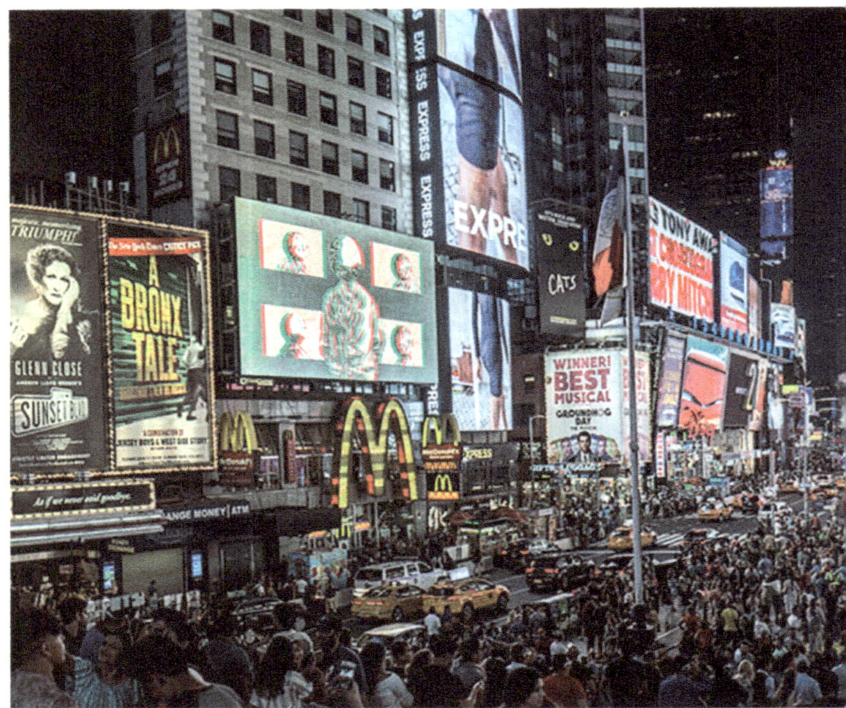

SUN XUN, *TIME SPY*, AUDEMARS PIGUET COMMISSION, PRESENTED BY TIMES SQUARE ARTS, TIMES SQUARE, 2017. PHOTOGRAPH COURTESY OF LOVIS DENGLER FOR TIMES SQUARE ARTS.

have become somewhat more sensitive to their Eurocentric tendencies and relatively more open to artists from what used to be referred to as the "periphery." But this change is also taking place as a result of the efforts of the artists themselves, demanding a spotlight be shone on their works without the filter of "Chineseness" or the label, "Chinese artist." The fictive artist in Yan Xing's *Dangerous Afternoon*, which opened at Kunsthalle Bern in June 2017, is a case in point. In this installation, Yan Xing invented an artist and a curator to stage an exhibition at the Kunsthalle, creating sculptures, drawings, and a film ostensibly authored by them to accompany the show. There was an elaborate backstory

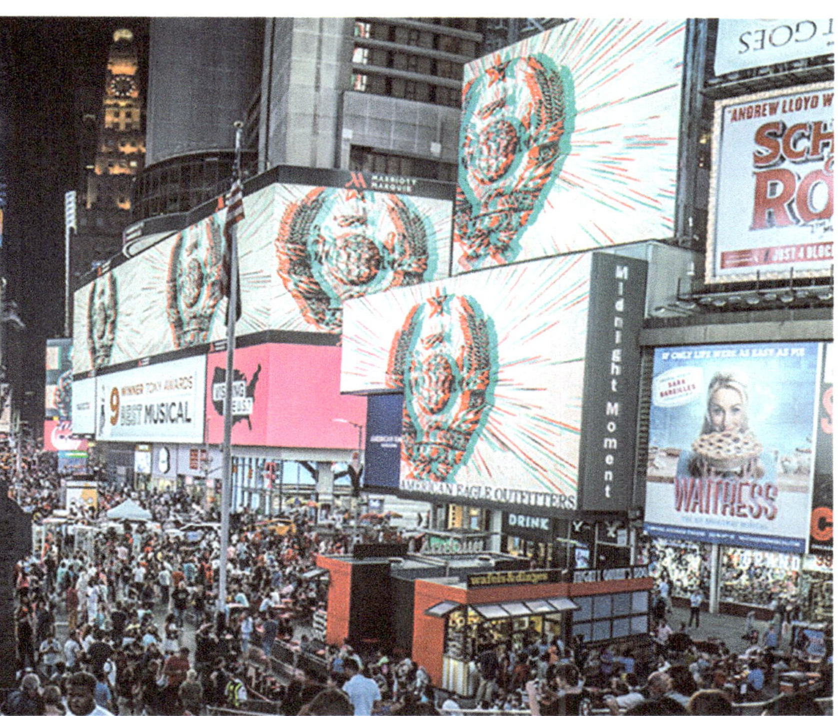

about the fictional curator, a fetishist who falls in love with a stranger's feet. When asked if the artist or the curator were Chinese, Yan Xing replied, "They are neither Western or Chinese. It doesn't matter." Likewise, most young Chinese artists that I encountered wanted their identity to remain irrelevant. By insisting on this, they have escaped the Chinese art ghetto and grasped the opportunity to emerge as artists in their own right.

The extent to which this "post-passport" strategy is effective has a great deal to do with the changing reception of Chinese contemporary art in the West. Tired of old techniques and trends, Western viewers presume that they are already familiar with

Chinese contemporary art and have no need to see more of the same. For many art connoisseurs in Europe and the USA, Chinese contemporary art has been mainly an auction phenomenon, producing record sales but few great artists. This is an audience that needs to be startled or shocked into seeing new art from China, a task that these younger Chinese artists are more than capable of fulfilling. Their desire to distance themselves from artists of the older generation, not only as a position statement but in their aesthetics as well, is feeding a new curiosity emerging in the West about the future of Chinese contemporary art and its place in global art movements.

But this could not be happening without the demonstrable role of young collectors and curators in creating an infrastructure for these young artists. Adrian Cheng has made inroads into prestigious Western institutions, from Palais de Tokyo to the Metropolitan Museum of Art, providing residencies and exhibition opportunities for many Chinese artists of this younger generation. After all, they are from his generation, and they share a belief system about Chinese identity and the need to transcend this limitation. Likewise, Michael Xu Fu Huang now sits on the board of the New Museum, while making his private museum in Beijing, M WOODS, a more international venue. Through platforms like these, young Chinese artists are not only afforded the chance to exhibit their work, they are given institutional validation which accelerates their reception in the West. This is not just some coincidental byproduct of the museum-building boom in China. It is the intentional goal of a handful of highly influential individuals operating in China and abroad.

There are still formidable barriers to acceptance of all Chinese artists, particularly in the USA, where residual Cold War politics and current concerns about China's rising power influence interpretation of the artworks. In this atmosphere, Western audiences embrace an artist like Ai Weiwei who challenges the Chinese government and fulfills their romantic notions of a lone hero standing up to an authoritarian society.

The vast majority of artists from China, by contrast, who do not take a political stand or choose to express their politics in more subtle forms, do not receive as much attention or accolades. Furthermore, Western viewers still complain about cultural differences, insisting, for example, that Chinese artists are difficult to remember because their names are impossible to retain. This widely held belief, as simplistic as it sounds, reflects the extent to which at least some forms of Eurocentrism still dominate the global art conversation.

But whether Western viewers are paying attention or not, young Chinese artists are moving into the mainstream and taking the lead in a global dialogue about the future of contemporary art. Whether we are looking at "post-internet art" or the more recent interest in a "post-truth" age, Chinese artists are at the forefront of these ideas, especially well-equipped to tackle these issues from their unique perspective developed from having grown up in China over the past 30 years. In the course of their lifetimes, they have witnessed the full effect of a country transformed by globalization. They have viscerally experienced the introduction of mega-brands—from McDonald's to Apple—into a society which once was dominated by Mao suits and Ming furniture. They have undergone a kind of reeducation, not at the hands of the state as their parents had, but through the introduction of smart phones and the internet. They have adopted an identity, framed by these circumstances, that is perfectly suited for transmigration and penetration of a global environment. In comparison to their peers in the West, who are either oblivious to these changes taking place around the world, or who live with them in more habitual ways, Chinese young artists have personally experienced these as shocks to their psyches and in turn, make artworks of astonishing impact and global reach.

As China ascends in the global arena, forever exploring new frontiers on which to exercise its formidable power, all eyes are on its millennial generation to see how the future of this once-isolated country might unfold. Much has been made of their unmatched privileges, leading some to call them "little emperors." Others conjecture that this new generation may demand political change, given their exposure to democracies in the West and the freedom afforded abroad. But I suggest that, rather than creating new stereotypes or trying to guess what these young people will demand from their country, it is best to familiarize oneself with this younger generation through their creative output and artistic production. For it is in the artworks themselves that you can see these minds at work, struggling to come to terms with the changes that they have grown up with and to devise identities that mirror this staggering transformation.

As China's new generation of artists eschew the label of "Chinese," they grow more acutely aware of themselves as spectators of a country that has undergone an unprecedented degree of change in the course of their lifetimes. It is not surprising that their artworks disclaim references of "Chinese-ness," given that their homeland is no longer a landscape dominated by temples, pagodas and statues of Mao, but a twenty-first-century nation of megacities housing 1.3 billion people. Chinese artists are no longer ambassadors from a strange, exotic land, but pioneers in the global experience. As such, they and their artworks tell us a great deal about the world in which we live and deliver messages too important to ignore.

NOTES

Introduction

1. Thelma Golden, *Freestyle*, Studio Museum of Harlem, 2001, pp. 14–16.
2. Li Xianting, "About the Stars Art Exhibition," *Contemporary Chinese Art: Primary Documents*, edited by Wu Hung (New York: Museum of Modern Art, 2010), p. 11.
3. Wang Nanming, "The Shanghai Art Museum Should Not Become A Market Stall in China for Western Hegemony," *Contemporary Chinese Art: Primary Documents*, edited by Wu Hung (New York: Museum of Modern Art, 2010), pp. 156–7.
4. Bernard Fibicher (ed.), *Mahjong: Contemporary Chinese Art from the Sigg Collection* (Ostfildern-Ruit: Hatje Cantz Publishers, 2005).
5. The re-evaluation of the notion of a universal culture can be found in a wide range of writings of postcolonial theorists, from Edward Said to Homi K. Bhaba.

1 The Last Chinese Artists

1. Gao Minglu (ed.), *Inside Out: New Chinese Art* (University of California Press, 1998).
2. Hou Hanru, "On the Mid-Ground," *Timeszone* 8 (2002), p. 26.
3. Hou Hanru, "On the Mid-Ground," p. 46.
4. Cai Guo-Qiang is referring to the exhibition *Inside Out: New Chinese Art*, which opened at Asia Society and PS1 in 1998.
5. Barbara Pollack, "Redefining Chinese Artists, in Qatar," *New York Times*, March 18, 2016.

3 Chinese Abstraction

1. Li Xu, *Calligraphic Time and Space: Abstract Art in China*, Power Station of Art, Shanghai, 2015.
2. Gao Minglu, *Chinese Maximalism: An Alternative "Metaphysical Art,"* Millennium Art Museum, 2003.
3. Li Xu, *Calligraphic Time and Space: Abstract Art in China*, Power Station of Art, Shanghai, 2015.
4. G. Roger Denson, "Colonizing Abstraction: MoMA's Inventing Abstraction Show Denies Its Ancient Global Origins," *Huffington Post*, February 15, 2013.
5. Wu Hung, *Contemporary Chinese Art* (New York: Thames and Hudson, 2014), pp. 178–9.
6. Maxwell Hearn, *Ink Art: Past as Present in Contemporary China*, Metropolitan Museum of Art, 2013, pp. 13, 139–53.

4 The Me Generation

1. Eric Fish, *China's Millennials: The Want Generation* (London: Rowman and Littlefield, 2015).
2. Jemimah Steinfeld, *Little Emperors and Material Girls: Sex and Youth in Modern China* (London: I.B.Tauris, 2015).
3. Fresh Air, "How China's One Child Policy Led to Forced Abortions and 30 Million Bachelors," National Public Radio, February 1, 2016, http://www.npr.org/2016/02/01/465124337/how-chinas-one-child-policy-led-to-forced-abortions-30-million-bachelors.
4. Elaine Jeffreys, *Sex in China* (Cambridge: Polity Press, 2015).
5. Alice C. Hu, "Half the Sky, But Not Yet Equal: China's Feminist Movement," *Harvard International Review*, August 22, 2016, http://hir.harvard.edu/china-womens-rights/.
6. Jonathan Kaiman, "In China, feminism is growing—and so is the backlash," *L.A. Times*, June 14, 2016, http://www.latimes.com/world/asia/la-fg-china-feminist-activists-20160614-snap-story.html.
7. Carol Hymowitz and Lauren Coleman, "A Skin-Care Ad Tackles Social Taboos in China," *Bloomberg News*, February 2, 2017, https://www.bloomberg.com/news/articles/2017-02-02/a-skin-care-ad-tackles-social-taboos-in-china.
8. Andrew Jacobs, "Taking Feminist Battle to China's Streets, and Landing in Jail," *New York Times*, April 5, 2015.
9. Didi Kirsten Tatlow, "Chinese Feminist Group's Social Media Account Suspended," *New York Times*, February 16, 2017.

7 Post-Internet Art

1. Zhang Peili, often described as the godfather of video art, founded the School of Intermedia Art at the China Academy of Art in Hangzhou in 2003.

His breakthrough artwork, *30 × 30*, created in 1991, is considered the first example of video art in China.

2. The number of people in China using the internet grew by over 40 million in 2016, with 95 percent accessing the internet through mobile phones. See China Internet Watch, *China Internet Statistics 2017*, https://www.chinainternetwatch.com/whitepaper/china-internet-statistics/.
3. *ON | OFF: China's Young Artists in Concept and Practice*, co-curated by Bao Dong and Sun Dongdong, Ullens Center for Contemporary Art, January 13 to April 14, 2013.
4. *Art Post-Internet*, co-curated by Karen Archey and Robin Peckham, Ullens Center for Contemporary Art, January 3 to May 11, 2014. From the accompanying catalog essay:

> Just as twentieth-century modernism was in large part defined by the relationship between craft and the emergent technologies of manufacturing, mass media, and lensbased imagery, the most pressing condition underlying contemporary culture today—from artistic practice and social theory to our quotidian language—may well be the omnipresence of the internet. Though the terminology with which we describe these phenomena is still nascent and not yet in widespread use, this exhibition presents a broad survey of art that is controversially defined as "post-internet," which is to say, consciously created in a milieu that assumes the centrality of the network, and that often takes everything from the physical bits to the social ramifications of the internet as fodder. From the changing nature of the image to the circulation of cultural objects, from the politics of participation to new understandings of materiality, the interventions presented under this rubric attempt nothing short of the redefinition of art for the age of the internet.

Participating artists and collectives included Aids-3D, Kari Altmann, Cory Arcangel, Alisa Baremboym, Bernadette Corporation, Dara Birnbaum, Juliette Bonneviot, Nicolas Ceccaldi, Tyler Coburn, Petra Cortright, Simon Denny, Aleksandra Domanović, Harm van den Dorpel, Ed Fornieles, Calla Henkel and Max Pitegoff, GCC, Josh Kline, Oliver Laric, LuckyPDF, Tobias Madison and Emanuel Rossetti, Marlie Mul, Katja Novitskova, Marisa Olson, Jaakko Pallasvuo, Aude Pariset, Seth Price, Jon Rafman and Rosa Aiello, Rachel Reupke, Bunny Rogers, Hannah Sawtell, Ben Schumacher, Timur SiQin, Hito Steyerl, Artie Vierkant, Lance Wakeling, Andrew Norman Wilson, and Jordan Wolfson.

5. The K11 Art Foundation is the brainchild of Hong Kong entrepreneur Adrian Cheng who has made inroads in many Western art institutions by underwriting exhibitions of young Chinese artists. His company, K11, operates shopping malls throughout China, all with an exhibition space located within its facility.

6. Barbara Pollack, "As China Evolves, the Artist Cao Fei Is Watching," *New York Times*, April 1, 2016.
7. WeChat is a social media application developed by Tencent, released in 2011. WeChat facilitates instant messaging, microblogging, and commerce, combining characteristics of texting, Facebook, Twitter, and PayPal. By 2016, it was one of the largest standalone messaging apps by monthly active users, with over 889 million active users spending 66 minutes a day on the app on average.
8. Michael Wines, "A Dirty Pun Tweaks China's Online Censors," *New York Times*, March 12, 2009.
9. Evan Osnos, "What is an iPad Doing On A Pedestal At A Chinese Museum?" *New Yorker*, January 18, 2013.

8 Movers and Shakers

1. "Mad About Museums," *The Economist*, January 6, 2014; B. Pollack, "Shangha's Tricky Museum Transformation," *ARTnews*, March 2014.
2. Amah-Rose Abrams, "Leaked Email Reveals that SH Contemporary Art Fair in Shanghai Has Been Called Off," artnet.com, July 8, 2015.
3. According to 2018 Art Market Report, compiled by Art Basel and UBS.
4. Justin Bergman, "An Arts Explosion Takes Shanghai," *New York Times*, November 5, 2015.

ARTIST BIOGRAPHIES

CAO Fei

b.1978, Guangzhou
Lives in Beijing

Guangzhou Academy of Fine Arts, 2001

Awards

2016 Best Artist, Chinese Contemporary Art Awards, Beijing, China
2016 Piedra de Sal, Cuenca Biennial, Cuenca, Ecuador
2010 Finalist, Future Generation Art Prize, Pinchuk Art Centre, Kiev, Ukraine
2010 Finalist, Hugo Boss Prize, The Solomon R. Guggenheim Foundation, New York
2006 Best Young Artist, Chinese Contemporary Art Awards, Beijing, China

Selected Solo Exhibitions

2016 *Cao Fei*, MoMA PS1, New York
2016 *Cao Fei*, The Center for Contemporary Art, Tel Aviv, Israel
2016 *Cao Fei: La Town*, Centre for Chinese Contemporary Art, Manchester
2015 *Cao Fei: Splendid River*, Secession, Vienna
2015 *Cao Fei: La Town*, Bonnefantenmuseum, Maastricht
2015 *Same Old, Brand New*, Art Basel Hong Kong, Hong Kong
2014 *La Town, Cao Fei's Solo Exhibition*, Lombard Freid Gallery, New York
2013 *Haze and Fog*, Tate Modern, Starr Auditorium, London

2011 *RMB City Opera*, The Nelson-Atkins Museum of Art, Kansas City
2010 *Cao Fei: RMB City*, Yerba Buena Center for the Arts, San Francisco
2009 *Utopia*, Institute of Modern Art, Brisbane, Australia
2008 *Cao Fei: RMB City*, Serpentine Gallery (2008–9), London

CHEN Tianzhuo

b.1985, Beijing
Lives in Beijing and Shanghai

Central Saint Martins College of Art and Design, 2009
Chelsea College of Art, 2010

Solo Exhibitions

2016 *ISHVARA*, Long March Space, Beijing
2016 *Tianzhou Chen*, chi K11 Museum, Shanghai
2015 *TIANZHUO CHEN*, Palais de Tokyo, Paris
2014 *PICNIC PARADI$E BITCH*, BANK, Shanghai
2013 *Tianzhuo's Acid Club*, Star Gallery, Beijing

Selected Group Exhibitions

2016 11th Shanghai Biennial, Power Station of Art, Shanghai
2016 *The Public Body*, Artspace, Sydney
2016 *WE: A Community of Chinese Contemporary Artists*, chi K11 Museum, Shanghai
2015 *Mankind.Machinekind*, Krizinger Projekte, Vienna
2014 *Tomorrow's Party*, Ullens Center for Contemporary Art, Beijing
2014 *PALE FIRE—Revising Boundaries*, M WOODS, Beijing
2014 *MEMOIRS OF AN AMNESIAC*, Maison Populaire, Paris

CHEN Zhou

b.1987, Zhejiang Province
Lives in Shanghai

Central Academy of Fine Arts, 2009

Selected Exhibitions

2015 *28 Chinese—Rubell Family Collection*, San Francisco Asian Art Museum and San Antonio Museum of Art
2014 *Kaufman*, AIKE-DELLARCO, Shanghai
2013 *I'm not not not Chen Zhou*, Magician Space, Beijing

2013 *ON | OFF: China's Young Artists in Concept and Practice*, Ullens Center for Contemporary Art, Beijing

CHENG Ran

b.1981, Inner Mongolia
Lives in Hangzhou

China Academy of Art, 2004

Solo Exhibitions

2016 *Diary of a Madman*, New Museum, New York
2016 *In Course of the Miraculous*, K11 Art Foundation, Hong Kong
2015 *In Course of the Miraculous*, Galerie Urs Meile, Beijing
2014 *A Telephone Booth Romance*, Leo Xu Projects, Shanghai
2014 *Immersion and Distance*, Ullens Center for Contemporary Art, Beijing

Group Exhibitions

2016 Yebisu International Festival for Art & Alternative Visions, Tokyo
2016 *Unlimited*, Art Basel, Switzerland
2015 14th Istanbul Biennial, Istanbul

CHI Peng

b.1981, Yantai
Lives in Beijing

Central Academy of Fine Arts, 2005

Solo Exhibitions

2015 *Chi Peng—Three Years*, m97 Gallery, Shanghai
2012 *Trading Pain*, Ludwig Museum, Budapest
2011 *Me, Myself, and I, Photoworks 2003–2010*, Groninger Museum, Netherlands
2010 *Chi Peng / Mood Is Hard to Remember*, Today Art Museum, Beijing
2010 *Chi Peng / Mood Is Never Better Than Memory*, White Space, Beijing
2005 *Naked Lunch*, Chambers of Fine Art, New York

CUI Jie

b.1983, Shanghai
Lives in Shanghai

China Academy of Art, 2006

Selected Exhibitions

2017 *Past Skin*, MoMA PS1, New York
2017 *The New Normal*, Ullens Center of Contemporary Art, Beijing
2016 *Cui Jie: Latter, Former*, Mother's Tanks Station, Dublin
2016 *Hack Space*, K11 Art Foundation, Hong Kong
2014 *Cui Jie: The Proposal for Old and New Urbanism*, Leo Xu Projects, Shanghai
2014 *My Generation: Young Chinese Artists*, Tampa Museum of Art and Museum of Fine Arts, St Petersburg

GAO Ling

b.1980, Jiangsu
Lives in Shanghai

Suzhou Art & Design Technology Institute, 2000
China Academy of Art, 2002
Florence Design Academy, 2004

Selected Exhibitions

2017 *The Body and the Theater*, Art Amoy Art Fair, Xiamen
2015 *The Contested Body*, Ray Art Center, Shanghai
2014 *WYNG Master Award*, Hong Kong
2012 *WOMEN*, Chinese Cultural Center of San Francisco
2010 *Who's Got It—New Femininity*, Downstream Garage, Shanghai

GUAN Xiao

b.1983, Chongqing
Lives in Beijing

Communication University of China, 2006

Solo Exhibitions

2017 *Living Sci-Fi, under the red stars*, Kraupa-Tuskany Zeidler, Berlin
2016 *Guan Xiao: Flattened Metal*, in association with K11 Art Foundation, ICA, London
2016 *Guan Xiao: Elastic Sleep*, in association with ICA London, K11 Art Foundation, Shanghai
2016 *Weather Forecast*, Jeu de Paume, Paris
2015 *Basic Logic*, Antenna Space, Shanghai
2014 *Something Happened Like Never Happened*, Kraupa-Tuskany Zeidler, Berlin
2013 *Survivors' Hunting*, The Magician Space, Beijing

Selected Group Exhibitions

2017 *Viva Arte Viva*, 57th Venice Biennale, Venice
2017 *Mutations*, The High Line, New York
2017 *Hybrid Layers*, ZKM, Karlsruhe
2016 9th Berlin Biennale for Contemporary Art, Feuerle Collection, Berlin
2016 *She: International Women Artists Exhibition*, Long Museum, Shanghai
2016 *WE: A Community of Chinese Contemporary Artists*, chi K11 Museum, Shanghai
2015 *Hugo Boss Asia Art – Shortlist Exhibition*, Rockbund Art Museum, Shanghai
2015 13th Biennale de Lyon: *La vie moderne*, Curated by Ralph Rugoff, Lyon
2015 *Triennial: Surround Audience*, New Museum, New York

Bill HE Ho King Man

b.1988, Xuwen
Lives in New York

Fordham Law School, 2012

Selected Exhibitions

2017 *Ho King Man: Stiff Cotton Brain Stone*, SALTS, Basel
2017 *Mosquitos, Dust and Thieves*, 47 Canal, New York
2016 *LORETTA*, Practice, New York

HUA Shangyu

b.1990, Zhejiang
Lives in New York

Fudan University, 2012
Maryland Institute College of Art, 2014

Selected Exhibitions

2016 *Brick Wall Biennale*, GradEx, MICA, Baltimore
2016 *MICA Grad Show*, Fox 3 Gallery, MICA, Baltimore
2016 *More Like You*, Gallery Four, Baltimore
2015 *Research Remix Exhibition*, Johns Hopkins University, Baltimore
2012 *Art Bye Bye*, SIVA, Shanghai
2011 *The Mild Spicy and Little Numb*, SIVA, Shanghai
2011 *Harmonious Differences*, Central Academy of Fine Arts, Beijing/Shanghai

JIN Nv

b.1984, Qinhuangdao
Lives in Beijing

Central Academy of Fine Arts, 2007

Selected Exhibitions

2016 *i sauce: the 11th Anniversary of Star Gallery*, Beijing
2016 *SHE: International Women Artists Exhibition*, Long Museum, Shanghai
2013 *Warmth and Heat: Jin Nü Solo Show*, Star Gallery, Beijing
2011 Solo Exhibition, Star Gallery, Beijing

JIN Shan

b.1977, Jiangsu
Lives in Shanghai

East China Normal University, 2000

Solo Exhibitions

2015 *Divine Ruse*, BANK, Shanghai
2012 *There Is No End to this Road*, Masters & Pelavin, New York
2012 *My Dad is Li Gang*, Brown University, Providence
2011 *It Came From the Sky*, Spencer Museum, Lawrence, Kansas

Mo KONG

b.1990, Heilongjiang
Lives in New York

Fen Qia University, 2011
Ji Lin University of Communications, 2012
Rhode Island School of Design, 2015
Skowhegan School of Painting and Sculpture, 2017

Selected Exhibitions

2017 *Please be the world you promised you would be*, solo exhibition, Artericambi Gallery, Venice
2015 *Black dirty my skin, eat my body, kill my soul*, solo exhibition, Chashama 461, New York
2015 *It's never as it seems*, Flux Factory, New York
2015 *Perspective*, Hillyer Art Space, Washington, DC
2015 *Fever Dream*, Gellman Gallery, Providence

LI Liao

b.1982, Hubei
Lives in Shenzhen

Hubei Institute of Fine Arts, 2005

Selected Exhibitions

2017 *After Us*, chi K11 Museum, Shanghai
2016 *The Art? Contemporary Art From China*, curated by Cai Guo-Qiang, Qatar Museum, Doha
2016 *Dragon Liver Phoenix Brain: Eight Emerging Artists*, OCAT Contemporary Art Terminal, Shanghai
2016 *HACK SPACE*, K11 Art Foundation, Hong Kong
2015 *Triennial: Surround Audience*, New Museum, New York
2013 *Hugo Boss Asia Art*, Rockbund Art Museum, Shanghai
2013 *ON | OFF: China's Young Artists in Concept and Practice*, Ullens Center for Contemporary Art, Beijing

LIANG Shuo

b.1976, Jixian
Lives in Beijing

Central Academy of Fine Arts, 2000

Solo Exhibitions

2017 *Lai Xi Xi*, New Century Art Foundation-Ceramic House, Shanghai
2015 *Temple of Candour*, Beijing Commune, Beijing
2014 *The Story of Beginning*, Space Station, Beijing
2014 *Art Peddler*, Yangte River Space, Wuhan

Selected Group Exhibitions

2016 *HACK SPACE*, K11 Art Foundation, Hong Kong
2015 *Fervant China*, Mons, Belgium
2014 *Landscape: The Virtual the Actual the Possible?*, Time Museum, Guangzhou; Yerba Buena Center for The Art, San Francisco
2014 *The Armory Show*, New York
2013 *Fuck Off 2*, Groninger Museum, the Netherlands
2012 *Reactivation—9th Shanghai Biennale*, Power Station of Art, Shanghai

LIANG Yuanwei

b.1977, Xi'an
Lives in Beijing

Central Academy of Fine Arts, 1999
Central Academy of Fine Arts, 2004

Solo Exhibitions

2017 *Behind the Curtain*, Palazzo Pisani-Conservatorio de Musica, Venice, Italy
2015 *OVAL*, Xi'an OCAT, Xi'an
2014 *The Tension between a Bow and an Elephant*, Pace, London
2013 *Pomegranate Liang Yuanwei*, Beijing Commune, Beijing

Selected Group Exhibitions

2016 *Chinese Whispers-Uli Sigg Collection*, Kunstmuseum Bern, Switzerland
2015 *My Generation: Young Chinese Artists*, Orange County Museum of Art
2013 *ON | OFF: China's Young Artists in Concept and Practice*, Ullens Center for Contemporary Art, Beijing

Pixy LIAO

b.1979, Shanghai
Lives in New York

University of Memphis, 2008

Selected Solo Exhibitions

2017 *Lady and Gentleman*, Galleri Vasli Souza, Malmö, Sweden
2016 *Venus as a Boy*, Leo Xu Projects, Shanghai
2016 *Some Words Are Just Between Us*, First Draft Gallery, Sydney
2015 *Experimental Relationship*, Circuitous Succession Gallery, Memphis
2013 *Let's Make Love*, Camera Club of New York, New York

Selected Group Exhibitions

2017 *A New Ballardian Vision*, Metro Pictures, New York
2017 *NSFW: FEMALE GAZE*, Museum of Sex, New York
2016 *Out Frames*, Museum of Modern Art in Bologna, Bologna
2016 *Bagsim*, chi K11 Museum, Shanghai
2016 *WECHAT—A Dialogue in Contemporary Chinese Art*, Asia Society Texas, Houston

LIN Ke

b.1984, Wenzhou
Lives in Beijing

China Academy of Art, 2008

Selected Exhibitions

2016 *Addicted to the Screen: Lin Ke Solo Project*, Goethe Institute, Beijing
2016 *Jian Ce & Lin Ke: I am not a Robot*, Galerie Philine Cremer, Dusseldorf
2016 *The 11th Shanghai Biennial: Why Not Ask Again*, Shanghai
2016 *Performing the Shot: Video Works from the Collection of Wang Bin*, New Century Art Foundation, Shanghai
2016 *Turning Point: Contemporary Art in China Since 2000*, Minsheng Art Museum, Shanghai
2016 *Screen Test: Chinese Video Art Since 1980s*, CAFA Art Museum, Beijing
2016 *Peepshow*, Long March Space, Beijing
2015 *Jing Shen*, Pac Padiglione D'arte Contemporanea, Milan
2015 *Works in Progress: Photography from China*, Museum Folkwang, Essen
2014 *OCAT-Pierre Huber Art Prize Shortlist Exhibition: The Truth About Entropy*, OCAT Contemporary Art Terminal, Shanghai

LIU Di

b.1985, Ankang
Lives in Beijing

China Academy of Art, 2007
China Central Academy of Fine Arts, 2009

Selected Exhibitions

2017 *Liu Di: Break with Convention*, Pékin Fine Arts, Beijing
2017 *Periphery-Centre Line: Contemporary Art Photography and Video in China*, Dimona Municipal Art Gallery, Shfaram, Israel and Wilfrid Israel Museum of Asian Art and Studies, Tel Aviv
2016 *The World of Fantasy*, Jacob Javits Center, New York
2015 *My Generation: Young Chinese Artists*, Orange County Museum of Art
2014 *My Generation: Young Chinese Artists*, Tampa Museum of Art and Museum of Fine Arts, St Petersburg
2012 *I See China*, Pékin Fine Arts, Beijing
2012 *Art Novo 100*, Today Art Museum, Beijing
2010–2015 *reGeneration2: Tomorrow's Photographers Today—A Travelling Exhibition*, Musee de l'Elysee, Lausanne
2010 *History Lessons*, Pékin Fine Arts, Beijing

LIU Wei

b.1972, Beijing
Lives in Beijing

China Academy of Art, 1996

Solo Exhibitions

2016 Lehmann Maupin Gallery, New York
2016 *PLATEAU*, Samsung Museum of Art, Seoul
2015 Ullens Center for Contemporary Art, Beijing
2014 Museum Boijmans Van Beuningen, Rotterdam
2011 Minsheng Art Museum, Shanghai

Selected Group Exhibitions

2016 *What About Art? Contemporary Art from China*, curated by Cai Guo-Qiang, Qatar Museum, Doha
2016 *Bentu, Chinese artists at a time of turbulence and transformation*, Fondation Louis Vuitton, Paris
2015 *La vie Moderne*, La Biennale de Lyon, Lyon
2013 *28 Chinese*, Rubell Family Collection, Miami
2013 *Re:emerge: Towards a New Cultural Cartography*, Sharjah Biennial 11
2012 4th Guangzhou Triennial, Guangzhou
2010 Rehearsal, Shanghai Biennale 2008 Expenditure, Busan Biennale
2005 51st Venice Biennale, Venice

LU Yang

b.1984, Shanghai
Lives in Beijing and Shanghai

China Academy of Art, 2010
China Academy of Art, 2007

Selected Solo Exhibitions

2017 *Lu Yang: Delusional Mandala*, MOCA, Cleveland
2017 *Delusional Mandala*, Space Gallery, Portland
2016 *Shanghainese in Yokohama*, Zou no Hana Terrace, Yokohama
2016 *Lu Yang / Delusional Mandala*, Société, Berlin
2016 *LuYang Delusional Crime and Punishment*, NYU Shanghai Art Gallery, Shanghai
2016 *Delusional Mandala*, Interstitial, Seattle

2015 *LuYang Delusional Mandala*, Beijing Commune, Beijing
2015 *ANTI-HUMANISME*, Ok Corral, Copenhagen
2014 *Lu Yang Arcade*, Wallplay, New York
2011 *11th Winds of Artist in Residence Part 2—Lu Yang*, Fukuoka Asian Art Museum, Fukuoka
2011 *The Anatomy of Rage (Wrathful King Kong Core)*, Ullens Center for Contemporary Art, Beijing

MA Qiusha

b.1982, Beijing
Lives in Beijing

China Academy of Art, 2005
Alfred University, 2008

Selected Solo Exhibitions

2016 *Wonderland*, Beijing Commune, Beijing
2015 *BKMQ*: Bettina Krieg & Ma Qiusha, SMAC, Berlin
2013 *Ma Qiusha: Raw*, Beijing Commune, Beijing
2013 *Ma Qiusha*, Chinese Arts Centre, Manchester
2011 *Ma Qiusha: Address*, Ullens Center for Contemporary Art, Beijing

Group Exhibitions

2016 *Utopia & Beyond*, Castello Di Rivara, Torino, Italy
2016 *Tall Tales: women artists' playful exploration of the human experience*, Freud Museum, London
2016 *We Chat: A Dialogue in Contemporary Chinese Art*, Asia Society Texas, Houston
2015 *On Curbstone Jewels and Cobblestones*, Daimler Contemporary, Berlin
2015 *Global Control and Censorship*, ZKM, Germany
2015 *My Generation: Young Chinese Artists*, Orange County Museum of Art

MIAO Ying

b.1985, Shanghai
Lives in New York and Shanghai

China Academy of Art, 2007
Alfred University, 2009

Selected Exhibitions

2017 *The New Normal*, Ullens Center for Contemporary Art
2017 *After Us*, chi K11 Museum, Shanghai

2017 *.com/.cn*, K11 Art Foundation, Hong Kong
2016 *Miao Ying: Chinternet Plus*, New Museum, New York
2016 *Content Aware*, Madein Gallery, Shanghai
2015 *Holding a Kitchen Knife to Cut the Internet Cable*, an online exhibition for the Chinese Pavilion, La Biennale di Venezia

QIU Xiaofei

b.1977, Harbin
Lives in Beijing

China Academy of Art, 2002

Selected Solo Exhibitions

2016 *Qiu Xiaofei: Double Pendulum*, Pace Gallery, New York
2014 *Qiu Xiaofei: Apollo Bangs Dionysus*, Pace, Beijing
2013 *Qiu Xiaofei: Rauschenberg Said, "The Walking Stick is Longer than the Maulstick, After All,"* Beijing Commune, Beijing
2013 *Qiu Xiaofei: Repetition*, Minsheng Art Museum, Shanghai

Selected Group Exhibitions

2014 *My Generation: Young Chinese Artists*, Tampa Museum of Art and Museum of Fine Arts, St Petersburg
2014 *Focus Beijing—The De Heus-Zomer Collection*, Museum Boijmans Van Beuningen, Rotterdam
2014 *Myth/History: Yuz Collection of Contemporary Art*, Yuz Museum, Shanghai
2013 *Criss-Cross: Artworks of Young Chinese Contemporary Artists from Long Collection*, Long Museum, Shanghai

TAO Hui

b.1987, Yunyang
Lives in Beijing

Sichuan Fine Arts Institute, 2010

Solo Exhibitions

2016 *Now & Then*, Galeria UNTILTHEN, Paris
2015 *New Directions: Tao Hui*, UCCA, Beijing
2015 *1 Character & 7 Materials*, AIKE-DELLARCO, Shanghai
2013 *Sightseers*, Space Space, Chengdu

Selected Group Exhibitions

2017 *Reciprocal Enlightenment*, CAFA Art Museum, Beijing
2017 *Talk, Talk*, Surplus Space, Wuhan, China
2017 *The mulberry forest becoming ocean*, Esther Schipper, Berlin
2016 *Performance in Mirror*, New Century Art Foundation, Shanghai
2016 *Hack Space*, chi K11Art Space, Shanghai
2016 Act, OCAT Shenzhen, Shenzhen
2016 *Why Not Ask Again*: 11th Shanghai Biennale, PSA, Shanghai
2016 *The Exhibition of Annual of Contemporary Art of China 2015*, Beijing Minsheng Art Museum
2016 *Art Basel 2016: Film Sector*, agnès b. CINEMA, Hong Kong Art Centre

WANG Xu

b. 1986, Dalian
Lives in New York

Central Academy of Fine Arts, 2010
Columbia University, 2013

Group Exhibitions

2017 *Seeds of Time*, Shanghai Project Chapter 2, Shanghai
2017 *Mosquitoes, Dusts, and Thieves*, 47 Canal, New York
2016 APEC, 67 Ludlow Street, New York
2016 *This one is smaller than this one*, GALERIST, Istanbul
2016 *This one is smaller than this one*, Postmasters, New York
2015 *In Response of Repetition and Difference*, Jewish Museum, New York
2015 *Under Foundations*, SculptureCenter, New York

Jennifer WEN MA

b.1973, Beijing
Lives in New York

Oklahoma Christian University of Science and Arts, 1993
Pratt Institute, 1999

Selected Exhibitions

2017 *Jennifer Wen Ma: Eight Views of Paradise Interrupted*, Sandra Gering Gallery, New York
2016 *Exhaustive*, Ink Studio, Art021 Art Fair, Shanghai

2016 *Paradise Interrupted*, Lincoln Center Festival, New York; Singapore International Arts Festival, Singapore
2015 *The Art of the March: Cues from Sun Tzu's Art of War*, Michigan State University football game half-time show, East Lansing, MI
2015 *Paradise Interrupted*, Spoleto Festival USA, Charleston, SC
2015 *Paradise Interrupted preview*, Temple of Dendur, The Metropolitan Museum of Art, New York
2015 *A Winter Landscape Cradling Bits of Sparkle*, Public Art Commission at Market Square, Pittsburgh
2014 *Paradise Interrupted: Disintegration*, Mikimoto, New York
2013 *Nature and Man in Rhapsody of Light at the Water Cube*, permanent new media public art, National Aquatic Center, Beijing
2013 *Forty-Four Sunsets in a Day*, Hanart Gallery, Hong Kong
2012 *Hanging Garden in Ink*, Ullens Center for Contemporary Art, Beijing

Cici WU

b.1989, Beijing
Lives in New York

City University of Hong Kong, 2012
Maryland Institute College of Art, 2015

Selected Exhibitions

2017 *A Disappearing Act*, Triangle Gallery, New York
2017 *Mosquitos, Dust and Thieves*, 47 Canal, New York
2016 *Not Really Here*, Platform Gallery, Baltimore
2012 *Andrei*, solo exhibition, Museum of Ideas, L'viv

XU Zhen

b.1977, Shanghai
Lives in Shanghai

Solo Exhibitions

2016 *Xu Zhen*, James Cohan Gallery, New York
2015 *Xu Zhen*, Long Museum, Pudong, Shanghai
2014 *Xu Zhen: Blissful As Gods*, ShanghARTGallery, Shanghai
2014 *ShanghART Supermarket*, ShanghART Singapore, Singapore
2014 XU Zhen, Commission Artist, The Armory Show, New York
2014 *XU Zhen: A MadeIn Company Production*, Ullens Center for Contemporary Art, Beijing
2013 *The Most Important Thing is not the Contract*, OCT Contemporary Art Terminal, Shanghai

2013 *Movement Field, XU Zhen—Produced by MadeIn Company*, Long March Space, Beijing

YAN Xing

b.1986, Chongqing
Lives in Los Angeles and Beijing

Sichuan Fine Arts Institute, 2009

Selected Solo Exhibitions

2017 *Dangerous Afternoon*, Kunsthalle Basel, Basel
2016 *Yan Xing*, Eli and Edythe Broad Museum, Michigan State University, East Lansing, MI
2016 *Nuit et Brouillard*, Galerie Urs Meile, Lucerne
2016 *Performance of a Massacre*, Stedelijk Museum, Amsterdam
2015 *Thief*, Galerie Urs Meile, Beijing
2014 *Standard Exhibition*, Galerie Urs Meile, Lucerne

Selected Group Exhibitions

2017 *Spectrosynthesis*, Museum of Contemporary Art, Taipei
2017 *Constellation*, The National Gallery, Georgian National Museum, Tbilisi
2017 *The Man Who Never Threw Anything Away*, Times Museum, Guangzhou
2016 *Annual Exhibition of Contemporary Chinese Art*, Minsheng Museum, Beijing
2014 *Kabinett*, Art Basel, Miami Beach
2014 *My Generation: Young Chinese Artists*, Tampa Museum of Art and Museum of Fine Arts, St Petersburg
2013 *28 Chinese*, Rubell Family Collection, Miami
2013 *ON | OFF: China's Young Artists in Concept and Practice*, Ullens Center for Contemporary Art, Beijing

YANG Dongxue

b.1984, Shenyang
Lives in Beijing

Guangzhou Academy of Fine Arts, 2003

Solo Exhibitions

2014 *Regarding the Silent Majority*, Pékin Fine Arts, Beijing
2013 *Got Used to Consume Today's Achievement with Achievement Habitually*, Yan Club Arts Center, Beijing
2012 *Romance in a Humble Moment*, Yan Club Arts Center, Beijing

2010 *Tell Me How To Be Sad*, Yan Club Arts Center, Beijing
2009 *"Disorder" Symphonic projects in the world*, First Live Art Space, Guangzhou

Group Exhibitions

2014 *New Works*, OCAT, Shenzhen
2014 *Memo*, White Space, Beijing
2013 *New Paper*, Pékin Fine Arts, Beijing
2013 *The Sun*, Shanghai Institute of Visual Art, Shanghai
2011 *Infinitely Close to the Front*, Guangdong Museum of Art, Guangdong

YE Funa

b.1986, Kunming
Lives in Beijing

China Academy of Art, 2008
Central St Martins College of Art, 2010

Selected Exhibitions

2017 *An Alternative Cinema*, Metro Pictures at 83 Pitt Street, New York
2016 *Nailhenge*, Space Station, Beijing
2016 *Zero for Conduct*, Tabula Rasa Gallery, Beijing
2016 *We*, chi K11 Museum, Shanghai
2015 Curated Nail Residency, MOCA Shanghai
2014 *Zha Golden Flowers—News from Nowhere*, V Art Center, Shanghai
2013 *Where are we from? Where are we going?*, Contemporary by Angela Li, Hong Kong

YU Ji

b.1985, Shanghai
Lives in Shanghai

Shanghai University, 2011

Solo Exhibitions

2017 *Prec(ar)ious Collectives*, project by K11 Art Foundation and Palais de Tokyo, Athens
2016 *Black Mountain*, Beijing Commune, Beijing
2016 *Dairy of Sulfur Mining—Pataauw*, Mind Art Set Center, Taipei
2014 *Never Left Behind*, C-Space, Beijing
2013 *In the Skin*, Mind Set Art Center, Taipei
2012 *Not Moss*, Artists Special Project, Gillman Barracks, Singapore

Selected Group Exhibitions

2016 *Snakes*, Power Station of Art, Shanghai
2015 *We*, chi K11 Museum, Shanghai, China
2015 *Inside China*, Project by Palais de Tokyo, chi K11 Museum, Shanghai
2015 *Nocturnal Friendships*, Lehmann Maupin, Hong Kong
2015 *Myth/History II: Shanghai Galaxy*, Yuz Museum, Shanghai
2014 *Inside China—L'Intérieur du Géant*, Palais de Tokyo, Paris
2014 *You Can Only Think About Something, If You Think About Something Else*, Time Museum, Guangzhou

ZHANG Ding

b.1980, Gansu
Lives in Shanghai

Northwest Minority University, 2003
China Academy of Art, 2004

Solo Exhibitions

2015 *Black Substance*, Shanghai Museum of Glass, Shanghai
2014 *Orbit of Rock*, ShanghART, Beijing
2014 *Orbit*, The Armory Show, New York
2013 *Gold & Silver, Zhang Ding*, Galerie Krinzinger, Austria
2012 *Buddha Jumps Over the Wall*, Top Contemporary Art Center, Shanghai
2011 *Zhang Ding*, ShanghART H-Space, Shanghai

ZHAO Yao

b.1981, Sichuan
Lives in Beijing

Sichuan Fine Arts Institute, 2004

Solo Exhibitions

2016 *The Last Egg*, Beijing Commune, Beijing
2015 *Painting of Thought*, Pace Hong Kong, Hong Kong
2013 *Spirit above All*, Pace London, London
2012 *Zhao Yao: You Can't See Me, You Can't See Me*, Beijing Commune, Beijing
2011 *Zhao Yao: I Am Your Night*, Beijing Commune, Beijing

Group Exhibitions

2017 *Any Ball*, CAFA Art Museum, Beijing
2016 *Turning Point: Contemporary Art in China Since 2000*, Minsheng Art Museum, Shanghai
2016 *A Beautiful Disorder*, Cass Sculpture Foundation, West Sussex
2016 *Mountain Sites: Views of Laoshan*, Sifang Art Museum, Nanjing
2015 *Adventures of the Black Square: Abstract Art and Society 1915–2015*, Whitechapel Gallery, London
2014 *Inside China*, Palais de Tokyo, Paris, France
2014 *For Armory Focus: China*, The Armory Show, New York
Museum of Fine Arts, St Petersburg
2013 *28 Chinese*, Rubell Family Collection, Miami
2013 *Move on Asia-Video Art in Asia 2002 to 2012*, ZKM, Karlsruhe
2013 *ON | OFF: China's Young Artists in Concept and Practice*, The Ullens Center for Contemporary Art, Beijing

ZHAO Zhao

b.1982, Xijiang Province
Lives in Beijing

Xinjiang Institute of Arts, 2003

Solo Exhibitions

2016 *Lighter, Fragments, Untitled and Safe*, Tang Contemporary Art, Hong Kong
2015 *Constellations II*, Chambers Fine Art, New York
2015 *Zhao Zhao*, Carol Kostyál, Stockholm
2015 *Zhao Zhao: OMNIPRESENT*, Roberts & Tilton, Los Angeles
2014 *Zhao Zhao: Uncertainty*, Chambers Fine Art, Beijing
2013 *Zhao Zhao: Constellations*, Chambers Fine Art, New York
2013 *Nothing Inside II*, Alexander Ochs Gallery, Berlin
2013 *A Sense of Security II: China Likes Me and I Likes China*, Platform China, Beijing
2012 *Nothing Inside*, Alexander Ochs Gallery, Beijing
2011 *According to Zhao Zhao: New Works*, Chambers Fine Art, Beijing

LIST OF ILLUSTRATIONS

Introduction

INDEX

Note: Page numbers in *italic* refer to images and accompanying captions